ULTIMATE HEALING

Ultimate Healing
The Power of Compassion

ॐ

LAMA ZOPA RINPOCHE

Foreword by Lillian Too

Edited by Ailsa Cameron

WISDOM PUBLICATIONS • BOSTON

Wisdom Publications
199 Elm Street
Somerville, MA 02144 USA

Library of Congress Cataloging-in-Publication Data
Thubten Zopa, Rinpoche, 1946–
    Ultimate healing : the power of compassion / Lama Zopa Rimpoche ;
edited by Ailsa Cameron ; foreword by Lillian Too.
       p.   cm.
    ISBN 0-86171-195-5 (alk. paper)
    Includes bibliographical references and index.
    1. Spiritual life—Bka'-gdams-pa (Sect) 2. Healing—Religious aspects—
Buddhism. 3. Meditation—Buddhism. 4. Compassion (Buddhism)
I. Cameron, Ailsa. II. Title.
BQ7670.6.T5 2001
294.3/444—dc21   2001016531

ISBN 0-86171-195-5

06 05 04 03 02
6   5   4   3   2

Design by: Gopa and Ted2
Typeface: Sabon 10.5/14
Cover image: The Eight Medicine Buddhas
Painted by Peter Iseli 1997. 17.5 x 11.5 feet. Photo © John Bigelow Taylor

Contents

ᘇ

Publisher's Acknowledgment

The Publisher gratefully acknowledges the kind generosity of Richard Gere and the Gere Foundation in contributing toward the printing of this book.

Foreword

ᔕ

Tʜɪs, ᴛʀᴜʟʏ, is an awesome book. From its pages emanate such soothing wisdom, so much healing light—manifesting the presence, the words, and the teachings of one of the world's foremost high lamas. Here is a book that focuses the heart on the spiritual cure for those in pain; a book that directs the attention of the mind to the special wisdom of cures that cause permanent healing to take place; a book for the sick, the unhappy, and the injured.

Yet *Ultimate Healing* is more than a book of prayer to alleviate our physical ills. The teachings and practices contained herein lead the mind toward a more profound understanding of life and death and of impermanence and suffering. Such an understanding allows us to begin to see illness and disease in a broader perspective. Within this perspective, the concepts of karma, reincarnation, and the quality of rebirth take on new meanings that have the power to comfort, and ultimately to heal us.

Lama Zopa Rinpoche is a spiritual teacher whose compassion, kindness, and incredible humility is legend to his thousands of students and disciples around the world. He was recognized at the age of four as the reincarnation of a a sage and meditator who lived in the Lawudo region of the Nepalese Himalayas.

I had the greatest good fortune to meet Rinpoche in India in February 1997, a meeting that forever changed the way I look at life. I brought to that meeting the negative baggage of a lifetime's worth of posturing and self-cherishing. I smoked like a chimney then—easily puffing two packs of cigarettes a day. I had been smoking for thirty years! In India, I was politely requested not to smoke in the presence of such a high lama, and so I recall slinking to the back of the building to light a desperate cigarette every few hours. I felt very silly, but as everyone who has ever been addicted to smoking will explain, it is not by choice that we smokers behave like addicts. After a lifetime of cigarettes it is not easy to give up.

And here's the wonderful thing: After returning from India I never touched another cigarette, and I have not smoked since then. I remember it was several months before I realized my quitting had something to do with meeting Rinpoche. His blessings had helped me succeed in quitting when every effort I had ever made to stop had failed. Yet when I attempted to thank him, Rinpoche would not even acknowledge he had anything to do with it. He simply ignored all references to it—that is the extent of Rinpoche's humility.

The practices compiled here are especially vital for those suffering from life-threatening illnesses. The practice of the Medicine Buddha is particularly powerful in that it can bring seemingly miraculous healing in our life and in the lives of those afflicted with chronic ailments and sicknesses. Lama Zopa Rinpoche's kindness is infinite in transmitting this knowledge and these teachings to the world.

So be prepared for cures, but also make an effort to penetrate the veil of ignorance and disappointment that prevent the mind from accepting when cures do *not* take place. Cut through karmic ignorance by meditating on these teachings, performing the visualizations, and reciting the mantras. Rinpoche shows us how, by understanding the true nature of existence, we are able to view every suffering as containing the seeds for happiness. Herein lies the superior wisdom of this wonderful book.

May anyone who reads the words of my teacher have happiness forever. May their sufferings be softened and alleviated, and may all their ailments, sickness, and disease be instantly cured.

Lillian Too
July 2001

Editor's Preface

જ્જ

Lama Zopa Rinpoche, spiritual director of the Foundation for the Preservation of the Mahayana Tradition (FPMT), had been helping people with health problems for more than twenty years when he decided to hold his first healing course in August 1991 at Tara Institute, the FPMT center in Melbourne, Australia. As well as traditional Tibetan herbal medicine, Lama Zopa had prescribed meditations, mantras, and various other Tibetan Buddhist healing practices to thousands of people. Feeling that there were more and more people in need of help and that Tibetan Buddhism had so much to offer them, especially those with incurable diseases, Rinpoche organized a one-week healing course.

Advertised as "Methods and Meditations to Help Heal Mind and Body," the course made no promises of miracle cures. Lama Zopa insisted that only those with a life-threatening disease could attend the course, and in the end just six people were accepted for the course: four with cancer, one who was HIV+, and one with multiple sclerosis. In addition, the course was attended by six people selected to organize the course or to run future healing courses.

On the morning of August 28, 1991, the course participants gathered in the meditation hall of Tara Institute for the first session. Dispensing with the traditional style of teaching from a throne, Lama Zopa sat in a comfortable armchair facing the six participants, also seated in armchairs. Rinpoche greeted them by saying, "I would like to thank all of you for coming here. Together we will help each other to develop our mind and, the most important thing in life, our good heart. In this way we can benefit other living beings better and more deeply. I would like to thank you very much for providing this opportunity."

All the people in the group, including Lama Zopa, then briefly introduced themselves and talked a little about what they expected from the course. Rinpoche later commented that he had initially been planning to concentrate on doing meditation during the course, but when the participants introduced themselves, he was surprised to find that they were more interested in finding peace of mind than in curing their disease. This encouraged Rinpoche to go more deeply into Buddhist philosophy in his discourses.

During the seven days of the course, Rinpoche taught twice daily, morning and afternoon, usually quite short sessions because of the physical limitations of the participants. He carefully avoided using Sanskrit terms and instead tried to use language with a more universal meaning. In addition to the discourses, there were gentle exercises each morning, guided meditations, and general discussions. Rinpoche introduced basic Buddhist philosophy, with special emphasis on thought transformation; he gave each person a signed copy of his book *Transforming Problems into Happiness*, pointing out that the book covered the fundamental topics to be discussed during the healing course. Rinpoche also led white light healing meditations; chanting of mantras and deity meditation, particularly that of Logyönma; circumambulations of stupas, relics, and texts; and the blessing of water, which was drunk at the beginning and end of sessions. Toward the end of the course, Rinpoche saw each person to discuss their individual situation and to give advice on personal practices. In his room he also performed pujas for them.

Although one young woman left the course after the second day because she needed further pain relief, the others commented that they felt much better by the end of the course, noting a lessening of pain and an increase of peace of mind.

To conclude the course, Rinpoche gave the *jenangs,* or permission to practice, of Medicine Buddha, Singhanada, and Sitatapatra. He also composed "Purification Practice for Cancer or AIDS" (see page 215) and translated a brief healing practice by Padmasambhava (see "The Healing Buddha," page 165). Rinpoche gave each person practices for after the course. Later he explained that he would prefer people with life-threatening illnesses to continue their spiritual practice, thus becoming closer to the end of all suffering and its causes, rather than to simply recover from their disease and then do no further spiritual practice. They might be healthy, but they would be wasting their lives.

Although the Tara Institute course has been the only healing course taught by Lama Zopa, in February 1993 Rinpoche gave three talks on "Healing Mind and Body" in Auckland, New Zealand. To these talks he brought a small notebook in which he had written outlines for healing courses that he described as "the very essence of healing." Unable to cover all the topics in Aukland, Rinpoche finished explaining them during subsequent teachings at Mahamudra Centre, also in New Zealand. Though the outlines were never mentioned during the healing course at Tara Institute, it was clear that they provided the framework for the discourses.

They also form the framework of Part One of this book. The first topic, covered in the first two chapters, is encouraging confidence in the benefits of meditation techniques by relating stories of people who have recovered from disease through this practice. Chapter 3 develops the second topic, the need to break the fixed concept of permanence. This means accepting that having a life-threatening disease and not having such a disease are the same in that death can happen to anyone at any time.

The third topic, explained in chapter 4, involves consideration of the ultimate purpose of life, which is not just to be healthy and live for a long time but to free other living beings from suffering and bring them happiness. This subject is further elaborated in the next three chapters.

The fourth topic, that everything comes from the mind, has two divisions. The first, related to the process of mental labeling, is covered in chapters 8 and 9, while the second, related to karma, is discussed in chapter 10.

Next comes the key subject of thought transformation, in which problems are transformed into happiness by thinking of their benefits. This is discussed in the following three chapters. The final topic, the taking and giving meditation (*tong-len,* in Tibetan), is explained in chapter 14.

Part Two contains various meditations and healing practices, many of them translated or composed by Lama Zopa himself. Chapter 15 offers meditations on white light healing, compassion, and taking and giving. Chapter 16 explains the benefits of Medicine Buddha practice and has the translations by Lama Zopa of two Medicine Buddha texts by Padmasambhava. Two chapters on animal liberation follow, the first explaining the benefits of circumambulations, recitation of mantras, and the blessing of water (the main practices involved in animal liberation), the second being the actual animal liberation ceremony composed by Rinpoche. Chapter 19 presents three techniques that can be applied to cure depression. Chapter 20 begins with a brief explanation of the remedy of the four powers and then gives a simple purification practice composed by Rinpoche at the end of the first healing course. The next two chapters offer a simple Chenrezig meditation for blessing water and a glimpse of practices involved in dealing with nagas and spirits—nonhuman beings implicated in causing disease. Chapter 23 introduces Rinpoche's attempts to find an herbal cure for AIDS, and chapter 24 has a translation of a famous healing prayer that Rinpoche recommended be recited during healing courses. The final chapter contains the three dedication prayers Rinpoche recited at the conclusion of the discourses and meditations during the Tara Institute course.

While structuring *Ultimate Healing* was relatively simple because Lama Zopa had already provided the basic outlines of the book, various decisions had to be made when choosing relevant material from more than six hundred pages of unedited transcript of Lama Zopa's teachings on healing. In addition to the three main teachings already mentioned, more than thirty other teachings of varying lengths were examined, plus excerpts from personal advice given to students in 1998 and 1999.[1] While most of the teachings were given in the early 1990s, they range from early 1981 to mid-1999.

During the Tara Institute course, the healing deity chosen for the group through Rinpoche's divination was Logyönma, a female deity usually practiced to counter contagious disease. Rather than try to include an exhaustive number of healing deity practices in this book, I elected to concentrate solely on Medicine Buddha, primarily because it is closely connected with healing and also because it can be practiced to bring general success. If you have an illness, it is best to check the healing deity with whom you have a strong karmic connection with a qualified lama and then pursue that practice. For further information on specific healing practices, please contact the FPMT Education Services.[2]

While some of the practices contained in this book can be adapted whether one is a Buddhist or not, many practices assume that the practitioner has taken refuge in Buddha, Dharma, and Sangha. Particularly with the deity practices, it is advisable to first train in the preliminary meditations of the graduated path to enlightenment, or lamrim, before attempting the visualizations and mantra recitations. Again, instruction from a qualified teacher is ideal for gaining the most benefit from these methods.

These practices are not magical or miraculous but rather a patient planting of real inner causes for health and happiness. As with Buddhist practice more generally, the results one receives depend on one's past karma and one's present conditions. For example, Rinpoche explains at many points the marvelous benefits of reciting various mantras, sometimes suggesting that reciting a mantra only one time can cut off the possibility of rebirth in the lower realms. Such explanations of inconceivable benefits encourage faith and perseverance. He also notes, however, that "the benefits you receive depend on how perfectly you recite the mantra, which is determined by your motivation and by the quality of your mind."

I sincerely thank the many people who helped with this book. I especially thank Lama Zopa Rinpoche for his infinite kindness and patience; Claire Atkins for her generous financial support; Ven. Robina Courtin for her generous advice; Nick Ribush of Lama Yeshe Wisdom Archive (LYWA) for his support; Wendy Cook of LYWA for her quick dispatch of tapes and transcripts; Ven. Connie Miller of FPMT Education Services for her generosity with advice and materials; Ven. Lhundrup Damchö for supplying materials; Ven. Thubten Gyatso, Ven. Pende Hawter, and Murray Wright for their transcribing and early editing work; and the many transcribers of tapes, including Ven. Wendy Finster, Ven. Yeshe Chodron, Ven. Kaye Miner, Ven. Thubten Wongmo, Chris Naylor, Katarina Hallonblad, Tracy Ho, Sally Barraud, Su Hung, Julia Hengst, Gareth Robinson, Segen Speer-Senner, Diana Velez, and the late Inta McKimm.

May everyone who reads *Ultimate Healing* be freed immediately from all their disease, spirit harm, negative karma, and obscurations and quickly achieve the peerless happiness of full enlightenment. May this book become medicine for all living beings, not just temporarily curing their physical suffering, but ultimately healing their body and mind so that they never have to experience suffering again.

PART ONE

Healing Psychology

1 *The Healing Power of the Mind*

࠾

The Nature of the Mind

SINCE HEALING essentially comes from our mind, not from our body, it is important to understand the nature of the mind. The intrinsic nature of the mind is pure in the sense that it is not one with the faults of the mind, with the disturbing thoughts and obscurations. All the faults of our mind—our selfishness, ignorance, anger, attachment, guilt, and other disturbing thoughts—are temporary, not permanent and everlasting. And since the cause of our suffering, our disturbing thoughts and obscurations, is temporary, our suffering is also temporary.

The mind is also empty of true existence, of existence from its own side. This quality of mind, known as Buddha-nature, gives us the potential to free ourselves completely from all suffering, including disease, and the causes of suffering and to achieve any happiness we wish, including the peerless happiness of enlightenment. Since the mind has all this potential, we do not need to feel depressed or hopeless. It is not as if we have to experience problems forever. We have incredible freedom to develop our mind in any way that we wish. It is simply a question of finding the right way to use the potential of our mind.

The mind and the body are two distinct phenomena. Mind is defined as that which is clear and perceives objects. Like reflections appearing in a mirror, objects appear clearly to the mind, and the mind is able to recognize them. Whereas the body is substantial, the mind is formless, without color or shape. Whereas the body disintegrates after death, the mind continues from life to life. It is not uncommon to hear of people in both the East and the West who are able to remember past lives and to see future lives, not only their own but also those of others.

Some are born with this capacity; others develop it through meditation. Some people can remember lives hundreds or even thousands of years ago. When Lama Yeshe, who guided me for many years, visited the pyramids in Egypt, he was able to remember that he had lived there in a past life.

The point is that even though many people do not believe in past and future lives, no one has actually proved that past and future lives do not exist. On the other hand, many people have realized that past lives exist because they remember them very clearly, just as we remember what we did yesterday. They realize the truth of reincarnation because they have the capacity of mind to see past and future lives.

Knowledge of the nature of the mind is more important, and also a vaster subject, than knowledge of the nature of external phenomena. And unless we understand the nature of the mind, there is no way that we can correctly understand the conventional and ultimate nature of other phenomena. Even in worldly terms, it is only through understanding the mind that we can define and understand precisely how external phenomena exist.

Generally speaking, developing knowledge of our mind is the practical solution to our problems. We first have to identify the root of our problems, for only then will we have the possibility of ending our problems and of ensuring that we never experience them again. We also have to recognize the full extent of our problems; otherwise, if we see only part of our problems, our concept of liberation will be limited.

Healing the Mind

Healing our mind is crucial, because otherwise our problems, which are beginningless, become endless. We may use medicine or some other external means to heal a particular disease, but the disease will return unless we heal our mind. If we do nothing to heal our mind, there is always the danger that we will again create the cause of the disease, that we will repeat the actions that caused us to become physically unhealthy. We will then experience the same illness in future lives, or even in this life.

Curing disease through external means is not the best solution because the cause of disease is not external. Bacteria, viruses, spirits, and so forth may act as external conditions for disease, but disease itself has no external cause. In the West, however, the external conditions for a particular disease are usually regarded as its cause. The cause of disease is not external; it is in the mind—or we could say, it is the mind. Disease is caused by our self-cherishing, ignorance, anger, attachment, and other delusions and by the negative actions motivated by these negative thoughts. Our negative thoughts and actions leave imprints on our mind, which then manifest as disease or other problems. The imprints also make it possible for disturbing thoughts and negative actions to arise again.

A physical sign necessarily has a physical cause, but the physical cause arises because of the inner cause, the imprints left on the mind by negative thoughts and actions. To fully understand disease, we have to understand this inner cause, which is the actual cause of disease and which also creates the physical conditions for disease. As long as we ignore its inner cause, we have no real cure for disease. We must study its development and recognize that its cause is in the mind. Once we recognize this, we will automatically understand that the healing of disease also has to come from the mind.

What I have been describing accords not only with Buddhist teachings but with our life experience. Research has also shown that health has very much to do with a person's attitude in daily life, with the ability to keep the mind positive. In *Uncommon Wisdom,* for example, Fritjof Capra interviewed well-known doctors and psychologists about the cause of cancer. From their research, they had concluded that the source of cancer lies in negative attitudes and that it can be cured by generating positive attitudes.[1] This scientific view is approaching the philosophy of Buddha.

A problem is a particular creation of mind. If the cause of a problem exists in our mind, the problem will definitely manifest unless we purify that cause. If the inner cause of a problem exists, the external conditions for the problem will also exist, because the inner cause creates them. In other words, outer obstacles come from inner obstacles. Even the external conditions for a problem are created by our mind. External factors become conditions for a problem because of the inner cause within our mind; but if there is no inner cause, even if the external factors are present, they cannot become conditions for the problem. Without the inner obstacle, there is no outer obstacle.

Take the example of skin cancer. It is commonly believed that skin cancer is caused by prolonged exposure to the sun. However, if sunlight is the main cause of skin cancer, everyone who sunbathes should develop it. The fact that not everyone who sunbathes develops skin cancer proves that sunlight is not its main cause. Exposure to sunlight is a condition for skin cancer but not its main cause. The main cause of skin cancer is internal, not external. The main cause is the mind. For people who have the cause of skin cancer in their mind, exposure to the sun does become a condition for the development of skin cancer. For those who don't have the internal cause, however, exposure to sunlight won't become a condition for them to develop skin cancer.

As I have already mentioned, the root of our problems is within our mind. It is our unskillful ways of thinking. We have to recognize the right ways of thinking, which bring happiness, and the wrong ways of thinking, which bring suffering. With one way of thinking, we have problems in our life; with another way of thinking, we don't. In other words, happiness and suffering come from our own mind. Our mind creates our life.

Meditation Is the Medicine

While external medicine can be taken to heal a physical sickness, inner medicine needs to be taken to heal the cause of disease, and to ensure that we never experience disease again. What is this inner medicine? Meditation. Meditation is using our own mind, our own positive attitudes, to heal ourselves. And we shouldn't restrict our definition of healing to recovery from one particular disease, but expand it to include the healing of all problems and their causes. Since disease and all our other problems are caused by negative imprints left on our mind, healing ourselves of the causes of our problems also has to come from our mind. "Meditation" is simply a label for what we do with our mind, and it is the best treatment because it has no side effects.

Since happiness and suffering come from our own mind, meditation is the essential key to healing. It is the only way to stop the cause of suffering and to create the cause of happiness. We cannot accomplish this through any external means; we have to accomplish it through our mind. Medicine alone or a simple visualization might heal a particular disease, but it is not sufficient to heal the mind. There is no way to heal disease as well as its cause other than through meditation.

In meditation, our own positive attitudes become the inner medicine that heals our mind and cures the cause of all our problems. Successful healing requires development of the good qualities of our mind. Certain ways of thinking are peaceful and healing; others are disturbing and harmful. Disease and all the other problems in our life are caused by unhealthy minds. An unhealthy mind is any mental action that disturbs us and makes us unhappy, and an unhealthy body comes from an unhealthy mind.

Meditation not only heals disease but brings great peace to the mind. It is the nature of positive thoughts to make us feel calm and relaxed. The best positive thoughts for healing are loving kindness and compassion. Loving kindness is the wish that others have happiness and the causes of happiness; great loving kindness is taking the responsibility upon ourselves to bring others happiness and its causes. Compassion is the wish that others be free from suffering and the causes of suffering; great compassion is taking the responsibility upon ourselves to free others from suffering and its causes. Generating these positive attitudes can heal disease.

Compassion is the best healer. The most powerful healing comes from developing compassion for all other living beings, irrespective of their race, nationality, religious belief, or relationship to us. We need to feel compassion for all living beings, every single one of whom wants happiness and does not want suffering. We need to develop not only compassion, the wish to free everyone from all suffering, but great compassion, which means taking upon ourselves the responsibility for doing this. This brings deep and powerful healing.

The nature of loving and compassionate thoughts is peaceful and healthy, quite different from the nature of ignorance, anger, attachment, pride, or jealousy. Even though a compassionate person feels genuine concern for others and finds it unbearable that anyone is suffering, the essential nature of their mind is still peaceful.

On the other hand, the mind of ill will, the wish to harm others, is not calm; it is like having a sharp thorn in our heart. Attachment also has its own pain; it is tight, squeezed, and very painful when we have to separate from the object of our desire. Attachment also obscures our mind, creating a wall between us and reality. When we are attached to a particular person, or even to a particular animal, we cannot see the reality of that being's suffering or feel compassion for them from our heart because attachment obscures our mind. Attachment gives us no space to feel compassion. Even if we help them, we always have an expectation of getting something in return. Our help is not given simply because they are sick or in danger, but with the expectation that they will reward us in some way in the future.

When our mind is invaded by attachment, we find it difficult to feel compassion. If we check, we find that when we are overwhelmed by strong attachment, we care only about what we want. Our main aim is our own happiness. Even if we help others, it is because we want something in return. Our mind is disturbed and obscured. We cannot see that the person for whom we feel strong attachment is at least as important as we are; we cannot cherish them and sincerely offer them help.

By healing our mind with great compassion, we will be able to solve all our own problems and those of others. The positive thought of compassion will not only help us to recover from sickness but bring us peace, happiness, and satisfaction. It will enable us to enjoy life. It will also bring peace and happiness to our family and friends and to the other people around us. Because we will have no negative thoughts toward them, the people—and even the animals—we deal with will feel happy. If we have loving kindness and compassion, our prime concern will always be not to hurt others, and this itself is healing. A compassionate person is the most powerful healer, not only of their own disease and other problems, but of those of others. A person with loving kindness and compassion heals others simply by existing.

Ultimate Healing

Each time we meditate on compassion for all living beings, we accumulate infinite merit, the cause of all happiness and success; each time we practice meditation for the benefit of all living beings, we perform ultimate healing.

Developing our compassion also helps us to develop wisdom, especially the wisdom that realizes emptiness, the ultimate nature of the I, the mind, and all other phenomena. This wisdom gradually thins the clouds of obscurations that temporarily obscure the mind until the mind becomes as pure as a clear blue sky flooded with sunlight. This wisdom directly purifies the mind. It liberates the mind from ignorance, anger, attachment, and all the other disturbing thoughts; from the seeds of these disturbing thoughts; and even from their imprints. All obscurations, even the very subtle ones, are completely purified by this wisdom.

With full development of compassion and wisdom, the mind becomes completely free from gross and subtle obscurations. At that time the mind is omniscient, or fully knowing. An omniscient mind is able to directly see all of the past, present, and future; it is able to see the minds of all sentient beings and to know the methods that will free them from their problems and bring them happiness, including the highest happiness of full enlightenment.

At the moment, our knowledge is very limited. Even to know the state of our own health we have to rely upon doctors, machines, blood tests, and so forth. Even in the small area of medical treatment, we cannot understand the problems of other beings, their causes, and the solutions that would suit them. Our understanding is very limited, as is our ability to help others. Our ability to see the future is also very limited. We can't tell what is going to happen next year, next month, next week, or even tomorrow, let alone what will happen next life.

The power of our body, speech, and mind is limited because of our mental obscurations. When we free our mental continuum from all gross and subtle obscurations, however, there will be no limitation of our power. Not only will our mind be able to directly see all the past, present, and future, but it will pervade everywhere. Without any resistance, our mind will be able to go to any object that we think of. When our mind is fully enlightened, which means free from all gross and subtle obscurations, we will be completely free from both the gross mind and the gross body. At that time we will not be limited by anything. This is ultimate freedom.

When the sun rises, it is spontaneously reflected everywhere. It is reflected in every uncovered body of water on the earth—in every ocean, stream, lake, and even dewdrop. In a similar way, since all the gross and subtle obscurations are eliminated, the omniscient mind naturally pervades everywhere. Whenever the positive imprint of a living being ripens, the omniscient mind can immediately manifest in a form that suits the level of mind of that particular being. If they have a pure mind, it manifests in a pure form to guide them; if they have an impure mind, it manifests in an impure form. Because the omniscient mind sees all existence at all times, whenever a positive imprint ripens in the mind of a being, it can manifest at once to help guide that being from happiness to happiness, to the peerless happiness of full enlightenment. This is the meaning of perfect power.

Knowledge and power alone are not enough, however. Compassion is needed. Even though an omniscient mind sees everything, the main source of help for living beings is compassion. For example, even if someone is very knowledgeable, it doesn't necessarily mean that they will use their knowledge to help others. Knowledge and power can even become obstacles to helping others if the person has no compassion; even if they know how to help and have the power to do so, there is a possibility that they might not help you even if you ask them. Someone with compassion, on the other hand, will always help you when you ask them for help.

It is compassion that helps us to perfect our wisdom and our power. Compassion urges us to develop our mind for others. We need to generate compassion and perfect it, developing compassion for all living beings, so that we can increase all other positive qualities. With perfect compassion, knowledge, and power, we can then really help others.

This transformation of the mind is ultimate healing. I may be the one saying all this, but the actual healing has to come from you, from your own mind. The healing comes through your meditation, through your positive thinking, which basically means through your own wisdom and compassion. Meditation on emptiness and on loving kindness and compassion ends the need for healing. Through this ultimate healing, you will never have to experience disease again.

2 *Successful Healing*

‿℈つ

SINCE SOME DISEASES have no cure or are difficult to cure, people are experimenting with various healing methods, especially those involving the power of the mind. Recovery from cancer and other diseases through meditation is now almost as common as recovery through standard medical treatment. As I have already explained, the best way to cure ourselves of disease is through meditation, through using our own mind. We then become our own doctor, our own psychologist, our own guru.

In my experience, those who sincerely try to practice meditation definitely have some result; even if they are not cured, they at least live longer. This is because our health has to do with our mind, with our way of thinking. I would like to tell you a few stories about people who have healed themselves through meditation.

Alice

My very first experience of cancer being healed through meditation was with Alice,[1] a successful fashion consultant. When Alice discovered that she had cancer, she sent a message through a friend of hers, a student at Vajrapani Institute in California, to ask for advice about meditation practice. I suggested that she meditate on Vajrapani, a wrathful aspect of Buddha that is powerful in healing cancer. I simply advised her to visualize Vajrapani above the crown of her head, emitting nectar beams to purify her. I also advised her to buy animals that were in danger of being killed and to then free them in a safe place, thus enabling them to have longer lives.

Alice was in hospital when she received my advice to do these two basic practices. When she explained to her doctors that she wanted to leave the hospital to carry out these instructions, they advised her to stay, but said that if she really believed in the methods, she could leave. She then left the hospital.

Alice saved many animals from restaurants and other places where they were going to be killed. Although I advised her to liberate animals equal in number to her age in years, she actually freed two or three thousand animals, mostly chickens, fish, and worms. She had the chickens taken care of on a farm, and she freed the fish in open water. She also bought one or two thousand worms, because they were cheap and readily available, and released them in the garden outside her home. Liberating worms is a good idea as they go straight under the ground when they are released. Since they have some protection there from predators, they have a chance to live longer. It is less certain that animals freed in forests, lakes, or the ocean will live long because they have natural enemies in those places.

When Alice returned to the hospital for a checkup after doing these practices, the doctors could not find any trace of the cancer. They were very surprised. This was the first time they had seen anyone cured of cancer through meditation. They wanted to write a book about her case as her recovery was a fascinating new phenomenon to them, but she told them that she would write the book herself.

Alice later came to Nepal to thank me in person for my help; she said that I had given her the rest of her life as a present.

Even though her cancer had been cured, I was curious as to whether it would return, so from time to time I would check with Alice about the state of her health. For some years she was fine, but after about five years she contracted a viral illness, and the cancer recurred. She told me that it happened because her life had become very messy and out of control. For a long time she had maintained discipline in her spiritual practice, but at that time she had stopped doing the practices, and her life had become very confused.

Alice's experience shows that healing the mind is much more important than healing the body. Her cancer returned because she stopped doing the practices and stopped disciplining her mind; she did not protect her mind by practicing the meditations. Disciplining your life means disciplining your mind. Her cancer quickly disappeared when she again meditated on Vajrapani, saved the lives of animals, and took the Eight Mahayana Precepts, one-day vows to abstain from eight specific negative actions.[2] When she then went for a checkup, her doctors said that the cancer had completely gone again. After her recovery, she was interviewed on TV many times about her personal experience of curing cancer through meditation.

We can recover from disease through meditation, but if we don't protect our mind, our life will again become confused, and our problem will return. If we simply allow our body to follow self-cherishing, attachment, and other delusions, our mind has no protection, and we simply create the cause for our problems to return.

Alan

I have seen several other cases of people's lives becoming confused and their physical condition deteriorating when they discontinued their meditation practice. This happened to Alan, who died of AIDS many years ago. When he was living at Chenrezig Institute, a meditation center in Australia, Alan was very disciplined and practiced the various meditations that had been recommended to him. I guess there isn't much choice in such an environment—there isn't much else to do.

Alan did meditation sessions every day, focusing mainly on Medicine Buddha but also doing other deity practices. Such deities are very powerful, and their mantras are also very blessed, so meditating on them is very effective. His practice definitely strengthened his mind and inspired him. External appearance reflects the mind, and Alan looked radiant and relaxed because of his healthy mind. When our mind is happy because we are meditating and leading a disciplined life, this is also expressed externally in our body. After all this meditation practice, Alan looked as if he had no sickness at all and was able to help in various activities around the meditation center.

Alan would stay in the meditation center for some weeks or months, but then the thought would come to return to the city with the intention of helping other people with AIDS. The problem was that whenever he went to the city he couldn't continue his practice, his life became confused, and his physical condition deteriorated. He was busy in the city, but I think that his health suffered not so much because he was busy, but because he was unable to continue his meditation practice. He would then return to the meditation center to try to regain his strength and inspiration. Once he had, however, he would again return to the city to help others, and the cycle would repeat itself. He went through this cycle several times.

Wishing to help others is, of course, a precious thought. Though I haven't observed it as frequently in those with cancer, people with AIDS are often especially concerned about helping others with AIDS. Their personal experience of the suffering involved causes them to feel strongly for other people undergoing the same experiences. Despite their own problems, they seem to naturally want to help others. There is no doubt that this is a beautiful attitude, and the mere generation of this blissful thought is a cause for celebration. The point of concern, however, is that the person's own health often deteriorates because they are unable to maintain the necessary level of discipline and practice.

The last time I saw Alan before he died, he was very weak and could walk only with the support of two friends. He sat in a chair and listened as I talked to him for an hour or more about how he could use thought transformation to see his illness as positive and meaningful rather than as negative and hopeless. I told Alan that he was very fortunate to have AIDS because his illness gave him an incredible opportunity to develop his mind in the spiritual path, in the path to enlightenment. His sickness opened the door to enlightenment and to all other happiness. I talked to him about the benefits of having AIDS. For example, having AIDS can be a quick and powerful way to develop compassion, because having the illness makes it easy for you to feel compassion for others who have it, as well as for those with other kinds of suffering. And using sickness to generate loving kindness and compassion brings very powerful purification. I don't remember every single thing that I said to Alan, but the essence was that his illness could bring him to enlightenment more quickly. I wanted him to see his having AIDS as positive; I wanted him to see the incredible benefit he could gain from having his sickness.

We need thought transformation, because healing has very much to do with our way of thinking. We have to learn to look at our disease as something we need, not as something we don't need. We have to look at our disease as an ornament that represents the suffering of all living beings. Rather than seeing disease as an obstacle, we should use it to develop our loving kindness, compassion, and wisdom. Like using poison as medicine, we should use our disease as a path to happiness. By transforming our mind, we can make our experience of disease meaningful not only for ourselves but for every living being. Using our disease to develop the precious human qualities of loving kindness and compassion enables us to bring peace and happiness to every single living being.

Since we have to experience the disease in any case, we might as well make it beneficial by using it to bring happiness, both temporary and ultimate, to ourselves and to all other living beings. This is the skillful way to experience illness.

After we had talked about thought transformation in this way, Alan felt much better. At the beginning he was slumped back in his chair, but after I had talked to him, he was able to lift his body and stand up unaided. He was surprised at the sudden improvement in his health. He waved his arms in the air, saying, "Oh, look! Look! Now I can stand by myself!"

Alan experienced an immediate improvement in his health, but of course it was not enough just to have his mind in that state at that time; he had to continue to keep his mind in that state. This would have helped him to stay healthy longer.

You can see from this how the state of the body has very much to do with the state of the mind. This is particularly true in the case of AIDS. If people with AIDS can make their minds strong and healthy, they can live longer and also have stronger, healthier bodies, even though their illness may not go away.

Lucy

Many years ago when Lucy, an Australian student, told me she had cancer, I suggested that she do several *nyung-näs*. A nyung-nä is a purification practice related to Chenrezig, the Buddha of Compassion. Each two-day retreat involves many prostrations and some fasting; one meal is eaten on the first day, but there is no eating and no drinking on the second day. Fasting itself is nothing special; in fact, it is simply a form of torture. However, this fasting practice is done with a special motivation of compassion, in which you take the responsibility upon yourself to free all living beings from suffering and to bring them happiness. Lucy did a few nyung-nä retreats in Bodhgaya, the holy place in India where Shakyamuni Buddha became enlightened.

I also suggested that she bless water by reciting three malas of the middle-length Chenrezig mantra[3] and then blowing on water. She then drank the blessed water several times a day. She continued the practice of blessing water even after she had returned to Australia from India.

When I later met her at a teaching in London, she was very healthy and looked radiant. I also met her recently in Australia, and she remains healthy. Each time I see Lucy she mentions that it was the practice of the Buddha of Compassion that helped her to recover from her cancer.

Luke

When Luke, a Chinese student from Singapore, went to the hospital for a checkup, he was told by his doctor that he had AIDS. A very devoted person, he then sent a letter to his guru, Rato Rinpoche, a very high lama who lived in Dharamsala in India but has now passed away. He had the good karma to receive meditation instructions from his guru. Even though Rato Rinpoche himself was showing the aspect of sickness at that time, Rinpoche kindly sent Luke a special meditation on loving kindness and compassion called tong-len, or taking and giving.

In the taking and giving meditation, to train in compassion, we take upon ourselves all the suffering, including disease, of other living beings and use it to destroy our own self-cherishing, which is the root of all our suffering. This meditation practice directly opposes our usual wish not to receive disease from other people. To train in loving kindness, we then offer other living beings our own body, possessions, happiness, and positive energy. This practice is not secret or rare. It is a common meditation from the teachings of the graduated path to enlightenment.

After receiving the instruction from Rato Rinpoche, Luke did the meditation for just four days. He then went to the hospital for another checkup, and the doctors could not find any trace of the HIV virus at all. When I asked him how much meditation he had done, I was shocked when he said that he had meditated for only three or four minutes each day. I was expecting him to say that he had meditated for many hours. The point to understand is that his few minutes of meditation were extremely powerful. During his meditation he had no thought of himself, of his own disease. It was as if his own problems did not exist. He thought only of the suffering of others, especially of those with AIDS, and generated intense compassion. Tears streamed down his face every time he did the meditation, not because he was concerned about his own situation but because he felt so much compassion for the other people with AIDS and for those with other problems. He was much more concerned about them than about himself. He had strong devotion, and during the meditations he also felt that his guru was with him and was guiding him.

Recovery from a serious illness takes a long time if you take small doses of weak medicine; but recovery is quick if you take powerful medicine, even if you take only a little and take it only a few times. Luke's quick recovery came about through the power of his own mind, through the power of the compassion he felt even during such short meditations. He quickly recovered because the strong compassion he generated purified much negative karma and obscuration, the cause of his AIDS.

Luke has been back to the hospital many times for checkups, but he remains well. This is my only personal experience of complete recovery from AIDS through meditation.

I asked Luke to give me a copy of the exact meditation he did, so that I could show it to other people as evidence when I tell his story. (See page 143.)

The tong-len meditation is the heart of healing. Once we understand this meditation, we can apply it to every problem in our life and transform all our problems into happiness. It is simply a question of whether or not we do the meditation. While we are doing it, it is impossible for us to feel depressed, because our problem is instantly transformed into happiness.

This special meditation is the best medicine, but its most important benefit is not that it heals disease but that it helps us to develop loving kindness, compassion, and *bodhicitta*, which is the main cause of enlightenment. Bodhicitta is the altruistic wish to achieve enlightenment in order to free all other living beings from their suffering and its causes and lead them to full enlightenment. Doing tong-len meditation can cure disease and transform problems into happiness, but most important it can help us to develop the realization of bodhicitta. The loving, compassionate thought of bodhicitta is the best medicine for the mind and for the body.

Mr. Lee

Mr. Lee, a Chinese businessman from Singapore, has used meditation to heal himself of stomach cancer. When I first met Mr. Lee at a teaching I gave in Singapore at a bowling alley, he was very thin and weak, and he had to lean on his wife to walk. His doctor had given him only a few months to live. In Singapore, Hong Kong, and Taiwan, sick people often attend the teachings and afterward come to see me to discuss their illness and ask for advice.

I advised Mr. Lee to meditate on Tara and especially to recite the *Twenty-one Praises to Tara*. Even though he was a businessman who traveled the world, Mr. Lee devoted himself to praying to Tara and quickly recovered completely from his stomach cancer.

When he later attended the one-month meditation course at Kopan Monastery in Nepal, Mr. Lee told me that he had not only cured his own stomach cancer but also healed his son's severe heart disease. In a dream he saw a wheel turning at his son's heart, and his son then recovered from his illness.

Mr. Lee has also healed many other people, especially those suffering harm from spirits and black magic. He uses blessed water to cure people possessed by spirits. One woman possessed by a spirit refused to come out of her room. When Mr. Lee went into her room, he saw her in the aspect of a spirit with bared fangs. The alterations in her face and voice reminded him of a medium entered by a spirit. As he sprinkled blessed water on her, however, she gradually became peaceful.

As a result of his success in healing, Mr. Lee has become very busy, with many sick people waiting to see him when he returns home from work each day. I have also asked him to lead healing sessions at Amitabha Buddhist Centre, the FPMT center in Singapore, so that all the students there, even though they are healthy, can help to pray for the recovery of those who are ill. There is more healing power when a group of people pray together.

The point to understand is the source of Mr. Lee's healing power. Even though it looks as if Mr. Lee's ability to heal himself and other people comes from an external object, Tara, in fact it comes mainly from his own positive attitude. His power to heal is the result of his strong devotion to Tara and his pure ethics.

The essential point is that we all have the potential to heal. By enhancing the power of our positive actions, we can heal ourselves and others of cancer, AIDS, and other diseases. However, it is far more important to remove the cause of disease, because otherwise any stopping of disease will only be temporary. Even if we heal someone's disease, we have only temporarily cured one problem in their life, and if the cause remains, the problem will return.

Meditation can generally heal disease, but simply meditating on a deity and reciting mantras is not enough. We need to change our attitudes and our actions. If we do not decrease our negative actions, which harm others and ourselves, once we have recovered we will again create the cause of disease. The vital point is to stop creating the cause of disease.

3 Breaking Fixed Concepts

༄

SOME OF OUR COMMON CONCEPTS do not accord with reality. We tend to think that we will die soon only if we have cancer, AIDS, or some other life-threatening disease, and that otherwise we can expect to live for a long time. We associate death with these diseases and as a result feel no personal connection with death. The very first thing we must do is give up our fixed idea that we will die soon only if we have a life-threatening disease and that otherwise we will live for a long time. This is completely wrong. Many people who are completely healthy will die today. Actually, more healthy people die each day than sick people. Every day hundreds of thousands of healthy people, people who do not have cancer or AIDS, die in car accidents, wars, and other situations. The reality is that cancer and AIDS are not the only conditions that result in death; death can happen in so many ways.

Your concept that you won't die soon because you don't have a life-threatening disease is wrong. If you do have cancer or AIDS, your belief that you'll die soon only because you have cancer or AIDS—and that otherwise you would live for a long time—is also wrong. This fixed idea tortures you by making you anxious and afraid. You need to shatter this wrong concept by recalling that even if you did not have cancer or AIDS, many other conditions could lead to your death. Accepting this brings peace to your heart. Having cancer or AIDS becomes less disturbing, less frightening. Once you see that many other conditions could cause your death, you find there is nothing exceptional about having cancer or AIDS. It doesn't bother you as much.

In our daily life we need to be aware of impermanence and death. Death is a natural phenomenon. After birth comes death, just as plants grow and then die. Trying to ignore something that is the reality of our life results in many negative emotions, including depression. Since death is something that we all have to experience, we need to be conscious of it and prepare for it.

We must break the concept of our own permanence, which is cheating us, and open our heart to the idea that not having a life-threatening illness is the same as having one: death can happen to any of us at any time. Whether we are healthy or unhealthy, we can die at any moment. Accepting this immediately brings peace, because freeing ourselves from the concept of our own permanence allows us to relax. This change of attitude is fundamental to healing because it reduces worry and fear. This change of attitude is important for everyone, of course, not just for people with a life-threatening disease.

We have to accept the reality of death, that we could die at any time and that many conditions other than disease could cause us to die soon. We should especially remember that we can die at any time—this month, this week, or even today—when we are overwhelmed by worry and fear or caught up in unfulfilled expectations. Because of our self-cherishing and our attachment to this life, we have many expectations about gaining happiness, wealth, power, and fame, and we experience worry and fear when these expectations are not being fulfilled. Remembering that we could die today, even within the next hour, immediately eliminates all our confusion and expectations. Remembering death enables us to see that none of these things has any meaning. As soon as we remember impermanence and death, we immediately find peace, happiness, and satisfaction because we eliminate all the unnecessary expectations that bring us only problems.

We need to be aware of the actual nature of our life, our body, our family and friends, and our possessions. They are all causative phenomena, which means they are transitory in nature. We need to be aware of their real nature and not cheated by the concept of permanence, which wrongly sees them as permanent and wishes them to be permanent. We then cling to these things and get angry at the thought of our death, when we will have to separate from them. This simply means that we are getting angry with the nature of phenomena, and this refusal to accept the nature of things makes our death even more terrifying.

Death is not the problem; our concept of it is the problem. Death is not frightening from its own side; our mind makes death frightening and difficult to accept. Our attachment clings to the appearances of this life—our body, our family and friends, and our possessions—but this is like being attached to the things that appear in our dreams, because our attachment is based on a hallucinated concept. Although all these things are merely labeled by the mind, we see them as real, independent, inherently existent. We do not see them as dependent on parts, on causes and conditions, or on the mind, label, and base. All these things appear to us to be inherently existent, and we believe this false appearance to be true.

On the basis of this hallucinated concept, we exaggerate the good qualities of our body, our family and friends, and our possessions and then cling to our projections. For example, we cling to a beautiful object as if its beauty existed externally from its own side, and had nothing at all to do with our own mind; and this attachment interferes with our acceptance of the realities of life, with our acceptance of impermanence and death. Attachment to this life does not allow us to accept death and instead makes us see death as frightening and difficult even to think about. There is, however, no real death from its own side, no frightening death from its own side. Death is a creation of our own mind. Therefore, our mind can also make death enjoyable; we can use our mind to transform death into a happy, exciting experience. Because we have the potential to transform death from something frightening into something enjoyable, we can use our death to develop our mind, so that the experience becomes beneficial for us and for all other living beings.

Discovering how our concepts create problems for us, including our fear of death, is an essential and very practical meditation, and I will discuss this in more depth later.

All of us are basically the same. When our stomachs are empty, we feel hungry and want to eat. At one point you may not be hungry but someone else will be; at another time you may be hungry and someone else will not be. It is the same with disease. You might have had a recent medical checkup and believe that you are free of disease, but it is simply a question of time. It certainly doesn't mean that in the past you have never experienced the diseases that other people are experiencing at the moment nor that you will never experience them in the future. You have experienced every possible disease on this earth, as well as every other problem, numberless times in the past. None of this is new. Sometimes you recover, sometimes you don't. However, when you leave behind your physical body, you also leave behind your disease. Your mind continues, but since the mind does not carry physical disease, you do not reincarnate with the disease.

Even though from the Western point of view a certain disease might be regarded as new, from the Buddhist point of view it is not. In the Buddhist explanation of the mind and of the whole experience of samsara, or cyclic existence, each of us has gone through every experience numberless times. It's completely natural, like a sprout coming from a seed. The point to understand is that if we don't do something right now to improve our mind, we will go through these experiences numberless times again.

We should feel happy that we have been able to live as many years as we have, and we should rejoice especially in having the opportunity to develop our mind and to transform all our experiences into happiness. Even if we have what doctors call disease, we still have an incredible opportunity to make spiritual progress, to develop our wisdom, compassion, and other positive qualities. We have the opportunity to use our disease to go from happiness to happiness, to the ultimate happiness of full enlightenment, which means to be released forever from all problems and their causes.

Our mind can bring us to the end of death and rebirth, to the end of all suffering. In the meantime, while we are developing our mind toward this goal, we should make illness and everything else we experience worthwhile not only for ourselves but for every other suffering living being. We should use our disease to free all other beings from suffering and to bring them temporary and, especially, ultimate happiness.

Since we have such an incredible opportunity to develop our mind and to bring happiness to other living beings, it is extremely important not to waste the precious years, months, weeks, days, hours, minutes, or even seconds that we have left. It is our attitude that determines whether our life is meaningful or meaningless. If our attitude is unhealthy, we waste our time and lead a meaningless life. If our attitude is healthy, if our wish is to bring peace and happiness to other living beings, we make our life most meaningful.

4 *The Purpose of Life*

～

THE PURPOSE OF OUR LIFE is not simply to be healthy, live a long life, become wealthy, get educated, or win many friends. None of these is the ultimate goal of life. Whether we are healthy or unhealthy, rich or poor, educated or uneducated, our ultimate goal is to benefit other living beings. The purpose of being alive, of continuing our present association of body and mind, is to benefit others, to use our body, speech, and mind to bring happiness to others.

All our past, present, and future happiness is received through the kindness of other living beings, and our self-cherishing is the source of all our problems, including disease. Instead of renouncing others and cherishing ourselves, we need to cherish others and renounce ourselves. Rather than working only for ourselves, we have to live only to bring happiness to others. This exchanging of self for others is the fundamental psychology that eliminates the very root of all our problems. It is also the source of healing.

Cherishing other living beings immediately heals our mind by curing it of self-cherishing, the major creator of our problems. Cherishing others also heals us by transforming our attachment to just this life, as well as our ignorance, anger, pride, jealousy, and other unhealthy thoughts, which are the cause not just of disease but of all our problems. These unhealthy thoughts give us no peace of mind. As soon as we generate bodhicitta, the healthiest mind, we find satisfaction and peace of mind. We then transform our mind from being the creator of suffering into the creator of happiness

The purpose of our life is not simply to solve our own problems and find happiness for ourselves but to free all living beings from suffering and its causes and to bring them not only temporary but ultimate happiness. And in terms of ultimate happiness, we need to lead others not just to liberation but to the highest happiness of full enlightenment. The purpose of our breathing every day, every hour, every minute, every second, is as vast as infinite space, because other living beings are numberless and the purpose of our life is to bring happiness to every single one of them.

With this goal constantly in our heart, all depression and problems are stopped, and happiness and satisfaction naturally follow. Real happiness in life comes when we dedicate our life to other living beings. Benefiting others brings us real peace of mind and satisfaction. It is the best way to enjoy life. We experience so much depression in our life basically because we have not changed our attitude to one of living for others. Switching our goal from finding happiness for ourselves to bringing happiness to others immediately reduces the problems in our life. This new attitude transforms all the undesirable things in our life into happiness. Rather than seeing problems as disturbing, we can come to see them as beneficial.

Many of our problems have to do with our expectations concerning the purpose of our life. Health, wealth, education, fame, and power are very limited goals. If we have a disease and our goal is nothing more than to be healthy again, this is nothing special. This limited expectation actually creates problems by causing us worry, fear, and depression, because if our goal is simply to be healthy, we become depressed and frightened when we are sick.

Being healthy is not the main consideration. The main consideration is making everything that happens to us beneficial for other living beings. If we are healthy, we should use our good health to benefit others; and if we are unhealthy, we should still use that experience to benefit others.

When we focus on the real goal in life, benefiting others, being healthy becomes incidental. Even having cancer or AIDS no longer disturbs us, because we can experience our illness on behalf of all sentient beings. Whether we are healthy or unhealthy, rich or poor, living or dying, our main goal is to benefit other living beings. This is the essential source of happiness in life. With this attitude, we enjoy everything we experience in our life. With this attitude, we make our life meaningful twenty-four hours a day.

Western culture emphasizes material success as the source of happiness. Happiness is thought to come from being wealthy, living in a luxurious home, owning property, and so forth. Wealth alone, however, cannot bring us happiness and satisfaction. Even if we become a millionaire, with enough money to last for fifty lifetimes, our wealth still cannot bring us peace of mind. And no matter how many friends we have, they too will not bring us peace of mind. Nor is academic success the source of happiness. In fact, it can bring us constant dissatisfaction, anger, pride, and so forth. Besides not bringing us satisfaction and peace of mind, our wealth, friends, and education can actually become problems for us.

If we see health, wealth, education, fame, or power as our goal, we are simply clinging to the happiness and comfort of this life. Even if we achieve our goal, we will never find satisfaction because our attitude is one of attachment to this life. We have been following this attachment throughout beginningless rebirths and have never yet found satisfaction. No matter how long we follow desire, we can never find satisfaction, and we can never really stop our problems. Following desire is not the way to stop dissatisfaction.

If our goal is to benefit others, however, being wealthy becomes worthwhile, because we can use our wealth to help others. With this attitude, the more power and fame we have, the more we can benefit others. With this goal in life, everything we do benefits others, and when we benefit others, there is no doubt that we also benefit ourselves.

Being healthy and not being healthy become the same to us if we use everything we experience to benefit other living beings. If we have problems, we use them to benefit others. This gives meaning to our life. Even if we do not have any problems, we still make our life beneficial for others.

Unhealthy thoughts, such as self-centeredness and attachment, are the source of all our problems, and we need to transform them into healthy thoughts, such as the intention to bring happiness to others. This transformation, or healing, of the mind is the general solution to the problems in our life. For example, it immediately reduces the fear that comes with a diagnosis of cancer or AIDS. With this attitude, no problem can disturb our mind, and we can use any problem to benefit others.

It is extremely important to be clear about our ultimate goal in life.

If recovery from a particular disease is our ultimate goal, we have missed the point, because even if we recover from our illness, nothing will have changed. We will still have the same old attitudes and do the same old actions. We will continue to create the cause of problems because our actions will create negative karma. In other words, we will again create the cause of disease.

Changing our attitude is actually far more important than curing our disease. If our ultimate goal is to benefit others, this positive attitude will prevent us from creating further negative karma, the cause of disease, and enable us to create positive karma, the cause of happiness.

Our wish to use our life to bring happiness to other living beings naturally ensures that we do not harm others. When the happiness of others is our ultimate goal we will enjoy incredible success, because this attitude brings all happiness, including the peerless happiness of enlightenment, and stops all suffering. The real definition of success in life is to be able to benefit others.

Even if we cannot cure our disease through medical treatment or meditation, we will still accomplish the most profound healing if we are able to transform our attitude to life into a pure wish to benefit others. This brings profound healing because it creates the cause of a healthy body and a healthy mind by cutting the wrong concepts that cause disease and creating the positive attitudes that cause happiness.

When we analyze the benefit we receive from the wish to help others, it is not a great failure if we are unable to cure our disease. On the other hand, experiencing a miracle cure does not mean very much if we have not been able to change our attitude to life, because we will simply create the cause of disease again. Being able to stand up after spending twenty years in a wheelchair means little if there is no change in our mental attitude. The real miracle is when someone is able to stop the cause of suffering and create the cause of happiness by learning that their own mind is the source of their suffering and happiness. The real miracle is to transform our mind, because this will take care of us for many lifetimes. Our positive attitude will stop us from creating the cause of problems, thus ensuring our happiness not only in this life but in hundreds, or even thousands, of future lives up to enlightenment. This is the greatest success.

Why We Need to Become Enlightened

To accomplish the vast work of bringing all living beings happiness, especially the peerless happiness of full enlightenment, we need to become enlightened. To guide others perfectly, we need to develop the inner qualities of our mind, especially omniscient wisdom, compassion for all beings, and the perfect power to reveal the methods to help others. These qualities are vital in healing ourselves and all other living beings. Enlightenment means cessation of ignorance, anger, attachment, and all other unhealthy thoughts, as well as cessation of even their subtle imprints, and completion of all realizations. And enlightenment is achieved through mental development. We need to develop both compassion and wisdom. We need to develop not only the wisdom that understands conventional reality, especially the causes of happiness and suffering, but also the wisdom that understands ultimate reality, because it is only then that we can eliminate the ignorance that is the root of all suffering and its causes and achieve liberation.

Normally, before we can teach others about literature, philosophy, science, or handicrafts we ourselves need to be qualified to teach. For example, before doctors can train other people to become doctors, they must have the knowledge and clinical skills needed to diagnose even obscure diseases. In a similar way, we cannot lead all living beings to the state of full enlightenment unless we are perfectly qualified through development of the positive qualities of mind, especially compassion and wisdom. Only then can we really help others.

The purpose of our life is to heal every single living being's body and mind of all suffering and its causes and to bring every one of them to the ultimate, everlasting happiness of full enlightenment. Developing our inner qualities of wisdom and compassion is the way to heal our own mind and body, and through this we will then also be able to heal others.

Making Every Day Meaningful

First thing in the morning when we get up, we should remember the purpose of our life, which is to free all living beings from all suffering and to bring them happiness. We should feel that the happiness of all living beings is our personal responsibility. To be able to help others, we need good health and a long life, and it is for this reason that we wash, eat, drink, and perform our other daily activities. Each time we eat and drink throughout the day, we should remember the purpose of our life. And it is the same when we go to sleep. To fulfill our universal responsibility we need good health and a long life, so this is why we sleep. In this way, we use all our daily activities to serve all living beings.

Before going to work, we should again remember the purpose of our life, that we are responsible for the happiness of all living beings. It is simply a question of changing our attitude from one of going to work because we are seeking our own happiness into one of working for others. Even if we cannot consider the happiness of all living beings, we should at least consider that of our employers, who need people to work for them. By doing our job, we are serving our employers in a practical way by bringing them the profit and happiness that they are seeking. We should at least remember that it is through our efforts that they are fulfilling their wishes. We are offering our employers all the profit, comfort, and happiness they receive through our work.

While we are working, we should think of the purpose of our life in relation to all the people around us, and even the animals. We are there to serve everyone, even strangers; we exist for the sake of all living beings. Remembering the purpose of our life immediately brings us happiness. As soon as we change our attitude, we find peace and contentment. We suddenly find that we are enjoying our life and our work.

When we think only of ourselves, we become tense, and prolonged tension is stressful. We become depressed about our problems, and think over and over again, "I have this problem, I have that problem. When will I be happy?" The physical expression of our self-concern is that our face looks tense and unhappy.

Our tension is released, however, as soon as we stop thinking about ourselves and become concerned about others. Like reciting a mantra, we should think over and over again, "I am here to serve others, I am here to serve others, I am here to serve others," or "I am here to bring happiness to others, I am here to bring happiness to others, I am here to bring happiness to others." These powerful mantras will make us happy and enable us to see our life as worthwhile. Sit somewhere and recite these phrases for ten minutes, or even an hour. This excellent meditation will immediately release the tension in our heart and bring happiness into our life.

We lock ourselves into a prison of self-cherishing, but cherishing others is the key that releases us. We can immediately feel the freedom. Our mind is no longer sharp and hurtful like a thornbush or rough and hard like a rock, but smooth and blissful like cream. Our heart feels open and spacious, and we immediately experience peace and happiness. This is the result of cherishing other living beings.

With this attitude all the activities during our eight hours of work become positive, the cause of happiness, because our motivation for doing them is unstained by self-cherishing. With this positive attitude, all our everyday activities—working, walking, sitting, eating, sleeping—become the cause of success and happiness, and nothing we do becomes the cause of suffering. Our actions also become causes of the highest happiness of full enlightenment.

From when we get up in the morning until we go to sleep at night, we should do everything for others. Through living our life for others we become happy, and our happiness will not be just some temporary excitement but deep peace in our heart. The best way to enjoy life is to freely dedicate ourselves to others—not because someone forces us but because of the freedom our loving kindness, compassion, and wisdom give us. There is suddenly happiness and meaning in our life. Life is worth living. We have incredible freedom to use our own mind to stop problems and to achieve happiness. We make everything that happens to us meaningful, and we do not waste our precious human life. Otherwise, even if we stay healthy for thousands of years, we have had an empty, meaningless life.

Having the happiness of others as our ultimate goal makes a huge difference, because it no longer matters to us whether we are healthy or unhealthy. Even if we have cancer, since being healthy is not our main goal, we are simply concerned about using our experience of cancer to bring happiness to others. This makes a huge difference psychologically and brings us much happiness. Sacrificing ourselves to give something to others rather than constantly taking from them and using them for our own happiness gives great meaning to our life. This new way of thinking transforms our life.

Happy or miserable, healthy or unhealthy, we should use whatever we are experiencing to benefit other living beings. Even if we are dying, we should make our experience of death beneficial for all living beings.

5 The Nature of Compassion

⟋⟍

COMPASSION IS THE SOURCE of happiness in life. It is the essential means of ensuring our own happiness and the happiness of society. Without loving kindness and compassion, there is no peace or happiness in the family, the society, the country, or the world. Compassion is also the source of a healthy mind and a healthy body. Generating compassion is the most powerful way to heal ourselves and other living beings.

Compassion is essential because it is the cause of happiness, success, satisfaction, and enjoyment in life. Practicing compassion means not harming others but only helping them, and helping others is the cause of our own success. If we are loving and compassionate, we make our life worthwhile by bringing happiness to others. Seeing that we are making others happy then makes us happy. His Holiness the Dalai Lama often says that if we are going to cherish ourselves, we should do it in an intelligent way, and the intelligent way to cherish ourselves is to cherish other sentient beings. In this way, even if we don't expect anything for ourselves, our own success is the natural result of bringing happiness and success to others.

Compassion makes everyone our friend. If we have loving kindness and compassion, we see everyone as our friend; we feel close to everyone, even if they are physically distant from us. If we don't have loving kindness and compassion, we don't feel close to anyone, even if they are in the same room as us. If we lack compassion, we have difficulty finding friends, and when we do manage to find some, sooner or later they become our enemies. Even the members of our own family can become our enemies.

Without compassion, life is miserable. People who are only concerned about themselves and whose hearts are empty of affection and compassion for others have no real peace or happiness. Unless we have compassion, no matter how much wealth, education, or power or how many friends we have, we have no peace or happiness, and we cannot enjoy life. Lack of affection and compassion for others brings loneliness, depression, and many other problems. When asked about depression in an interview, His Holiness the Dalai Lama replied that depression basically comes from not having affection for others. This makes sense because self-concern brings worry and fear.

If we don't have compassion, no matter how many friends or how much wealth we have, we have no real peace or satisfaction in our life. Even if we become the richest person in the world, our wealth won't bring us any satisfaction if we lack the precious human qualities of loving kindness and compassion. We won't be able to enjoy life, and our heart will be like a hot, barren desert. If we lack these precious qualities and our attitude to life is selfish, our wealth actually brings us a lot of worry and fear and unfulfilled expectations. This is especially true if we succeed in obtaining all the material wealth and comfort we want, because we can never find satisfaction. We will also be afraid that one of our competitors will become richer than us. Our wealth can actually create problems in our life, bringing us enemies and even endangering our life.

Self-cherishing and lack of loving kindness and compassion make the lives of wealthy people unhappy and unsatisfying. They can be unhappier than a beggar who has to beg for his food each day, because even though they have every possible material comfort, they still cannot find satisfaction. This exacerbates their mental problems, and they experience much depression and dissatisfaction in their lives.

On the other hand, because they are warmhearted and compassionate, many people who live in primitive conditions are happy and contented. Take the villagers who live in Solu Khumbu, the Himalayan region where I was born. Compared to wealthy people in the West, these villagers have nothing; they live in bare stone houses and possess one or two changes of clothes, a few pots, and just enough food to survive. However, even though they live very simply and primitively, these villagers are often very happy and peaceful because of their warm hearts.

Also, no matter how much education and intellectual knowledge we have, we will have no peace in our heart if we lack loving kindness and compassion. Even if we spend our whole life studying, our education will only cause us problems if we are motivated simply by self-concern. Instead of bringing us happiness and satisfaction, our education will cause pride, anger, and other unhealthy thoughts to arise. We will not enjoy life or see any meaning in it. If we don't have compassion, there is a danger that we will use our education and intelligence to harm others, even to destroy ourselves and the world. Take atomic power, for example, which can be used destructively if there is no motivation of compassion. But with compassion, we will use our education to bring happiness to others, which is the best way to bring happiness to ourselves.

Why Others Need Our Compassion

Our compassion is the source of peace and happiness in our own life and in the lives of others. It is the source of happiness for every other living being, starting with the people and animals around us.

We can understand this by considering how our happiness depends upon the people, and even the animals, around us in our daily life. We are affected by how other people think of us and behave toward us. It can make us happy or depressed. We are delighted when someone, even a stranger, smiles at us affectionately or treats us kindly. On the other hand, we are not happy when someone frowns at us or treats us unkindly. The sight of someone walking along the street single-mindedly focused on themselves and their problems depresses us. Their mind is busy and their whole body is tense.

In the same way, the way we think and behave affects the people and even the animals around us. Others feel relaxed around us when they sense that we have no intention to harm them. Even mice can sense kindness. At first they are hesitant about whether or not to trust you, but once they discover that you have no wish to harm them, they become comfortable and relaxed around you. You can even see a change in their faces, which become soft and relaxed.

I have a lot of karma with mice. Even if there were previously no mice in a place, they usually appear soon after I arrive. When I was doing a retreat in Adelaide, Australia, several mice would appear late at night. They would climb up next to me on the bed and then duck behind one of the pillows, where I think they had made a nest in the warmth. One night one of the mice tried many times to climb up onto the table in front of me, and he managed it only once. The mouse didn't climb up because I am kind or good-hearted, of course, but he must have sensed that I had no intention of disturbing him. This small mouse sat there, looking up into my face, his face very soft and happy-looking. After some time he went away.

Although the mouse wasn't able to climb up onto the altar in my retreat room, he could climb onto another altar in the next room. He climbed up there a few times to drink water from the offerings bowls and nibble at the food offerings. I especially filled a large bowl with nuts and *tsampa* and put it where the mouse could climb up, but he didn't actually eat much of the food—perhaps I didn't have enough merit. He would eat just a little and then run away.

One night a whole stack of large plaster *tsa-tsas* on the altar collapsed backward. I think the mouse must have been caught in between a couple of the tsa-tsas when they fell. He took a little while to come out, and when he did, he was very frightened and distressed. He looked like someone who had been badly beaten. When I made a small sound, he jumped straight down from the altar and ran away. From that time, he never went back on the altar.

The point I am trying to make is that the happiness of the people and animals around us depends on us, on how we think of them and act toward them. Each one of us is responsible for the happiness not only of everyone around us in our daily life but of all the numberless other living beings; and that happiness depends on our mind, on our compassion. It is completely in our own hands. Whether or not we offer peace and happiness to others depends on what we do with our mind. We hold the full responsibility.

If we do not practice compassion, out of our self-cherishing thought and other delusions we will harm numberless other living beings either directly or indirectly, and from life to life. Since the happiness and even the lives of others depend on us, we can endanger other living beings. By not having compassion, one person can use their power and influence to endanger even the whole world.

It has happened many times in the history of the world, in the past and even recently, that millions of people—and even more animals and insects—have been killed because one person in power did not practice compassion. If that one powerful person had been compassionate, all those millions of people would not have been tortured and killed, nor would an uncountable number of animals and insects have suffered. In a war or an atomic explosion, only the number of people killed are counted; the dead animals and insects are ignored. Even if that one powerful person had done nothing special to help others but had simply practiced compassion and stopped harming others, all those numberless beings would have received much happiness and peace. Instead they received terrible harm, and even after many years they still harbor the hurt in their hearts.

On the other hand, because of their compassion, individuals such as His Holiness the Dalai Lama and Mahatma Gandhi have been major sources of peace in the world. His Holiness's books and public talks have brought peace to millions of people by teaching them about compassion and wisdom. If the people in power have compassion, they can use their power to bring happiness to many millions of people; if they lack compassion, however, they can use their power to endanger the world.

When I was traveling in Amdo during my second visit to Tibet, a two-month pilgrimage with more than seventy students from various countries, the thought occurred to me that the essential mistake in China was that millions of people, whether freely or through being forced, had followed Mao Zedong's philosophy without really analyzing it. This mistake of blindly believing in one person's ideas resulted in the suffering of millions of people. Not only did Mao Zedong himself not practice any religion, but he rejected all religions and did not allow anyone else to practice them. Not allowing other people this freedom was his huge mistake.

Someone with compassion will not be a danger to others no matter how many weapons they have. Someone without compassion is dangerous to others even if they have no weapons; they will always find ways to harm others with their body, speech, or mind.

We have just seen how one powerful person may hold great responsibility for the lives of many living beings; the peace and happiness of many millions of beings can depend on this one person's mind and level of compassion. It is exactly the same with each of us. Each one of us is responsible for the happiness of every other living being, whether or not we can see them. We are responsible for the happiness of every human, every animal, every tiny insect, every spirit. Every living being is the same in wanting happiness and not wanting suffering, and we are responsible for the happiness of every living being, not just of our friends but also of strangers and our enemies.

When we practice compassion, the very first thing we do is stop harming other living beings, starting with the people and animals around us. This means that others receive peace from us. Absence of harm is peace. For example, if we had a bad headache yesterday and the headache is not so bad today, even though it hasn't completely disappeared, we tell other people, "Oh, I feel better today!" We are happy because of the absence of the additional pain we had yesterday, and because of the absence of that pain we call ourselves "better."

Or take the example of someone who is threatening to shoot us. If, by reasoning with the person, we can get them to change their mind, they bring us peace and happiness simply by deciding not to shoot us. By changing their mind, they free us from fear and the danger of being killed, and they actually prolong our life. In reality, the person helps us by refraining from harming us. It is similar when we practice compassion. We are helping others when we refrain from harming them. The absence of our harm means that numberless other living beings receive peace from us.

On top of this, when we are compassionate, we feel generous and sympathetic toward others, so we also try to help them. When we feel strong compassion for a being, whether a person or an animal, not only do we not harm them but we do whatever we can to help them. This is our normal response to people who are very sick or poor, even strangers, and to wounded animals. According to our understanding of the situation and our capacity, we try to help them. Not harming others and, on top of this, benefiting them encapsulate the entire philosophy of Buddhism.

Whether others receive help or harm from us depends upon whether or not we are compassionate. It is clear that if we are compassionate, we will help others or, if we cannot help them, at the very least we will not harm them. The more compassion we have, the more we will dedicate our lives to helping others. All other living beings will then receive peace and happiness from us, either directly or indirectly. Whether others receive this benefit from us depends on whether or not we practice compassion. This is how each of us is responsible for the peace and happiness of each and every living being. The happiness of all living beings depends on our own mind, on whether or not we generate compassion.

If we do not generate compassion but live with a self-centered mind, then anger, attachment, jealousy, and other delusions will arise quickly and strongly. These negative thoughts will constantly lead us to harm other living beings, either directly or indirectly, and from life to life. Lack of compassion will bring so much unhappiness and so many problems into our lives and those of others.

You Are Just One Person

It doesn't matter whether other people show compassion for you. Even if everyone dislikes you and, on top of that, verbally abuses or physically harms you, it is nothing to be depressed about because you are just one person. It is nothing to be alarmed about because just one living being is involved, and that being is only you. Even if you are born in hell, it is nothing to be depressed about because you are just one living being. And even if you achieve liberation, it is nothing to be excited about because you are just one person.

However, if you, this one living being, do not practice compassion, there's a danger that you could harm all living beings, directly or indirectly, and from life to life. As I have already pointed out, even in this life there is a possibility that you could harm millions of people. For this reason, generating compassion should be your prime concern; it should be the first thing you think about and try to practice. Numberless living beings want you to feel compassion for them, to help them and not to harm them. Even though you also want everyone to love you and to help you, because you are just one person you are completely insignificant when compared to the numberless others whose happiness depends upon your compassion.

It is more important for you to show compassion for others, who are numberless, than for others to show compassion for you, just one person. And, whether or not others behave compassionately toward you, you should initiate the practice of compassion for the reason I have already mentioned: if you generate compassion, you benefit numberless other beings; and if you don't generate compassion, you endanger numberless other beings. For this reason, even if others are not practicing compassion, you should still do so.

It is common for us to think, "Why should I practice compassion if other people don't?" but this argument comes from self-cherishing rather than from wisdom. This argument has not been thought through, because it does not take into account even our own happiness and peace of mind. Our self-concern argues this way in the hope of profit, but in reality it incurs only loss, because its interpretation of profit is false. Self-cherishing defines profit as causing others to lose and taking the victory for ourselves; others have to lose for us to be happy. Dharma wisdom, on the other hand, understands the actual evolution of happiness and suffering, that they both come from our own mind. Positive attitudes and actions bring happiness and negative ones bring suffering. This wisdom also knows that defeating others and taking the victory for ourselves is actually a loss, because in reality we are creating the cause to experience loss ourselves in this life and in many thousands of other lifetimes.

Whether or not we realize it, by harming others we create problems for ourselves. Our happiness and our problems have a natural evolution, just as a medicinal plant grows from the seed of a medicinal plant and a poisonous plant grows from the seed of a poisonous plant. The seed of a medicinal plant cannot bring forth a poisonous plant, nor can the seed of a poisonous plant bring forth a medicinal plant. Harming others creates the causes of problems that will be experienced by us, and not harming others creates the causes of happiness that will also be experienced by us.

Self-cherishing is solely concerned with our own immediate happiness, but the methods it uses to secure this happiness are not skillful. Defeating others and taking the victory for ourselves is actually childish because its result is contradictory to its aim. We mean to take medicine, but in reality we take poison.

When we act with Dharma wisdom, we offer the victory to others and take the loss upon ourselves. The loss is only apparent, however; in fact we profit immensely from this one positive action, since for many thousands of lifetimes we are able to enjoy victory, or success. This is why we ourselves should practice compassion, regardless of whether others do.

Why It Is Possible to Generate Compassion

We all have some compassion. We might not feel compassion for all living beings, but we do for at least some of them. There are other people who have much more compassion than we do. There are even people in the world who feel compassion for a vast number of suffering beings. And, following this same line of reasoning, there are beings whose compassion is fully developed and embraces every suffering living being.

The main thing that makes it possible for us to generate compassion is the nature of the mind itself. As I explained earlier, the very nature of our mind is pure; it is not one, or mixed, with the faults of the mind. Since the very nature of the mind is not one with disturbing thoughts and obscurations, some people actually call this nature of the mind "Buddha" and regard it as fully enlightened.

The pure, clear light nature of the mind, called Buddha-nature, gives us the potential to develop our mind in any way we wish; it gives us the possibility to generate compassion and to develop it. We can train our mind and develop perfect compassion for all living beings.

Compassion is not an independent phenomenon. It doesn't exist from its own side; it is not inherently existent. Our mind labels "compassion" on the peaceful, positive thought that wishes other beings to be free from suffering. In other words, compassion is something that we create with our own mind. Compassion is a dependent arising; it arises in dependence upon causes and conditions. For example, compassion arises in dependence upon the condition of our seeing the suffering of another being, whether a starving Ethiopian child or a wounded animal, and wishing that being to be free from their suffering. It is the very nature of the mind that makes it possible for us to generate and develop compassion. The mind itself is also a dependent arising; it exists in dependence upon causes and conditions.

As we know from our own experience, when we feel even a little compassion for someone, we wish that person to be free from problems and we do what we can to help. As our compassion becomes stronger, we assume the responsibility to free more and more living beings from suffering. When we have perfected the development of compassion, we dedicate our life to all living beings; we live solely to free each of them from their suffering and its causes and to bring them happiness. At that time we continuously accumulate merit, the cause of happiness and success, as infinite as space.

How to Generate Compassion

We can now see that generating compassion is of the utmost importance for us and especially for all other living beings. We need to develop compassion for every living being in order to free them from all suffering and its causes and lead them not only to temporary happiness but to the ultimate happiness of full enlightenment. But compassion doesn't drop miraculously from the sky or come simply by saying over and over, "I need compassion, I need compassion, I need compassion." Just as we study various subjects and progress through different classes in school, we have to develop compassion step by step, beginning with the preliminary meditations.[1] Otherwise, our compassion will not be stable. We might feel compassion for a friend or a wounded animal for a few days, but then it will disappear.

We need to develop perfect compassion, which means feeling for every living being the same compassion that a mother feels when her one beloved child is in danger. If her child falls into a fire, a mother's only thought is to rescue it. This thought arises spontaneously and intensely, and she immediately drops whatever she is doing to rush to rescue her child. When we have developed perfect compassion, we feel exactly like this about the suffering of every living being, whether friend, enemy, or stranger.

With great compassion, we do not simply wish every living being to be free from all suffering, but we wish to free them from this suffering ourselves. It is called *great* compassion because we take upon ourselves the responsibility for freeing them. When we have great compassion, we bring peace and happiness not only to ourselves but to every living being. It makes our life profoundly meaningful. We need to develop this compassion for all living beings, every single one of whom wants happiness and does not want suffering. We need to feel compassion not just for those who are sick or poor but even for healthy, wealthy people.

To generate compassion for every living being, we need extensive knowledge of all the different types of problems that living beings experience. Every problem, whether individual, national, or global, is a reason for us to generate compassion. Each person and animal that we see suffering, even if it is only on TV, is a reason for us to generate compassion. Every suffering being is begging us to generate compassion. We see animals in incredible suffering, overwhelmed by fear, anger, desire, and ignorance. They attack each other, not understanding that by harming others they are creating the cause to receive harm later themselves.

Many animals, especially birds, cannot relax even for a moment because they live in constant fear. When they find food, they cannot eat it in a relaxed manner because they have to listen constantly for every sound and watch every direction. Their lives are so uncertain. All of them have enemies that could attack and kill them. Whether they are flying in the air or sitting on the ground, they are constantly afraid. We, on the other hand, take our safety for granted and generally lead comfortable, relaxed lives. When we go out of our house, we trust that the people around us have no intention of harming or killing us. In reality, however, danger is just a second away. It's simply a question of one person changing their attitude. If one person becomes violent, our life is immediately in danger. We can see again how dependent we are on others.

The Three Types of Suffering

To feel compassion fully for other living beings we have to be able to see the three types of suffering that they experience: suffering of suffering, suffering of change, and pervasive compounding suffering. And to understand the suffering of others we first have to understand our own suffering. We have to recognize clearly that we ourselves are experiencing these three types of suffering and generate the determination to free ourselves from not only the suffering of suffering, but also the suffering of change and pervasive compounding suffering.

Otherwise, if we do not recognize all our own suffering, we will not be able to see all the suffering of others. Our understanding of suffering will be limited, and any compassion we generate will be limited. We will feel compassion only for those whose suffering we are familiar with. For example, we might think of suffering in terms of just one disease.

If our understanding of suffering is limited, our idea of liberation will also be limited. If we understand the three levels of suffering, however, we will be able to generate compassion more deeply and extensively, because our compassion will then encompass all living beings. Otherwise, our compassion will be limited to only those who are in pain.

The *suffering of suffering* is easy to recognize and refers to birth, old age, sickness, death, and all the other mental and physical problems. Disease, like a single atom compared to all the atoms of the earth, is just one of the thousands of problems in the category of the suffering of suffering.

The second type of suffering, the *suffering of change,* is more subtle and more difficult to recognize. It can only be understood through analytical reasoning. The suffering of change refers to the temporary pleasures we experience; these pleasures do not last, and when we try to make them last, they change into the suffering of suffering.

In relation to the temporary pleasures that we experience, we label "pleasure" on a feeling that is actually suffering. Because the suffering nature of the feeling is not noticeable to us as gross suffering, we label it "pleasure," and it then appears to us to be pleasure. The underlying suffering becomes noticeable as the pleasure decreases, however. Continuing the action—whether it is eating, walking, sitting, or sleeping— merely intensifies the discomfort. The suffering becomes more noticeable, and we experience less of what we had labeled "pleasure." There is no pleasure from its own side; there is simply what we label "pleasure." We label "pleasure" on a base that is not pure pleasure but is actually unrecognized suffering.

For example, if we have less pain today than we had yesterday, we say that we feel better, but it doesn't mean that we have no pain at all. There is just less pain. We label "happiness" on the lessening of any problem that we have, but the basis of our labeling is not the complete absence of the problem. We still have a problem, but it is smaller. It is the same with the temporary pleasures of samsara.

When we are sitting, the longer we sit, the more uncomfortable and tired we become. The discomfort of sitting is soon noticeable, and when it becomes unbearable, we stand up. At that time the unbearable discomfort of sitting ceases because the action that exacerbates that discomfort, sitting, has ceased. But as soon as we stand up, the action of standing immediately starts to aggravate the discomfort of standing. Even though the discomfort of standing starts at once, it is so small that we don't notice it; but as we continue to stand, the discomfort of standing gradually increases. After some time, when the discomfort of standing becomes gross, we become aware of it. At that time it becomes the suffering of suffering. We label "pleasure" on the feelings of discomfort that are so small that we do not recognize them as discomfort, and we continue to label them "pleasure" until the discomfort becomes noticeable.

When a previous gross feeling of suffering stops, we say that we are experiencing pleasure, but this is not pure, or ultimate, happiness. Just as we say that we feel better when we feel less pain, we label "pleasure" on a base that is actually suffering. It appears to be pleasure because we label it pleasure, but in fact it is not pure happiness. We can label something pure happiness only if it is free from all three types of suffering: not only free from the suffering of suffering and the suffering of change, but also free from pervasive compounding suffering.

The third form of suffering, *pervasive compounding suffering,* is the most subtle one and the most important to understand. It is the fundamental suffering, because without it we would not experience the suffering of suffering and the suffering of change. We need to have a strong determination to be free from this suffering.

What is pervasive compounding suffering? It is this samsara, this association of body and mind, which is under the control of karma and disturbing thoughts and is contaminated by the seeds of disturbing thoughts. Beings in all three realms—the desire, form, and formless realms—all experience this third type of suffering. Hell beings, hungry ghosts, animals, human beings, and the worldly gods that live in the desire realm experience all three types of suffering. Worldly gods in the form realm do not experience the suffering of suffering, though they do experience the other two kinds of suffering. Gods in the formless realm, who have consciousness but no substantial body, do not experience the suffering of suffering or the suffering of change; they do, however, experience pervasive compounding suffering, because they are still under the control of karma and delusions.

Because the seeds of disturbing thoughts contaminate our consciousness, we generate disturbing thoughts when we meet ugly, beautiful, or indifferent objects. These disturbing thoughts then motivate karma, which leaves an imprint on our consciousness, and this imprint later becomes the cause of our future-life samsara, our future-life association of body and mind, which again is not free from suffering.

Every action motivated by a disturbing thought leaves a negative imprint on our consciousness; then, like a sprout coming from a seed, that imprint manifests future aggregates of the same type, which means in the nature of suffering. Just as the original corn plant does not return but a similar corn plant grows from its seed, aggregates of a similar type arise from the imprint, in the sense that the new aggregates are also not free from suffering. Even though our body does not continue to the next life, our consciousness does migrate; it becomes associated with another body to become the future-life aggregates, or samsara. Our future-life aggregates are a continuation of our present aggregates, which is why samsara is said to be a cycle.

This third suffering is called "pervasive" because the association of body and mind is under the control of and pervaded by karma and disturbing thoughts, and "compounding" because the imprint produces aggregates of a similar type. Our present aggregates create future aggregates of a similar type, which again experience the three types of suffering. In other words, these aggregates compound another set of aggregates, the future-life aggregates, which are also suffering in nature, by compounding the cause, the imprint. This is why these aggregates are called pervasive compounding suffering.

If we remove the seeds of disturbing thoughts from our mental continuum, disturbing thoughts cannot arise, and without them there is nothing to produce the negative actions that leave imprints on our mind and create our future samsara—just as nothing can grow in a field that has no seeds planted in it. Without the cause, there is no result. This is how it is possible to be completely free from suffering. By transforming our mind through meditation, we can purify ourselves of the seeds of disturbing thoughts and free ourselves completely from the cause of suffering and, therefore, from suffering itself. We are then freed forever from rebirth and death and all the problems in between. Once we have purified our mind of the seeds of delusions, we are freed forever from suffering. This is how we can free ourselves completely from this third, fundamental suffering.

When we free ourselves from the aggregates—or, in other words, from pervasive compounding suffering—we also free ourselves from the suffering of suffering and the suffering of change. Ultimate liberation is total freedom from all three types of suffering. At that time we no longer have to reincarnate in such suffering aggregates. The happiness of liberation is everlasting because it is impossible for us to ever experience suffering again. This is ultimate liberation.

6 The Healing Power of Compassion

ぷ

ALOVING, COMPASSIONATE PERSON heals others simply by existing. Wherever they are, compassionate people are healing, because they do everything they can to help others with their body, speech, and mind. Merely being near a compassionate person heals us because it brings us peace and happiness.

Simply seeing the face of a kind, warmhearted person makes us feel happy. Even if we are worried about some problem, we become happy and peaceful when we see such a person. We want to talk to them and help them. We are happy to be visited by someone who is compassionate and warmhearted, because such a person brings joy to everyone. When they come into a room, we are happy. We are delighted even to hear their name.

My mother, who has now passed away, was a very compassionate person. Everybody liked and respected her, not because she was my mother, but because she was always concerned about others. Whenever I saw her and we had time to talk, she always talked about the problems of other people. I can hardly remember her ever bringing up her own problems. When she was blinded by cataracts, she did once ask me to recite mantras and blow on her eyes, but normally she would never discuss her own needs.

My mother would never let anyone leave her house empty-handed. She gave to people all day long. When we were driving along a road, she would become upset about the people who were walking along barefoot; she would be very concerned that they had no shoes.

My mother was once invited to Tushita Retreat Centre in Dharamsala, India, where every morning the cooks made pancakes for breakfast.

She would eat a little of her pancake then fold up the rest and put it in her pocket. Every day she would walk down from Tushita, which is high up on a mountain, to circumambulate the palace where His Holiness the Dalai Lama lives and also the nearby temple, and every day she would share her pancake among the many lepers who begged on the circumambulation path.

In many areas of the Himalayas in Nepal people have to travel on foot because there are no roads, and families stop along the way to make fires and cook their food. Whenever my mother went on pilgrimage with the rest of her family, after the food was cooked, she would give it away to other people. Because there would then be nothing left for the family, they would have to cook all over again.

At Kopan Monastery, when the young monks brought food to her, she would always say, "I don't deserve to be served by them—my stomach is empty." She didn't mean that her stomach was empty literally, but that her heart was empty of realizations. She was always concerned about other people and their difficulties, and not just about the people in her family. If anybody helped her or worked around her, she would be very concerned that they had to work so hard for her.

Because my mother was so compassionate, everyone was happy to meet her and talk to her. Whenever we see someone who seems generous and warmhearted, even if we don't know them, we feel like sitting down and talking to them. This is our natural response to compassionate people, to those who always put others before themselves.

There are many stories in the Buddhist scriptures of *bodhisattvas,* or saints, who sacrificed themselves for the happiness of others. *Bodhisattva,* a Sanskrit term, could be translated as "the hero of enlightenment." Bodhisattvas, holy beings who are not yet fully enlightened, have no thought of seeking their own happiness but think solely of cherishing and working for other living beings with their body, speech, and mind. They do not simply wish others to be happy, but take the full responsibility upon themselves alone for freeing all beings from suffering and for bringing them happiness. They vow to do this no matter how difficult the work is or how long it takes. Out of their great compassion, they take the responsibility for accomplishing this work not only upon themselves but upon themselves *alone.* It is the totally dedicated thought of an extremely brave heart. Any being with this kind of courage is the real hero.

Shakyamuni Buddha, before he became enlightened, was a bodhisattva in many hundreds of lifetimes during three countless great eons. Not only Buddhist saints have had this pure mind, however, but also many Christian ones, such as St. Francis of Assisi, the Italian saint who lived at the same time as Milarepa. Whether Christian, Hindu, Buddhist, or a follower of some other religion, anyone who has no thought of their own happiness but only the thought to free all other beings from suffering and bring them happiness is a saint, a holy being. Even an animal is a holy being if it has this attitude.

During his time as a bodhisattva, Shakyamuni Buddha sacrificed his holy body to other living beings hundreds of times. In hundreds of lifetimes Buddha gave his eyes to blind people and his limbs to those who wanted limbs. For example, he once gave his holy body to feed a family of tigers who were starving to death. Buddha prayed that the tigers, through the connection they made by eating his body, would be born as human beings in their future lives and become his disciples. He also prayed that he would reveal the path to enlightenment to them. Because of their connection to Buddha, the tigers were later born as human beings, heard teachings directly from Buddha, and then actualized the path to enlightenment.

In another lifetime as a bodhisattva, Buddha gave his blood to five *rakshas,* blood-drinking spirits, and prayed to be able to reveal the path to enlightenment to them in their future lives. When later born as human beings, the five rakshas became Buddha's first disciples. When he gave teachings for the first time, at Sarnath in India, Buddha taught them the Four Noble Truths.

In another of Shakyamuni Buddha's past lives, he and another hell being were pulling a carriage, in which were seated karmic guardians,[1] on the red-hot iron ground of one of the hot hells. He felt so much compassion for the suffering of the other hell being that he sacrificed himself and pulled the carriage by himself. He also prayed that he could substitute himself for all the sentient beings who had the karma to experience such suffering.

When he sacrificed himself to free the other hell being from suffering, the karmic guardians told him he was crazy and hammered him on the head. He was immediately liberated from the hell realm, and his consciousness was transferred to the pure realm of Tushita. It is said in the teachings that this was the first time Buddha generated great compassion.

In yet another of his past lives as a bodhisattva, Shakyamuni Buddha was the captain of a ship with five hundred traders aboard. The traders were crossing the ocean in pursuit of jewels. Through his clairvoyance, the bodhisattva captain discovered that one person on board was planning to kill all the other passengers. The captain then felt unbearable compassion for the would-be murderer and thought, "I don't care if I am born in hell because of it—I have to kill him." Completely renouncing himself, he was willing to be born in hell in order to protect the person from creating the heavy negative karma of killing all the other traders. With unbearable compassion, the bodhisattva captain then killed him.

Generally speaking, the action of killing is regarded as negative, and the captain's action should have resulted in his rebirth in hell. However, because his action was done out of great compassion, instead of causing the captain to be reborn in hell, it brought great purification and shortened his stay in samsara by one hundred thousand eons. In other words, because he completely sacrificed himself for that other person's happiness, his action of killing brought him closer to enlightenment.

There is also a story about the novice monk Tsembulwa, a disciple of the great yogi Krishnacharya, who had very high realizations. Krishnacharya, was on his way to Oddiyana, one of the twenty-four holy places of Vajrayogini, to perform a special tantric practice that is done just before the achievement of enlightenment. He came to a river, beside which was a woman whose whole body was disfigured by leprosy. She looked very ugly, with her skin blackened and oozing pus. When the leper asked Krishnacharya to carry her across the river, he refused.

When Tsembulwa later reached the same spot, the leper also asked him to carry her across the river. Although, as a monk, Tsembulwa would normally not touch a woman, he felt such unbearable compassion for the leper that without any hesitation he sacrificed himself, even taking the chance of contracting leprosy himself, and lifted the woman onto his back. In the middle of the river, however, the leper suddenly transformed into Vajravarahi, an aspect of Vajrayogini. Because of Tsembulwa's unbearable compassion and complete self-sacrifice in helping the leper, Vajravarahi took him in his human form to the pure land of Vajrayogini, where he had the opportunity to hear teachings and complete the path to enlightenment.

The point is that the leper was always Vajravarahi, but Tsembulwa saw her as a leper because of his karmic obscurations. It was only after he generated compassion and sacrificed himself to help her that he was able to see her as an enlightened being. During the moments he generated unbearable compassion for the leper, he completely purified the negative karma that caused him to see her as a leper and blocked his seeing her as an enlightened being.

A similar thing happened to Asanga, a great pandit and a lineage lama of the graduated path to enlightenment. Although Asanga meditated in a hermitage for twelve years in order to actualize Maitreya Buddha, he did not see Maitreya. At the end of each three years of retreat, Asanga would become discouraged and leave the hermitage. He would then encounter something that inspired him to return to the hermitage for another three years of retreat. He did this three times, but after twelve years still nothing had happened.

When Asanga abandoned his retreat and left the hermitage for the final time, as he was walking down the road he saw a wounded dog whose lower body was an open wound filled with maggots. On seeing the dog, Asanga generated unbearable compassion and was willing to sacrifice himself to help it. Deciding that the maggots would need food to live on once he had picked them out of the wound, Asanga cut flesh from his own thigh and spread it out on the ground. He then went to pick up the maggots, but not with his fingers because he was afraid of crushing them. He closed his eyes and bent down to pick up the maggots with the tip of his tongue, but he found that he couldn't reach them. There seemed to be nothing there. When he opened his eyes, he suddenly saw Maitreya Buddha.

Asanga then complained to Maitreya Buddha, "Why did you take so long to appear? I've been meditating on you for years!" Maitreya Buddha replied, "It's not that I wasn't there. I was there with you all the time, but you could not see me." Asanga had the habit of spitting in the hermitage, and Maitreya proved he had been in the room by showing Asanga the stains on his robes where he had spat on him. Maitreya Buddha said, "I was always there, but you didn't see me because of your karmic obscurations. These obscurations have now been purified by your compassion. This is why you are now able to see me."

That one moment of intense compassion that Asanga felt for the wounded dog completely purified his negative karma, and he was able to see Maitreya Buddha, a realization that had been denied him during twelve years of retreat.

Sacrificing himself for one living being—in Asanga's view, a wounded dog—made a huge difference. Cherishing even one living being, whether a person or an animal, and sacrificing ourselves to take care of them bring great purification, purifying all our negative karma, the cause of disease and all our other problems. It heals our mind and our body. Sacrificing ourselves even for one living being also accumulates incredible merit.

As I have already explained, until we are completely free from these aggregates, which are suffering in nature, we will have to experience illness and other problems again and again. Since we have to go through these problems, why don't we make them worthwhile? Why don't we follow the examples of these holy beings by renouncing ourselves and cherishing only others? The result for them was that they quickly became free from all problems and their causes, achieved full enlightenment, and then enlightened numberless other beings. Why don't we use our problems in the same way?

The amount of benefit we derive from experiencing our disease or any other problem on behalf of others depends on the strength of the compassion we feel. It depends on how much we cherish others and are willing to sacrifice ourselves to experience their suffering. Since numberless other living beings have the same problems as we do, we need to take all these problems upon ourselves and experience them on behalf of all other beings. The bodhisattva captain, the novice monk Tsembulwa, and Asanga sacrificed themselves to help just one living being. We too can achieve the greatest success by generating unbearable compassion and sacrificing ourselves for even one living being.

7 *Healers*

ॐ

MANY CAUSES AND CONDITIONS determine whether a person can be cured of an illness and how quickly it can happen. For example, it depends on whether the sick person has accumulated enough good karma from their past positive actions. It also depends on whether they have a positive karmic connection with the person who is healing them and whether the four elements of their body are harmonious with the healer's elements. However, three main factors are important in healing: faith, compassion, and morality.

The Power of Faith

Healing has a lot to do with faith, both the faith of the person who performs the healing and of the person who receives it. The power of the healer's mind is important, but so is their faith in the method they are using. Of course, this faith needs to be based on a sincere, compassionate attitude with little egotism. An egotistic attitude, as well as unhealthy thoughts such as anger and ill will, interfere with the ability to heal other people.

Faith is an important cause of success not only in healing but in any activity, including attaining realizations of the path to enlightenment. Sometimes the healing technique can seem ridiculous, but if the patients have strong faith in it, they can be cured.

This is illustrated by a story from Buxa Duar, in West Bengal, India, where I lived for eight years after escaping from Tibet. Buxa had been a prison when the British controlled India and was the place where

Mahatma Gandhi and Prime Minister Nehru were imprisoned. Tibetan monks from all four traditions who wanted to continue their monastic studies were sent to Buxa; most of them, however, came from the three large monastic universities near Lhasa: Sera, Ganden, and Drepung. Other monks went to various other places in India: some to work on roads. The long cell block where Prime Minister Nehru had been imprisoned accommodated the monks from Sera Monastery. The monks were crowded inside and out on the balcony, which was still enclosed with barbed wire; they simply covered the barbed wire with old clothes, bamboo, and other materials. The nuns were housed in the cell block where Mahatma Gandhi had been imprisoned. Nothing had changed. The cell blocks and barbed wire were still there—it was just that the people housed there were no longer called prisoners.

Buxa was a hot and unhealthy place, and many monks contracted tuberculosis or other diseases. Many monks became ill and died there, partly because they could not adjust to the Indian climate and food.

Each morning the monks of the four traditions of Tibetan Buddhism would gather together on a platform to do prayers and pujas.[1] Because it was so hot, everyone sweated a lot. One morning during puja one monk told the monk sitting next to him that he was sick and had a high fever. The other monk then rubbed the dirt on his body into a small ball and gave the ball of dirt to the sick monk, telling him that it was a blessed pill. The sick monk, believing that it really was a blessed pill, swallowed it and quickly recovered from his fever. The monk recovered not because of the pill itself but because of his faith in its healing power. The healing power came from his mind, from his faith in blessed pills.

The Power of Compassion

As I have already discussed, compassion is another source of healing. If our doctors are gentle and compassionate, we start to feel better when they simply talk to us or touch us; we feel happy and our pain lessens. Even if the medicine they prescribe is not the best quality, it will still benefit us. When doctors lack love and compassion, they become more concerned about their reputation and happiness than the suffering of their patients; even if such doctors prescribe the best and most expensive medicine, it will be difficult for them to benefit their patients.

Anyone who is involved in healing should meditate strongly on bodhicitta. Either in retreat or in their everyday life, they should do the step-by-step meditations of the graduated path to enlightenment to generate the realization of compassion. Everyone agrees that compassion is needed, but not many people actually know how to develop it.

The best healer of all is someone with the realization of bodhicitta, the altruistic thought to achieve enlightenment for the sake of all living beings. The whole body of a bodhisattva is blessed because of their pure altruistic mind, which is unstained by any thought of self-cherishing. Their mind is transformed because they have completely renounced any thought of working for themselves and work only for other living beings. Bodhisattvas do every single action—walking, sitting, sleeping, eating, and even breathing—for the sake of others.

Bodhicitta is such a pure, precious mind because bodhisattvas have renounced not only the gross mind of self-cherishing but even the thought of working for themselves. Even the vehicle of this holy mind of bodhicitta, the bodhisattva's body, is blessed. Bodhisattvas are meaningful to behold, which means that any being, even an animal, who sees, hears, or touches them is benefited. Simply seeing a bodhisattva is healing, because it calms the mind. Every single breath of someone with great compassion is medicine, as is the saliva, urine, feces, blood, and everything else that comes from their body. A sick person can recover simply from the breath of a bodhisattva touching their body. Being touched by a bodhisattva, or even by their clothing, brings great blessing. Drinking their urine or applying it to infections also has the power to bless and to heal.

Many stories of spiritual practitioners illustrate this. In Tibet, when someone faints or goes crazy, it is a common practice to burn the hair or clothing of a high lama and get the person to inhale the smoke. If the person has fainted, they quickly regain consciousness. In some Christian countries there is a similar practice with relics of St. Francis of Assisi and of other saints. Lama Yeshe and I observed this when we visited some Christian churches and monasteries in Italy. Some churches in Italy have preserved the clothing of certain Christian saints, and tiny pieces of the cloth are given to sick people, who burn or eat the cloth. They usually vomit immediately after eating the cloth and then gradually recover. It is said that the evil causing the illness leaves the person. The healing power comes from the saint's high attainments, especially their loving kindness and compassion.

In Solu Khumbu, Nepal, there is a monastery for both monks and nuns, though now that the head lama has passed away, not so many monks live there. The head of this monastery was a highly realized ascetic meditator who had escaped from Tibet. Earlier he had been the manager of a large Tibetan monastery, a branch of Sera Me College. His job was to collect grain and other food from the various villages connected with his monastery and sell the food to support the monastery. He failed as a manager, and his failure caused him to generate renunciation, the determination to be free from samsara.

After he gave up his job as manager of the monastery, he went to see a very learned high lama, Ling Tse Dorje Chang, from whom he received teachings on the graduated path to enlightenment. He then went to a solitary place in the mountains to meditate. For six or seven years he lived in a simple mud cave dug into a mountainside. Previously in Tibet the tops of many high mountains were riddled with holes, like ant nests; these were the caves of meditators who went to live in the mountains in order to actualize the path to enlightenment. They simply dug a cave into the mountain and covered its mouth. Nowadays very few remain.

This monk did retreat for six or seven years and realized calm abiding, or *shamatha,* and bodhicitta. He also achieved tantric realizations. With attainment of calm abiding, your concentration is single-pointed and immovable; once your mind is placed on an object, you can concentrate on it for as many months, years, or even eons as you wish. Your body and mind become extremely refined. Physical problems of disease, tiredness, and so forth do not become obstacles to meditation, and you experience physical and mental ecstasy.

Because he had actualized calm abiding, he became clairvoyant and was able to use this power to advise others about their problems. His attainments made him quite famous. He established a monastery for monks and nuns in Tö Tsang, in the upper regions of Tibet. When Tibet was invaded by the Communist Chinese, this lama and many of his monks and nuns escaped to Nepal. When he asked His Holiness the Dalai Lama whether he should come to India, His Holiness advised him to live in Solu Khumbu, where he built a monastery for monks and nuns on a mountainside below Lawudo Cave. Because of his achievements, he soon became famous also in Solu Khumbu.

This lama would tell his attendants to mix the residue of his butter tea with tsampa and make it into pills. He would then give the pills to the sick people who came to see him. Many were immediately cured by these pills.

From time to time, the lama would suddenly show the aspect of serious sickness and vomit blood, sometimes enough to fill a small pot. His disciples would then make pills by mixing the vomited blood with tsampa and give them to the sick. It was common for people to recover after taking the pills. Because of his bodhicitta, everything related to his body had healing power. People even used his leftover food, urine, and belongings to heal themselves.

Many sadhus in India have similar powers. There is one particular sadhu, with only a small number of followers, whose feces can cure leprosy when applied to the body. In India, people generally defecate in the fields, and this sadhu's feces have become very rare and very difficult to obtain because people rush to find them. Again, this healing power comes from his holy mind, from his compassion.

The teachings also mention the story of a family in Tibet with a daughter who had been possessed by a spirit for a long time. Even though they had invited many lamas to perform ritual pujas, their daughter had never recovered. One day when a very simple monk came begging at the house, the family invited him in and asked him to help their daughter. When the monk did a ritual for dispelling interferers that involved prayers and offering ritual cakes, he found that the spirit was reciting the same prayers.

The monk could see that the puja was not helping, so he covered his head with his shawl and meditated on compassion for the spirit. Only then did the spirit leave the girl. The spirit then apologized to the monk and said, "Show me the way." The stronger the good heart, the more powerful the healing.

If we ask bodhisattvas for help, they will help us because of their compassion. From our side, however, we need to have the wisdom and faith to rely upon them and ask for their help. If we have this wisdom and faith, bodhisattvas will be able to guide us.

The Power of Morality

Another powerful factor in healing is pure morality. Whether or not they have realizations, those living in pure morality have much power to heal. You do not necessarily have to be a monk or nun; for example, if you live a pure life by abstaining from the ten nonvirtuous actions, you can benefit others.[2] Your prayers have much power to eliminate disease and other obstacles and to bring success. If someone has become crazy because they are possessed by a spirit, you can order the spirit to leave the person; and because you are living a pure, truthful life, the spirit has to listen to and obey you.

Anyone with the realization of emptiness, the ultimate nature of phenomena, is also a powerful healer. The realization of emptiness gives the person more control over the elements and living beings, so they have power to heal people who are violent or crazy. If someone has a disease caused by a harmful spirit, a practitioner with the realization of emptiness can help to pacify the spirit. With this realization, you can also do the four types of tantric actions: pacifying, increasing, controlling, and wrathful. It also gives the power to bring and to stop rain.

Even if we don't have any of these realizations, it is essential to generate as much compassion as we can and to have strong faith in the healing methods that we are using. At the end of an instruction on how to bring and to stop rain, Lama Tsongkhapa emphasizes the importance of having strong faith in the instructions, bodhicitta, and some experience of emptiness. This advice also applies to healing. Strong compassion, realization of emptiness, and faith in the healing method are all necessary, but healing profits most from strong compassion and strong faith. The more we have of these qualities, the more we will be able to help others.

Miracle Cures

In Malaysia, Singapore, and also America, I have met many healers with stories of miracle cures. A person's ability to perform miracle cures has nothing to do with any external material phenomena. Their healing power generally comes from their own good heart; they are usually warm people with concern for others. There is no egotism involved, and they cherish others more than themselves.

In America I met a young Chinese man from mainland China who has performed many miracle cures. When he is giving a talk, he is able to cure sick people sitting in the audience even without touching them. People in wheelchairs are suddenly able to stand up and walk without assistance, even though they have not been able to walk for many years. He does not actually touch them; he simply makes a hand gesture at a distance, yet they immediately feel better and stand up unaided. He is a very kind and compassionate person, who is famous in China for his miraculous cures. He has an album with photos of the many people who have recovered after many years of sickness simply by seeing him.

In Malaysia, I have a friend called Tony Wong, a Chinese business-man, whose life is filled with stories of miracle cures. He is a devoted Buddhist and has arranged many tours of Malaysia by lamas from all four traditions of Tibetan Buddhism. As he doesn't have a separate place for his healing ceremonies, he uses his office. On one side of the room is his Buddhist altar and on the other his wife's altar. Every week-end, his office is filled to capacity with people wanting to be healed; some even sit on the steps outside.

Tony simply places a jar of water on the altar in front of a statue of Kuan Yin, a female aspect of the Buddha of Compassion, and then leads three or four hours of continuous chanting of Kuan Yin's mantra. Like Tibetans, but unlike Westerners, the Chinese are accustomed to chanting for many hours.

When I asked Tony whether he does any special meditation or visu-alization, he told me that he doesn't do anything at all; he simply places the water on the altar and leads the chanting. After the chanting he then distributes the water. Both he and his patients have strong faith that the water has been blessed, though those cured are not necessar-ily Buddhist.

Tony tells many stories of seriously ill people who immediately start to feel better after chanting the mantra and drinking the water. Some even recover completely by the next day. Someone with cancer will come in one day supported by two people because they are unable to walk. The next day, after drinking the blessed water, the person will walk into the office unassisted. Tony has witnessed many such miracle cures.

How do these miracles happen even though no special meditation is done? One factor is the power of Tony's mind. Tony himself is a very sincere and compassionate person who dedicates his whole life to serving others. He never refuses his help to anyone who asks for it, but tries to do what he can to help others. This is his spiritual practice. Another factor is his faith. He has strong faith that the water is blessed simply by being placed in front of the Kuan Yin statue. Much of the healing power comes from the faith in his mind and in the minds of the people who drink the water.

Water or another substance can be blessed, pure, and powerful, but the actualizing of its healing power depends on the person who gives the water and on the person who drinks it. Basically, its healing power depends on the mind; the mind has to make it work. Even though we like to believe in external healing power, there is no such thing; all the healing power comes from our mind, mainly from our faith. This is the case with Tony Wong, where no special visualization is done to bless the water, yet there have been many miraculous recoveries from illness. The individual's mind, especially the positive thought of faith, creates the blessing. It is a dependent arising.

While some people can be healed by drinking blessed water or taking other blessed substances, doing meditation, reciting mantras, or using conventional medical treatment, others cannot be helped by these simple means because they have heavy obstacles. Even if a doctor accurately diagnoses a disease and prescribes what should be the correct treatment, there is no guarantee that the person will recover. The treatment will not work if the person has many heavy obstacles. The person will have to put some effort into doing some purification practice. Only then can there be a cure.

Take one of my uncles, for example. For many years he could not sleep because he was in so much pain. He tossed and turned all night. Even though he went to Tibet and consulted many doctors, nothing helped. Finally, he went to see a meditator who lived in a cave not far from Lawudo Cave.

The meditator used divination to check my uncle's condition and then advised him that his disease was karmic. Of course, disease and every other problem that we experience is the result of our own negative karma, but the meditator meant that in my uncle's case simply taking medicine would not be sufficient to cure the problem and that he would need to do some practice of purification. He advised my uncle to recite hundreds of thousands of Vajrasattva mantras, a particular aspect of Buddha that brings powerful purification, and to do hundreds of thousands of prostrations. Just as doctors specialize in a particular field—a cardiologist specializes in curing heart problems, for example—different Buddhas have special functions; Vajrasattva specializes in purification. The practices of Vajrasattva and prostrations were recommended to enable my uncle to purify the actual cause of his disease, his past negative actions and the imprints left by them on his mind. Purifying the mind purifies physical disease because physical problems come from the mind.

My uncle did some of these practices in Lawudo Cave, then later built a small hermitage high on a rocky mountain. For the six or seven years he was doing these practices, he also took care of my grandmother, who was very old and blind. During all those years, he cooked her food and carried her outside to go to the toilet. As soon as he began the practices, his condition started to improve, and he gradually became healthier and healthier. In the end he recovered completely.

Even though medicine or blessed substances generally benefit people, they do not work with certain individuals whose heavy obstacles prevent recovery. Those who cannot be cured through such simple means have to use other methods, such as meditation or purification practices. After they do some practice, the recommended medicine is often able to work.

There are also many cases where taking what should be the correct medicine for a particular disease causes the person to contract a new disease or to experience unpleasant side effects, such as fever. Rather than curing the disease, the medicine makes it worse. Of course, in addition to the person's attitude and actions, external conditions such as diet, climate, and spirits can affect the course of an illness. Spirits can interfere by not allowing medicine to work. Certain pujas and meditation practices then need to be done to pacify the spirits, and once these are done, the medicine is able to work.

While some people can experience miracle cures simply by meeting or touching a great healer, not everyone can meet such a healer, and it is important to understand the reason for this. Those with great obstacles must do something to purify their mind, the real cause of their physical problems; someone simply touching or speaking to them will not be enough to heal them. This is why it is essential to practice meditation and purification. In this way we become the healer of our own mind and body.

8 Everything Comes from the Mind through Labeling

⤳

EVERYTHING COMES FROM THE MIND; everything is a creation of the mind. When a hundred people look at the same person, each one sees that person differently: some see the person as beautiful, some as ugly, others as neither. The differences come from the minds of the perceivers. The way any object appears to us comes from our own mind, not from the side of the object. It depends on how we look at the object, on how we interpret it, on how we label it.

That everything comes from the mind is a fundamental Buddhist principle, but Western scientists now agree that even the existence of an atom is related to the mind of the observer. Everything is a creation of the mind, including the mind itself. Since everything comes from the mind, the mind itself is fundamental to healing disease. Like the teachings of Buddha, Tibetan and Chinese medical texts explain that all diseases originate in the mind and relate sickness to the three fundamental delusions: ignorance, anger, and attachment. The very root of disease—and of all other suffering—is ignorance, specifically ignorance of the ultimate reality of phenomena.

To heal not just disease but all suffering, and to make it impossible for us to ever experience suffering again, we have to heal the causes of suffering, which are in our mental continuum. We have to completely cease actions motivated by delusions, the delusions themselves, and the seeds of delusion. The medicine we use is the realization of emptiness, the ultimate nature of phenomena. This is why it is important to understand emptiness and why Buddha gave many teachings on the subject of emptiness, the shortest of which is *The Essence of Wisdom*, commonly known as *The Heart Sutra*.

The Reality of a Flower

The reality of phenomena can be considered in various ways. One reality of a flower, for example, is that it is impermanent; it is changing, decaying, day by day, minute by minute. Even within each second, it is decaying. Why? Because it is dependent on other causes and conditions. It is only when the decay becomes gross and affects the color and shape of the flower, however, that we are able to notice it. We don't notice the subtle decay of the flower within each second.

The flower grows because of causes and conditions, and it decays because of other causes and conditions. The reality is that the flower changes within every second because of causes and conditions, and because of this subtle change, it changes every minute, every hour, every day. The subtle change leads to gross change, when we finally notice that the flower is decaying. Prior to this point, a lot of change has already happened but it was too subtle for us to notice. Because we are not aware of this change, the flower appears permanent to us. By apprehending this false appearance of permanence to be true, we create a hallucinated concept of permanence in relation to something that is impermanent.

Now consider the ultimate reality of a flower, which is extremely subtle. "Flower" is a name, a word, a label, that is applied to the base of a flower. We see a flower in dependence upon its base, and we don't label "flower" on just any base. When we see a vase or a book, for example, we don't call it a flower. Before we apply the label "flower" to something, we have to have a reason to do so; otherwise, we could apply that label to any object that we see. If you label yourself a flower, you might end up in hospital in a psychiatric ward. Before we choose the specific label "flower," we have to see a specific base, a material object that has grown in the ground and has the particular shape and color of a flower. Seeing such an object makes us decide to apply this particular label "flower." Seeing a vase, a book, or a table does not.

This is the process through which we see a flower. When we do not analyze our perception, it seems as if we see a flower from the very beginning, as if we see a flower without our mind labeling it a flower, but this is completely wrong. The actual process is that we first see the base of a flower, a specific material object; we label it *flower;* and a flower then appears to us. It is only after we label "flower" on the base of a flower that we see a flower. Until then, we don't see a flower.

The material object with the design of a flower is the base, and "flower" is the label. We first see the base and then the flower, so the base is not the flower. Even though this is the reality, our mind is not aware of it. It seems to our hallucinated mind that we see the flower, not the base of the flower, from the very first. In reality, we see the base first and see the flower only after we have labeled it.

The main point to understand at this stage is that the base and the label are not one; the base of the flower and the flower are different. They are not separate, however, because the flower does not exist separately from its base. The object that you first see is the base; it is not the label "flower." These two are different. Even if we don't know much about meditating on the emptiness of phenomena, it is essential that we understand the process of distinguishing the label from the base.

Also, there is no flower on the base of the flower. To us there appears to be a flower on the base, but it is a hallucination. It is what is known as "the object to be refuted"; it is what we have to realize is empty. There is no flower there—not in the sense that no flower exists, but in the sense that no flower exists on the base of the flower.

What we first see is the base of the flower, but it is not the flower. Where there is the base of a flower, a flower exists; but on the base of a flower, there is no flower at all. So, what happened to the flower? The flower is not nonexistent; the flower exists. By analyzing in this way, however, we can see that the flower is something completely different from what we believed it to be in the past.

What is the flower? The flower is simply what is merely labeled by the mind in dependence upon its base. In other words, the flower is created by the mind. This is the essential nature of the flower, and we can see that it is extremely subtle. The shortest way to express it is to say that the flower is merely labeled by the mind. To elaborate a little, we can say that the flower is merely labeled by the mind in dependence upon its base.

The flower is extremely subtle, like space. It is not that the flower doesn't exist at all; it exists, but in an extremely subtle way. Another way of expressing it is to say that the flower exists simply because the base of the flower exists. It's not that the flower doesn't exist at all. It exists, but it is so subtle that it is as if it doesn't exist.

From this analysis, we can see that the flower is completely empty of being a real flower in the sense of existing from its own side. The flower exists as a subtle dependent arising, being merely imputed by the mind. This is the ultimate reality of the flower that I mentioned earlier. Even though this is the way the flower actually exists, those who haven't realized emptiness do not see the flower in this way. The flower that appears real to us and in which we believe is completely false. That flower, which seems to exist from its own side, is a complete hallucination; it is completely empty.

Z Is a Label

When you were learning the alphabet as a child, before you were taught that the particular figure, Z, was called "Z," how did this figure appear to you? You simply saw some lines, not Z. Why not? Because you had not yet learned to label this figure "Z" and to believe that it was Z.

It was only after one of your parents or your teacher told you, "This is Z," and you believed that person's word, that you labeled this figure "Z" and believed it to be Z. Only after you apply the label "Z" to this particular figure and believe in that label do you see this figure as Z. In other words, Z is Z only after you label it "Z." Before you labeled this figure "Z," you didn't see Z. You can see how the appearance of Z comes from the mind.

You can also see that this figure with these specific lines is the base and "Z" is the label. These two factors, the base and the label, are not one; they are different. They are not separate, however, because Z doesn't exist separately from these lines, which are the base to be labeled Z. If these lines *were* Z—in other words, if the base were one with the label "Z"—why would you bother to label it at all? If the first thing you saw was already Z, there would be no reason for you to label it "Z." What would be the purpose of applying the label "Z" to something that was already Z? It means that the labeling process would be endless, because you would have to label Z again on top of that Z, then Z on top of that Z, and so on.

A second mistake occurs if you think the lines you see in the very beginning are Z and not the base to be labeled Z. It is clear that "Z" is a name, a label, so it has to come from the mind. If you see Z from the very first, and not the base to be labeled Z, why decide upon this particular label, "Z"? Since it does not depend upon your first seeing the base, these particular lines, you have no reason to choose the particular label "Z." This means you could call anything at all Z. You could even say that A or B is Z.

The point is that the base is not the label. The lines are the base. First you see these particular lines, the base, and it is only after you have labeled "Z" on this base that you see Z.

Also, there is no Z on these lines. Yet even though you cannot find Z on these lines, there is a Z on this page. Wherever the base of Z is, Z exists; but on the base of Z, there is no Z. Even though there seems to be a Z on these lines, you cannot find Z when you look for it. This real Z is the object to be refuted. It is a complete hallucination; it is completely empty.

I Is a Label

The point of using these examples of the flower and Z is to help us to understand the ultimate nature of the I. As I have already explained, everything that exists comes from the mind, is merely labeled by the mind. Without the mind that creates the label "I," there is no I. In other words, without the concept of I, the I doesn't exist at all. We must understand this point clearly.

The body is not the I, the mind is not the I, and even the association of the body and mind is not the I. None of these is the I. The association of body and mind is the base to be labeled I and "I" is the label. And as we have just discovered, there is no way that the base to be labeled and the label can be one; they have to be different.

So, what is the I? What is the I that walks, sits, eats, sleeps, and experiences happiness and suffering? That I is nothing other than what is merely labeled by the mind in dependence upon this particular association of body and mind, and the I that is merely labeled by the mind does exist. This is all that the I is—something merely imputed by the mind. If we are sitting somewhere and ask ourselves what we are doing, we reply, "I am sitting." Why do we believe that we are sitting? The only reason is that our body is sitting. Because of this, we make up the label, "I am sitting," and believe in our own label. It is merely an idea, a concept.

When we look for the merely labeled I, however, we cannot find it. Even though the merely labeled I exists, we cannot find it on these aggregates, on this association of body and mind. The merely labeled I does exist, because it performs all our activities and experiences rebirth, old age, sickness, and death; but when we specifically look for it on this association of body and mind, we cannot find even the merely labeled I anywhere.

This is not the correct way to meditate on the emptiness of the I, because it does not consider the inherently existent I, but it can be helpful.

First we have to understand clearly that the merely labeled I does exist, and second that we cannot find it anywhere on this particular association of body and mind, from the top of our head down to our toes. We cannot find the merely labeled I inside our head, our brain, our chest, our heart, our belly, our legs, or our arms. Nor can we find it on the surface of our body or outside our body. Even though it exists, because our mind has made up the label in dependence upon our aggregates, we cannot find the merely labeled I anywhere.

We normally believe that the I exists on the association of our body and mind, but we have to understand that there is no such I. When we do not check closely, it looks as if such an I exists. When we actually search for it, however, and cannot find it anywhere, we suddenly understand that it is not there. It is like thinking that the shadow of a plant on the ground at night is a scorpion. What looked like a scorpion in the dark cannot be seen at all when we shine a flashlight on the spot. In a similar way, as soon as we actually start to analyze, we discover that the I is not there on the association of our body and mind.

The I that we feel is inside our body somewhere does not exist; it is a complete hallucination. If it did exist, it should become clearer as we search for it, but instead we cannot find it at all. If we think we have some money in our purse, but when we check we cannot find any money there, it means the purse is empty. In a similar way, when we check for the I on the association of the body and mind, we cannot find it anywhere, from the top of our head down to our toes.

We now have to consider the real I, which appears to exist from its own side, to be unlabeled by the mind. When we are very upset—for example, when someone has criticized us or wrongly accused us of something—or when we are very excited about something, we feel that this independent, truly existent I exists inside our body. It seems to us that we can find this real I somewhere inside our body. However, if we cannot find even the merely labeled I on this base, how could we possibly find this real I? There is no way we could find it. Logically, there is no way this real I that has nothing to do with our own mind could possibly exist.

When we recognize a dream as a dream, we understand that the person we were talking to in our dream is not real; that person does not exist. However, if we don't recognize our dream as a dream, we believe the person in our dream to be real. In the view of wisdom, the person we see in our dream doesn't exist; but in the view of ignorance, the person exists. With one view, the object doesn't exist; with the other, it does. It is similar with this real I. In the view of wisdom, no real I exists; but in the view of the hallucinated mind of ignorance, that real I exists, because it appears to us and we believe it to be true.

We should now have some idea how the I actually exists. The I exists, but it is empty of inherent, or true, existence. It is empty of any existence that has nothing to do with our mind or with our aggregates. Our mind makes up the label "I" in dependence upon our aggregates, the association of our body and mind. This is all that the I is. No I exists that is more than what is merely labeled by our mind. Any I that appears to exist as more than this is a complete hallucination; it is completely empty. That I does not exist.

However, even though we have merely imputed the I, we are not aware of our creation. The I appears to us, not as merely labeled by our mind in dependence upon our aggregates, but as a real I that exists from its own side. In other words, the I that appears to us seems to have nothing to do with our mind. It appears to exist from its own side, to be truly existent. We simply create this false I, which is false in the sense that it does not exist at all. Not only does this I not exist on these aggregates, but it does not exist at all.

Allowing ourselves to believe this false I to be true is the ignorance that is the root of all suffering. It produces the other types of ignorance, as well as anger, attachment, and the other delusions, and these delusions then motivate the negative actions that result in all our suffering, including rebirth, old age, sickness, and death. When we allow ourselves to believe that the appearance of a real I that exists from its own side is true, we are creating the ignorance that is the root of all delusions and negative actions and of all suffering.

Realizing that the I is completely empty of existing from its own side is realizing the emptiness, or ultimate truth, of the I. Ceasing this ignorance that believes in the inherent existence of the I is the only way to liberate ourselves and all other living beings from all suffering and its causes. Everything depends on cutting this root ignorance, and the only way to do this is by realizing emptiness. We have to actualize the wisdom that realizes the emptiness of the I and of the aggregates.

Only the wisdom that realizes emptiness can eliminate the ignorance that is the root of all suffering. No matter how many other realizations we have, unless we have the realization of emptiness, we do not have the weapon that directly destroys the hallucinated concept of true existence. As long as we hold the concept of a truly existent I, other delusions will continuously arise and then motivate negative actions and produce problems for us.

The reality is that the I is merely imputed by the mind. Even though our mind merely labels "I" on the association of our body and mind, the I appears to us falsely, as if it exists from its own side. Our self-cherishing thought then cherishes and clings to this false I, which appears to be not merely imputed by the mind but inherently existent. We generate the thought of cherishing this false I, thinking that it is more precious and more important than all other living beings. For us, the most important thing in the world is that this particular I finds happiness and does not experience problems.

In reality, cherishing the self is cherishing a hallucination. It is like finding a million dollars in a dream and locking it in a safe because it is so precious. For as long as the dream lasts, we will see the million dollars, cherish it, and worry about keeping it safe. But when the dream is over, we won't see a million dollars; we won't see even one dollar. Cherishing this real I is like cherishing this million dollars. There is actually no inherently existent I to cherish. It is a complete hallucination. There is nothing there. As long as we are under the spell of the wrong concept that believes in true existence, a real I appears to exist and to be worth cherishing. In reality, however, the self-cherishing thought is cherishing an object that is completely empty.

Realizing the emptiness of the I is a powerful meditation for purification and healing; it is a powerful way to find peace, because it eliminates all our unnecessary worry and fear. By meditating on emptiness, we use our own skillful thinking to eliminate our disease and other problems.

9 Disease Is Just a Label

ॐ

THE EXAMPLES I have just mentioned help us understand the reality of cancer, AIDS, and even death. Meditating on the emptiness of cancer, AIDS, and other diseases is useful in breaking our fixed concepts of disease, which create worry and fear.

In reality, having a particular disease is one view of our mind. What appears to us is something that we ourselves have created. Or as the great yogi Naropa said, "When we are sick, the concept is sick." It is clear that it is our own concept that is experiencing disease. First our mind labels something, then we see it. This applies to sickness as well as to all other phenomena. All our sickness is the creation of our own mind. I have already explained that unless our mind makes up the label "I" there is no way that we can see the I. In the same way, unless our mind makes up the label "cancer" or "AIDS," there is no way that cancer or AIDS can appear to us.

Understanding how our illness and all our other problems come from our mind is an important point in healing, because if something comes from our mind, we can control it, we can change it. Since this means that our mind has the power to eliminate disease, we have no need to feel depressed or upset. Knowing how much freedom we have should inspire us and give us hope.

AIDS Is a Label

There is no real AIDS, no AIDS that exists from its own side. First a doctor finds that their patient is HIV+ and tells them that they may contract AIDS. Based on what the doctor says, the patient labels "AIDS" on their condition and believes in their label. The particular virus, HIV, which makes a person unable to resist disease, is the base and "AIDS" is the label. In reality this is all that the disease AIDS is: the mind makes up the label "AIDS" and applies it to a particular base. There is no AIDS other than this. There is no independent AIDS, no AIDS that exists from its own side. There is no AIDS from the side of the body; AIDS is merely imputed by the mind. The real AIDS that we believe in does not actually exist. That real AIDS is a complete hallucination; it is completely empty right there, right on its base.

Just as AIDS is completely empty, so are cancer and all other diseases. A thought transformation text says, "Suffering is a manifestation of emptiness." AIDS is a manifestation of emptiness, cancer is a manifestation of emptiness. The cancer that we believe is real, and not merely labeled by the mind, is completely empty. So, what is cancer? Cancer is merely labeled by the mind on its base.

Simply meditating on the ultimate nature of AIDS, cancer, and other diseases brings powerful healing, because it cuts off the hallucinated mind of ignorance and also eliminates fear, depression, and other negative emotions. Understanding how everything comes from the mind is itself meditation on emptiness, because it cuts straight through our usual hallucinations; it breaks our solid concept that everything exists from its own side. This hallucinated concept, which contradicts reality, is the fundamental sickness. We touch reality through understanding that everything comes from the mind.

Death Is Also a Label

Even death comes from our own mind. Death is a concept, something that comes from our mind, so our mind creates death. There is no real death, no death from its own side, as it appears to our hallucinated mind. That real death, which frightens us, does not exist; it is a complete hallucination.

As I explained earlier, death itself is not the problem; it is our concept of death that is the problem. We have a concept of death as something that exists from its own side, and it is this hallucinated concept that makes us frightened of death and does not allow us to relinquish our attachment to this life: to our body, our family, and our possessions. Death becomes terrifying because we see the objects around us as permanent, a way in which they do not exist at all, and we then feel attachment, anger, and other negative emotions in relation to these objects.

While life is defined as the association of body and mind, death is defined as the mind separating from the body under the control of karma and delusions. In other words, what is called "death" is created by our mind. Death is merely labeled by our mind in dependence upon its base, the consciousness leaving the body. This is all that death is. Therefore, there is no death that exists from its own side. There is no real death in the sense of one that exists inherently. It is a hallucination.

Death does exist, but the death that exists is the one that is merely labeled by our mind, not the inherently existent one that appears to us. The concrete, independent death that appears to us is a hallucination. Our mind is hallucinated because the object in which we believe does not exist. Death, which is created by our concept, appears to us falsely as something concrete and frightening from its own side. We then believe this wrong concept to be true. The great yogi Naropa said, "When we are born, the concept is born; when we are sick, the concept is sick; and even when we are dying, the concept is dying." In other words, everything is a concept. When we logically analyze what death really is, we find that the way it appears to us and the way we apprehend it to exist are false. Our false view and false conception of death are what frighten us.

The great yogi Saraha said that without the concept, there are no external enemies, no vicious tigers, no poisonous snakes. If we have anger, we find external enemies; if we have no anger, we cannot find any external enemies. If we have the concept of an enemy, we see an enemy; if we have no concept of an enemy, we don't see an enemy. If we don't have anger or the concept of an enemy, we cannot find an enemy, even if everyone is angry with us, criticizes us, or even kills us.

In *A Guide to the Bodhisattva's Way of Life,* the great bodhisattva Shantideva also mentions that subduing the inner enemy, anger, is like subduing all external enemies, because once this inner enemy is destroyed, we will never find a single external enemy. To help us to understand this point, Shantideva explains that if we tried to stop thorns entering our feet by covering all the thornbushes in the world with leather, we wouldn't have enough leather to do it; but if we wear leather shoes, no thorns will go into our feet.[1] Shantideva is basically addressing the same point: by cutting off the concept, we won't find anything external frightening.

If death itself were really the problem, it would be a problem for everybody. But this is not true. Many people even find death enjoyable. Whether or not death is a problem depends on the mind of the person who is dying. Death itself is not terrifying, but a person's concept of death can be terrifying.

Buddhist teachings explain that the best Dharma practitioners feel joyful when they are dying, as if going home to see their family after a long absence or going on a picnic. Death does not bother them at all. Less accomplished practitioners are happy and comfortable at the time of death and are fully confident that they will have a happy rebirth. And even the least accomplished practitioners die without worry or fear. Enjoyment of death, as well as fear of death, is created by the mind; it does not exist from its own side.

If we have lived our lives with compassion, we will have no regrets on the day of our death, because everything we did became Dharma, the cause of happiness, and nothing became the cause of suffering or of rebirth in the lower realms. Therefore, even when we are dying, our mind will be happy and content. People who have lived compassionate lives, even though they might not have followed a particular religion, will have no fear when they die, but will die with comfortable, happy minds.

Some people, even though they reject reincarnation and karma, feel insecure about what will happen after death and experience a lot of fear at the time of their death. The answer to this is simple and logical: if there is only one life and no life after this, they have no cause for worry because after death they will have no more problems.

Nurses who have taken care of dying people have told me that in their experience alcoholics have the most fear when they are dying. Why do alcoholics experience so much fear at the time of death? It is important for Western society to learn about this. Not everyone dies in the same mental state: some people die happily and peacefully; others die in fear. Some people experience terrifying deaths, screaming because they see many frightening things attacking them. Regardless of whether they believe in reincarnation, people who have done many negative actions during their life experience fear at the time of their death. The imprints left by their past negative actions produce terrifying hallucinations, their own mental creations. Just as we cannot see the dreams of other people, even of someone sleeping next to us, we cannot see the hallucinations of a dying person. Such fearful appearances are the result of negative karma and a sign that the person will reincarnate in one of the lower realms.

The time close to death is crucial. If we believe in reincarnation, we have no doubt that there will be another life after this present one, and the quality of our future life is largely determined by how we die. The way we think at the time of death is the immediate cause of our future life. Thinking in a positive way results in a happy life; thinking in a negative way results in a life with more problems than our present one. Whether or not we believe in reincarnation, it is essential to establish a positive attitude at the very end of our life, before the gross consciousness has absorbed, and to die with a happy, peaceful mind. We should use meditation and whatever other methods we have to reduce our attachment, anger, anxiety, and fear and to transform our mind.

One means of preventing a fearful death is to purify its cause, which is our negative karma and the imprints it has left on our mind. Once we have purified it, the prospect of our death will not bother us. Death will not be a big deal, because it will simply mean a change of body. Reincarnating will be like changing our clothes. Just as we leave our old, dirty clothes behind and put on a fresh, clean set, we will simply leave our present body, which has exhausted its potential, and take a new, young body in a family and place where we have every opportunity to develop our mind and generate realizations of the path to enlightenment. If we have created the cause, we can take a better body in order to continue to practice the path and to serve other living beings.

Another means of preventing a frightening death is to abandon harming others, which means abandoning negative actions as much as we can. Even if we cannot abandon them completely, we should lessen them as much as possible.

If we apply these solutions, death, rather than frightening us, can become an enjoyable challenge. If we can generate compassion, patience, faith, or awareness of the ultimate nature of phenomena, we can use our death as a meditation, as a spiritual practice. We can even use our death to develop realizations of the path to enlightenment and to bring all living beings to that state. Instead of death riding on us, we will ride on death. Instead of being frightened of death, we can use death to achieve ultimate happiness by ending the cause of problems. This is the real challenge.

The answer is to practice bodhicitta, which brings powerful purification of our past negative karma and our obscurations and automatically stops us from creating further negative karma. With bodhicitta, we naturally and happily abandon negative karma. This practice is the best preparation for death and ensures a happy, peaceful death. With this good heart, if we are sick, we experience our sickness on behalf of all living beings, and even if we die, we experience our death on behalf of all living beings. We experience everything that happens to us for other living beings. This brings us a life that is filled with peace, happiness, and satisfaction. And we have no regret, now or in the future.

10 *Everything Comes from the Mind through Karma*

や

A DEEPER EXPLANATION of how everything, including disease, comes from the mind is related to karma. External factors affect the body and the mind, but this doesn't happen without causes and conditions. Everything that happens to us is a result, or an effect, so its cause has to exist beforehand. In other words, nothing happens without a reason, which is the same as saying that nothing happens without causes and conditions.

From where does the reason come? It comes from our own mind. Whether the effect is negative or positive, it is caused by our own mind. If it is a negative effect, it is a creation of our own negative mind; if it is a positive effect, the cause has been created by our own positive mind. This is karma. Our whole life comes from our mind; our happiness and suffering is constantly coming from our own mind.

Without the mind nothing appears, and the purity or impurity of what appears to us depends on the purity or impurity of our mind. War, floods, droughts, famine, and other disasters are negative appearances, and all negative appearances are the products of negative imprints left on the mind by past actions motivated by negative attitudes. These appearances are the projections, or creations, of negative imprints.

Consider the example of Ethiopia, where many millions of people have died through drought, famine, disease, and civil war. At one point, Ethiopia had a critical shortage of drinking water because of prolonged drought. When drinking water was flown in from a neighboring country, however, it had become undrinkable by the time it arrived in Ethiopia. Even though the water was drinkable in its country of origin, in Ethiopia it appeared to be undrinkable. This impure appearance had to do with the minds of the Ethiopians.

A healthy environment in Ethiopia has to come from the minds of the Ethiopians, from their own positive thoughts. Otherwise, even when other countries try to help by flying in water or giving financial aid, it turns out badly. We have discussed how everything comes from our own mind through our labeling it in specific ways, but here we are talking about a longer and more complex process. Past negative actions leave imprints on the mind, and these negative imprints manifest as negative situations.

Unlike Ethiopians and many others, we live in a utopia. We have clean, comfortable houses; we enjoy delicious food; we see beautiful flowers. All the beautiful objects that appear to us are projections of our positive mind; they arise from the positive imprints left by our past actions, actions done with positive attitudes. In other words, all these sense objects are creations of our own mind.

Any action done with a motivation that is unstained by self-cherishing, ignorance, anger, attachment, or any of the other disturbing thoughts becomes virtue, the cause of happiness. The purest action is one done with a motivation that is unstained by self-cherishing thought. Any action that is done with a motivation of self-cherishing, ignorance, anger, attachment, or any of the other disturbing thoughts becomes nonvirtue, the cause of suffering.

Whereas Christianity has the Ten Commandments, Buddhism has the abandoning of the ten nonvirtues: three negative actions of body (killing, stealing, and sexual misconduct); four negative actions of speech (lying, slander, harsh speech, and gossip); and three negative actions of mind (covetousness, ill will, and wrong views). The point we have to understand is what makes the three actions of body and the four actions of speech negative. It is the mind. These actions become negative when they are motivated by ignorance, anger, attachment, or any other delusion. There is no negative action from its own side, no inherently existent negative action. There is no negative action that has not been created, or labeled, by our own mind. Even though negative actions appear to us to exist from their own side, and we believe them to exist in this way, in reality no such negative actions exist.

Take the action of killing, which is generally regarded as negative.

In reality, whether killing is actually negative depends on the mind of the person performing the killing. If the action of killing is motivated by self-cherishing thought or any other delusion, it becomes negative karma and the cause of suffering. But if the action of killing is motivated by bodhicitta, wisdom, or some other positive thought, it becomes good karma and the cause of happiness. Remember the story I told you earlier of Buddha's past life as the bodhisattva captain. The bodhisattva captain killed the trader who was planning to murder the other traders, but because the captain was motivated by unbearable compassion, his action of killing became only good karma.

In the West, people find it difficult to decide about what is right or wrong, whether it is a matter of parents disciplining children or governments introducing gun laws. Whether an action is right or wrong depends on the attitude of the individual who performs it and on its purpose. This is the only logical way to determine whether an action is right or wrong.

None of the physical and verbal actions I mentioned are negative if they are done with a pure motivation—for example, to bring happiness to others or to protect them from danger. An action does not become negative karma if we do it with strong compassion and with the wisdom that can see it will definitely benefit others; it becomes a positive action and the cause of only happiness.

The Laws of Karma

Guru Shakyamuni Buddha explained four laws of karma. The first is that karma is definite. This means that an action will definitely bring its own specific result, unless it meets an obstacle; a positive action will definitely bring its own result of happiness, and a negative action will definitely bring its own result of suffering. If someone has created a negative cause, unless they do something to purify it, the cause will definitely bring its own negative result, just as a seed that is planted will definitely result in a sprout as long as it is not eaten by birds and so forth. Once there is a cause, as long as there is no obstacle to that cause, it is natural to experience its result. The results of negative actions are definite unless we purify our past negative actions and remove their seeds by actualizing the remedy of the path to enlightenment in our mind.

Vajrasattva, the Thirty-Five Buddhas, and various other Buddhas manifest specifically to help us to purify negative actions, which are obstacles to realizations and are the causes of problems in this life and in future lives. Even if we are unable to generate the path in our mind, at least we can completely purify our negative actions by doing the practices of such deities and thus make it impossible for us to experience the resultant problems.

Karma is also expandable. From planting one tiny seed in the ground a huge tree with many branches, leaves, fruit, and seeds can grow. However, this external example cannot be compared to the expandability of the inner phenomenon of karma. From one small negative action we can experience problems for hundreds or thousands of lives. According to the teaching of the great pandit Nagarjuna, if we cheat one sentient being, we will be cheated by other sentient beings for one thousand lifetimes.

Because karma is expandable, we have to be careful to avoid committing even small negative actions. We can start to experience the results in this life of even small negative actions committed in relation to powerful objects, from our present parents up to our gurus, and then experience problems in many subsequent lifetimes. We shouldn't carelessly commit a negative action because we think it is so small that it doesn't matter. Protecting ourselves from negative karma, even if it is minor, will help us in this life and in many future lifetimes; we will be healthy, wealthy, live long, and experience few problems.

Even though we may be doing purification practices, if we continually create negative karma we are like an elephant that goes into a lake to wash itself and then comes out to roll in the dirt. Unless we stop creating negative karma, our practice of purification will never end.

The other two laws of karma are that one cannot experience a result without having created its cause; and, once created, karma is never lost.

The Negative Actions of Body

Killing. Any complete action of killing motivated by self-cherishing or any other delusion is nonvirtuous and results in four types of suffering. For an act of killing to be complete it must involve four factors:

base, thought, action, and goal.¹ If any of these four is missing, the action of killing is incomplete.

The first type of suffering, called the ripening aspect result, means we are reborn in one of the lower realms, as a hell being, a hungry ghost, or an animal. Generally, the heaviest negative karma brings rebirth in hell, lighter karma brings rebirth in the hungry ghost realm, and the lightest karma brings rebirth in the animal realm.

After an incredible length of time, when the karma to be in the lower realms is exhausted and the positive karma from other past lives becomes stronger, we are reborn in the human realm. As a human, we then experience the three other types of suffering. The second form of suffering, known as experiencing the result similar to the cause, means that we have a short life, perhaps dying in the womb or as a child. We are also harmed or killed by other human beings, spirits, or disease.

The third form of suffering, the possessed result, has to do with the environment. We are born in a dangerous place with much war or disease. The place we are born is also very dry and miserable. Food and drink are low in protein, difficult to digest, and can even cause disease. Medicine is also ineffective. Even though food and medicine are generally conditions that support life, because of our past negative action of killing, they become obstacles to our life and can even cause our death.

The fourth type of suffering, creating the result similar to the cause, means that because of the imprints left on our mind by the past action of killing, we again perform the action of killing when we are born as a human being. It is a habit from the past. Completing the negative action of killing once again results in our experiencing the four types of suffering from that particular cause. And unless we change our attitude and stop committing the negative action of killing, we will endlessly create the cause of our problems and continually experience suffering.

We can stop the process, however, once we transform our attitude and actions and take a vow not to kill. The complete action of keeping a vow not to kill results in four types of happiness. Once we know the results of the ten negative actions of body, speech, and mind, we will readily understand the results of the ten positive actions.

The ripening aspect result of having kept a vow not to kill is that we are born as a god or a human. Experiencing the result similar to the cause means that we live a long life. The possessed result is that we are born in a place where there is little fear or danger, where food and water are plentiful, where food is high in protein, easy to digest, and does not cause disease, and where medicine is potent. All these conditions lead to a long life. We are currently enjoying the results of our past positive actions of having kept vows not to kill.

Creating the result similar to the cause means that we again keep the vow not to kill. And from each complete action of not killing, we will again enjoy four types of happiness in future lives. Because karma is expandable, we can experience positive results for hundreds or even thousands of lifetimes from keeping the vow not to kill for even one day. Doing one positive action for just one day in our life can result in happiness in thousands of lifetimes.

Stealing. The second negative action of body, stealing, becomes negative karma when it is done out of self-cherishing or any other delusion, and again the complete action of stealing results in four types of suffering.

The ripening aspect result is rebirth in the lower realms. Experiencing the result similar to the cause means that even when we are again born in the human realm, we are poor, without the means to support ourselves. Even if we have some possessions, we don't have the full use of them, but have to share them with others. Our possessions are also confiscated or stolen by other people. Losing our possessions, or having them stolen, is the result of our past—and not necessarily past life—negative karma of stealing.

The possessed result of stealing is that we live in a place that experiences a lot of drought or a lot of floods. Even the crops that do grow are eaten by worms, insects, or animals.

We have to recognize that our experience of poverty and these other disasters comes from our past negative karma of stealing. The actual way to develop the economy of a country and to transform the environment is to change the minds of the people in that country. Only by changing their attitudes into positive ones can people perform positive actions, such as giving generously to others and taking vows not to steal; and it is through these positive actions that they can be wealthy in this life and in future lives. Only this change of attitude gives them the possibility to create the cause for economic development and a better standard of living.

Unless they change their attitudes and their actions, the problems will continue. On top of this, because of their hard life, the result of their past negative actions, they will again steal and harm others in order to survive. They will think that they are helping themselves by stealing, but in reality they are again creating the cause of the same problem.

Creating the result similar to the cause means that, having stolen, we steal again; and from each complete action of stealing we will again experience the four types of suffering. Unless we transform our mind and take vows not to steal, the process goes on indefinitely.

As I have already explained in relation to taking a vow not to kill, something positive starts once we transform our attitudes and actions by keeping a vow not to steal. The ripening aspect result is that we experience rebirth as a god or a human. Experiencing the result similar to the cause means that we are wealthy. The possessed result is that we live in a place where rain comes at the right time, crops are plentiful, and there is no scarcity of food. And creating the result similar to the cause means that we again keep the vow not to steal.

Sexual misconduct. As with killing and stealing, the negative action of sexual misconduct does not come from its own side but from the side of the mind. Sexual misconduct becomes negative karma, the cause of suffering, because of the mind; it becomes negative karma if it is motivated by self-cherishing, which then causes attachment and other disturbing thoughts to arise.

Sexual misconduct done out of self-cherishing is a negative action and results only in problems. On the other hand, if sexual misconduct is motivated by compassion and done purely to bring happiness to others, it is a virtuous action and results only in happiness. If done with a pure motivation, sexual misconduct can benefit both the person doing it and other living beings. It can purify many obscurations and shorten the person's suffering in samsara. It can bring the person closer to enlightenment.

A complete negative action of sexual misconduct again results in four types of suffering. The ripening aspect result is that we are reborn in the lower realms, and the length of time we have to experience this suffering corresponds with the heaviness of the negative action.

When we are again born in the human realm, we experience the result similar to the cause, which means that we experience disharmony in our relationships, with our partner often leaving us for someone else.

The possessed result of sexual misconduct is that we have to live in filthy or muddy places where there are harmful diseases and so forth. If we normally live in a clean place, we still have to travel through filthy or muddy places occasionally, and then we should remember that this is the possessed result of sexual misconduct.

Creating the result similar to the cause means that we commit sexual misconduct again because of our past habit. The imprints left by our past negative actions of sexual misconduct mean that we again perform sexual misconduct, and each complete action again results in the four types of suffering.

The Negative Actions of Speech

Lying. Telling a lie out of self-cherishing or any other delusion is a negative action, and a complete action of lying again results in four types of suffering. The ripening aspect result is that we are reborn in the lower realms. When we are again born as a human being, we experience the result similar to the cause: other people lie to us. When we meet people who lie to us, we need to recognize that it is the result of our own past negative karma of telling lies to others.

The possessed result of lying is that we are born in a place where there is a lot of fear and cheating and where we are unable to succeed. If we are a farmer, our crops fail. If we run a restaurant or retail business, we have no customers. If we drive a taxi, we cannot find passengers. All such failures are the possessed result of the past negative karma of telling lies. Creating the result similar to the cause of lying means that we tell lies again, and thus continue the cycle of suffering.

Slander. Motivated by self-cherishing or any other disturbing thought, slander is a negative action, and each complete action of slander results in the four types of suffering. The ripening aspect result is that we are reborn in the lower realms. When we experience the result similar to the cause, other people slander us and cause disunity between us and others—our partners, parents, children, or spiritual teachers.

The possessed result is that we live in a very unattractive place, with steep mountains and valleys. There is also much fear and danger in our life. Creating the result similar to the cause means that we engage in the act of slandering again, and the complete action of slander means that we again have to experience the four types of suffering. This makes the process endless.

Harsh speech. Speaking harshly out of self-cherishing or any other delusion is a negative action, and each complete action of harsh speech again results in four types of suffering. The ripening aspect result is that we are reborn in the lower realms. Experiencing the result similar to the cause means that other people will speak harshly to us. When we experience this in our life, we need to recognize that it is the product of our past negative karma of speaking harshly to others. Even if the words we say sound sweet, they constitute harsh speech if they hurt the person we are addressing.

The possessed result of harsh speech is that we live in a rough, ugly place with no greenery or water. It is full of rocks, thornbushes, or burnt trees, and it is a dangerous place where heavy negative actions occur. Creating the result similar to the cause means that we again commit the negative action of speaking harshly to others.

Gossip. Gossiping done out of self-cherishing or any other delusion is another negative action, and each complete act of gossiping results in the four types of suffering. As before, the ripening aspect result is that we are reborn in the lower realms. Experiencing the result similar to the cause means that our speech has no power. When we talk to other people, they don't listen to us and don't do what we say. When we ask other people for help, no one listens to us or helps us. The possessed result of gossiping is that we live in a place where trees either do not produce fruit or do not produce it at the right time. And even if the fruit appears good on the outside, inside it is unripe or full of worms. If crops do grow, they don't last long. The place is also full of fear and danger. Creating the result similar to the cause means that we will find ourselves gossiping again and again.

The Negative Actions of Mind

Covetousness. A complete action of covetousness results in suffering in the same way. The ripening aspect result is that we are reborn in the lower realms. Experiencing the result similar to the cause of covetousness means that we are very discontented; we cannot find satisfaction. Also, we do not get the material possessions that we want. If we want to buy a particular object, when we go to the shop, we find that someone else has already bought it. Or if we do manage to buy it, it quickly breaks.

The possessed result of covetousness is that the quality and availability of crops and other enjoyments in the place where we live steadily decreases. Crops either don't grow, are sparse, or are eaten by animals. An example of the possessed result of covetousness is finding that food tastes bad even though it looks good on the outside, though this can also be the result of other negative karma. And creating the result similar to the cause means that we continue to feel covetous.

Ill will. The ripening aspect result of ill will, the wish to harm others, is rebirth in the lower realms. Experiencing the result similar to the cause means that other people have ill will toward us. The possessed result of the negative karma of ill will is that we live in a place where there is a lot of fighting, contagious disease, and harm from spirits, poisonous snakes, scorpions, or biting insects. When we experience such conditions from time to time, we need to recognize that they are the result of our own past ill will, which has left negative imprints on our mind. These negative imprints then resulted in the appearance of these problems in the place where we live. These appearances are the creation of our own mind. Creating the result similar to the cause means that we continue to feel ill will toward others and act in ways that harm them.

Wrong views. Generating a wrong view means denying the existence of reincarnation, karma, emptiness, or something else that actually exists. The ripening aspect result of wrong views is rebirth in the lower realms. Experiencing the result similar to the cause means that it is difficult for us to understand Dharma. No matter how logically Dharma is explained to us, we have difficulty even comprehending the words. We also act with cunning, concealing our faults and cheating others.

The possessed result of wrong views is that we are born in a dirty place. If oil, gold, or jewels were once produced there, they no longer are. We also look at suffering as pleasure, unclean things as clean, and so forth. When we have problems, we cannot find anyone to help us. Creating the result similar to the cause means that we generate wrong views again.

If we want to be healthy and to have a long life, now and in all our future lives, we have to change our mind and our actions by taking vows to abandon these ten kinds of negative karma. This is the essential solution. Happiness in our future lives can only come from abandoning these negative actions.

Buddha taught that we are our own guide and our own enemy. When we create good karma, the cause of happiness, we are our own guide; when we create the cause of problems through generating negative thoughts, we are our own enemy. Because we are the creator of both our happiness and our suffering, we have incredible freedom. With so much freedom to make our life better, we can be full of hope. By understanding Buddha's teachings on karma, we know the causes of happiness and how to create them, and we know the causes of suffering and how to eliminate them. We have free will, because we can create the cause to achieve any happiness that we wish and we can stop our suffering by eliminating or reducing its causes. The more we understand karma, the more free will we have. Understanding karma does not imprison us; instead it liberates us from the prison of suffering, the prison of delusions. Understanding karma gives us the key to escape from the prison of negative emotions in which we are caught.

The Buddha's fundamental philosophy is that we are the creator of our own happiness and of our own problems, that there is no external creator. Everything we do, including reading this book, is our own decision; it has not been decided by somebody else. Everything we experience, every moment of every day, is the creation of our own mind.

11 *Transforming Illness into Happiness*

〜

T HE MAIN MEDITATION in thought transformation is looking at everything as positive rather than as negative, and we have incredible freedom to do this because everything comes from our own mind. Whether we are happy or unhappy, healthy or unhealthy, is determined by our mind, by the way we think.

By transforming our problems into happiness, we use them to benefit ourselves and all living beings. In other words, we use our problems to develop our mind and to bring happiness to others. If we can transform our problems into happiness, especially into the path to enlightenment, experiencing a disease can itself become medicine. This is the real medicine, because it does not just stop our suffering but removes the causes of disease and of all other suffering—the negative karma, delusions, and negative imprints in our mind. The psychology of thought transformation is essential in healing, because it enables us to use our disease not only to end all suffering but to achieve enlightenment.

By remembering the purpose of our life, that we are responsible for freeing all living beings from suffering and for bringing them happiness, we should experience every problem we encounter—whether cancer, AIDS, or even death—for the benefit of other living beings. When we have a problem, such as a particular disease, we should experience it on behalf of the other living beings who have the same problem and on behalf of those who have more and much worse problems. We should dedicate our experience of the problem to freeing the numberless other beings from all problems and their causes and bringing them ultimate happiness.

Experiencing our problems on behalf of others not only purifies the cause of our problems but brings us satisfaction. Transforming our problems into the path to enlightenment purifies unimaginable obscurations and accumulates extensive merit. In this way, we will find satisfaction no matter what problem we have. Even if we are experiencing depression, with this attitude we can enjoy it. Actually, depression disappears when we practice thought transformation.

We can transform all our problems into happiness, the happiness of this life and beyond this life. We can transform all our failures, whether in business, study, or spiritual practice. We can transform criticism, a bad reputation—and even death, from which we have been trying to protect ourselves since birth. Rather than rejecting death, many tantric practitioners accept it gladly and use it as a skillful means to generate realizations of the path to enlightenment and to be reborn in the pure land of a fully enlightened being. Many meditators pray during their life to be born in such a pure land and use their death as a means to achieve this goal because it is a quick way to reach enlightenment. A pure land, where there is no suffering at all, is like a utopia. For many years I mixed up the words "utopia" and "Ethiopia" and thought Utopia was a place with drought, fighting, and many other problems. I was seeing a pure land as hell and hell as a pure land.

We can transform any problem, even death, into happiness. The point is not so much to stop the experience of problems but to stop the conditions that we call "problems" from disturbing our mind, and instead use them to support the spiritual path that we practice. Our main aim is to not allow problems to become obstacles to the development of our mind in the path to full enlightenment.

Learning Not to Dislike Problems

When we have a problem, transforming it into happiness is accomplished through two thoughts. First, we have to eliminate the thought that looks at the situation as a problem and establishes the thought of disliking it. Second, we have to generate the thought that looks at the problem as positive and establishes the thought of liking it. When we are able to look at problems as a source of happiness, the thought of liking them will naturally arise.

How do we eliminate the thought that interprets a situation as a problem and dislikes it? We have to realize that if we heed this thought, our mind will become habituated to seeing situations as problems, until we will see almost everything that happens to us as a problem. Once we are accustomed to seeing undesirable conditions as problems and disliking them, even very minor things will become huge problems for us. In this way, our worry, fear, and emotional pain will increase, and it will be difficult for us to ever feel happy or relaxed.

Even such an insignificant thing as finding some mice or tiny insects—a few mosquitoes or fleas—in our room will become a huge problem for our mind. We won't be able to stand it and will have to move to another place. If our food is cold or not cooked exactly the way we like it, this minor thing will be a huge problem and make us very angry. Tiny things will drive us crazy.

When we are habituated to this pattern of behavior, we will be disturbed by almost everything that we see, hear, smell, taste, or touch. Almost everything we encounter will become a problem and will cause us to generate negative thoughts and perform negative actions. Everything that appears to us will appear to be our enemy. It will then be very difficult for us to find any happiness in life.

We have to recognize that all the problems in our life come from our own mind. There are two ways of looking at any situation, including having a disease: it might be a problem or it might not be a problem. With one interpretation we see a problem, with another we do not. When we dislike a particular situation, we interpret it as a problem, apply the label "problem" to it, and we then see it as a problem. Once we have applied this label, a problem appears to us. If we do not label something a problem, we do not see it as one.

In response to external factors we experience pleasant, unpleasant, or indifferent feelings—and we need to understand that even the external factors that affect our feelings come from our mind. When we encounter something desirable, we interpret it as being pleasant; it then appears to us to be pleasant, and we establish the thought of liking the situation and experience happiness. When we have to separate from that desirable object, our feelings change from pleasant to unpleasant. We interpret separation from the object as bad and establish the thought of disliking it. We also experience unpleasant feelings when we encounter an undesirable object. What makes the experience unpleasant? We interpret the situation as bad, label it "bad," and then establish the thought of disliking it.

Take the example of someone we regard as our enemy. We won't feel angry with the person unless we think, "They are bad because they dislike me and are trying to harm me." It is very clear that it is not the person but our own concept of the person that upsets us. We create the concept and that concept then makes us angry.

When we encounter this person we regard as our enemy, we don't think of their positive qualities or of the benefit we can derive from them. We can learn so much about the nature of our mind from someone who dislikes us and opposes the wishes of our attachment and selfishness. They can help us to develop patience, loving kindness, compassion, wisdom, and other precious qualities of mind. They can help us to develop the path to enlightenment.

Like using poison as medicine, we can gain infinite benefit from our enemy if we use them as an object of meditation in this way. If we use our enemy in a negative way, we will get only a negative result; but if we use that same person in a positive way, we will get only benefit. It is up to us; it all depends on how we look at and use our enemy.

Unless we realize that our problems are simply our own interpretations of situations, we will blame other people, the weather, or some other external factor as the cause of every problem we encounter. Our hallucinations about the causes of our problems will blaze up like a fire and increase the problems in our life. Our negative thoughts and actions will then fan the flames.

Consider paranoid schizophrenics, who see and hear strange things that other people do not. They hear people in the next room criticizing them, for example, even though there is nobody there. They create their own reality and then torture themselves with their belief in that reality. The anxiety and fear they suffer can cause many problems for them, including murder or suicide. Instead of blindly believing in their own perceptions, they should immediately check whether or not they are true. If they checked whether anyone was in the next room and found no one there, it would enable them to recognize that their perception was false and make it easier for them to distrust their perceptions in other instances. In the future they would have some doubt as to the reality of what they were experiencing. The initial experience would help them to recognize that what they think is happening might just be their own hallucination. But they will understand the true situation only if they do not completely trust their own perception. Complete trust in their own perception will block any opportunity to find out what is really happening.

Our mind is like a baby, and we are like the parent that protects it from danger. A major problem with schizophrenics is that they do not take responsibility for their own mind; they do not watch over their mind and analyze their thoughts, but blindly believe in and do whatever their mind suggests. We cannot blindly follow the impulses of our mind. We have to regard our mind as a baby, and constantly check what it is doing. We listen to the mind when it wants to do something beneficial, but we ignore it when it wants to do something harmful or unreasonable. It can be dangerous to listen to everything the mind suggests. Before we act on our ideas we have to analyze them carefully. The result of our analysis should be that we disregard the thoughts that bring problems and act on those that benefit us and others.

Schizophrenia is also quite common in the East. In Tibetan medicine schizophrenia is classified as *lung,* or wind disease, though there are many other types of wind disease. Stress is a type of wind disease, and severe stress can lead to schizophrenia. Some illnesses found in the West are not common in the East, but various types of wind disease are common. In Eastern philosophy, schizophrenia is easily explained in terms of its internal cause and external conditions. The main cause is a negative action motivated by a strong delusion, such as ignorance, anger, or attachment, which harms other living beings or holy beings. The person then fears the consequences of the negative action they have done; they are anxious because they feel they are in danger of being criticized or even physically harmed.

Performing a negative action opens the door to harm from other beings, human and nonhuman. The person becomes a target. Paranoid schizophrenia results when the inner cause of negative karma and delusions forges a connection with the external condition of spirits. Spirits are able to harm us only after we have created negative actions motivated by delusion. If we are free from such faults, there is no way we can receive harm from other beings. This is illustrated by the story of Buddha's enlightenment in Bodhgaya, India. On the morning of the day Buddha became enlightened, ten million spirits attacked him with thunderbolts and all kinds of weapons in an effort to prevent his enlightenment. When the weapons approached Buddha, however, they were all transformed into flowers, which rained down on Buddha's holy body. If the mind is pure, there is no reason to receive harm from anyone.

I once saw a TV program on schizophrenia, which featured a hostel where schizophrenic people lived together. One woman, who was crying and pleading for help, said that doctors could not explain either the cause of schizophrenia or the cure for it. The thought occurred to me that while certain medical treatments, such as surgical operations, are better in the West, the East has more to offer in the case of schizophrenia. Buddhism offers a variety of methods to treat schizophrenia.

The best solutions are thought transformation and purification practices, which purify the negative thoughts and actions that are the cause of the problem. It is best for people with schizophrenia to do these practices themselves, but other more qualified people can also be asked to perform certain pujas and meditations to control the external beings that are causing the problem. Some of these pujas involve ordering the spirits to liberate the person from their harm.

Many lamas living in the West are qualified to do these practices to benefit people with schizophrenia. Even without doing any additional pujas, these lamas help other people simply by doing their daily meditation practices and prayers. Healing someone of spirit harm usually requires more than knowledge of the appropriate meditation or mantra, and many of the qualifications are quite rare. For example, a person who lives with a pure morality has great power to heal and to control spirits. When such practitioners request help from enlightened beings or protectors, their pure moral conduct obliges the enlightened beings and protectors to assist them. Such practitioners work together with these higher beings to control the spirits.

Recovery from schizophrenia depends on various factors, including the heaviness of its cause. If it is caused by heavy negative karma, a powerful remedy is required. Not everyone can be cured through the methods I have mentioned, but it is a common experience in the East that some can certainly be helped.

The point to understand is that everything we see and hear comes from our own mind. If we recognize this, any strange things we see and hear will not bother or harm us. If we realize that they are caused by wind disease, we won't trust them. And when we don't trust them, but instead recognize them as hallucinations, they will not bother us. However, if we don't relate them to our own mind but believe that their source is solely external, we will be frightened and might even drive ourselves crazy.

Accepting Problems

When we encounter an undesirable situation, we should remind ourselves that there is no benefit in looking at it as a problem and causing ourselves worry and fear. In *A Guide to the Bodhisattva's Way of Life,* the great bodhisattva Shantideva advises that if a problem can be solved, there's no point in being unhappy about it.[1] If there is a solution to a problem, you simply apply the solution. It is ridiculous to be unhappy about a situation if you have a way to resolve it. If there's a solution, use it. Just do it!

Shantideva adds that if a problem can't be solved, again, what's the point of being unhappy about it? Even if we cannot manage to resolve a problem, there is no point in being unhappy about the situation. For example, becoming upset because we cannot turn our house into gold or the sky into the earth does not help at all. There are some problems that we cannot avoid, whether it is an incurable illness or an irrevocable breakdown in a relationship. In the case of an unavoidable problem that we simply have to endure, it doesn't help to be unhappy about it. We need to accept the situation rather than reject it.

During a retreat I did in Adelaide, I used to listen to the radio in the afternoon. One afternoon the program was on depression, and the guest was a female psychologist who had written books on the subject of depression. She seemed to have a controversial philosophy, which differed from that of most other psychologists. Her essential advice to people with depression was that they should accept their depression rather than reject it. She advised them to tell themselves, "I deserve to have this depression because I am weak."

Her advice was quite intelligent. It seemed that she had analyzed other methods of dealing with depression and found them unsatisfactory, whereas accepting depression immediately reduced the associated emotional problems of worry and fear and brought peace. Her advice to accept depression rather than reject it is controversial because it completely opposes our usual way of thinking. Our selfish mind wants to be free from depression, not accept it. The conclusion she reached represents a radical change of concept, but it accords with the philosophy of thought transformation.

This psychologist's advice, however, made no mention of the long-term management of depression. We accept today's depression and this month's depression, but what do we do about all our future depression? Is there a solution that ensures that we never have to experience depression again? Her initial idea was good, but she lacked an ultimate solution.

It is clear that there are many disadvantages to looking at situations as problems, and if we become habituated to this way of thinking, we will interpret even minor discomforts as huge problems. We have to remember these shortcomings and be determined that when anything undesirable happens to us, we will not look at it as a problem but instead welcome it as something pleasant. We have to be courageous and generate a strong intention to do this at the beginning of each day. If we can stop interpreting miserable conditions as problems and instead look at them as pleasant, even huge disasters will become insignificant and feel as light as cotton wool.

Next we have to consider how to see problems as pleasant, because once we do, the thought of liking them will naturally follow. To see problems as pleasant and like them, we have to meditate on the benefits of problems.

12 *The Benefits of Illness*

ञ

To TRANSFORM OUR PROBLEMS into happiness, we have to learn to see them as pleasant. Instead of disturbing us, our problems will then help us to achieve the realizations of the path to enlightenment, which is the ultimate healing of mind and body. We can then heal not only our own mind and body but those of every other suffering living being.

There is no benefit in assuming that a certain situation is necessarily a problem. It only tortures us and makes us miserable. It is wrong to be pessimistic and live in black fog, thinking that all we have are problems, for this is the view of only one of our many minds. In the view of this one mind, there is a problem in our life; but in the view of another mind, there is no problem. Out of ignorance or laziness we choose a dark view of things, but we could choose other views. In the view of the positive mind, there are no problems.

Rather than making a situation more painful, we can choose to see it as positive and even enjoy it, knowing that it is supporting us in actualizing the path to enlightenment. The basic psychology of thought transformation is to break our wrong concept of problems and to generate instead a happy mind that looks at every problem as positive. This basic process can eliminate depression, loneliness, and all the other problems that seem to have no solution.

To enjoy problems we have to reflect on their benefits as extensively and as effectively as possible. We should consider these benefits from many different angles. Various benefits are mentioned in the verses of *A Guide to the Bodhisattva's Way of Life* and in other thought-transformation texts, and we can elaborate on them drawing on our own wisdom and experience.

Using Illness to Train in Meditation

Problems can bring us joy by encouraging us to generate the path to enlightenment, which frees us completely from all suffering and its causes because it removes the seeds of delusions and their imprints. Once the delusions have ceased, we no longer perform actions motivated by them, so we no longer create the causes of suffering. We are then able to guide all other beings to the peerless happiness of full enlightenment.

The situations that we call "problems" actually oblige us to meditate, to develop our mind. Because of illness or another problem, we practice meditation and develop our inner qualities. In other words, by forcing us to practice meditation, our illness gives us the chance to end all our problems and their causes. It actually helps us to end not just disease but every single problem and its causes. We gain this ultimate benefit from illness if we practice meditation, which transforms poisons into nectar. According to our own capacity, our own skills in meditation, we transform the poison of our illness into nectar so that it helps us instead of harming us. Because our illness supports our development of the path to enlightenment, we should see it as a source of joy.

Using Illness to Eliminate Pride

One of the benefits of illness is that we can use it to destroy pride, which has many shortcomings. Each time pride arises it leaves an imprint on the mind, and when the imprint becomes thick, it is very difficult to free the mind from obscurations and achieve full enlightenment. This also applies to anger, attachment, and all the other delusions.

In the sutra teachings Buddha explains the results of pride as follows. "Ignorant ones under the control of pride will be reborn in the unfortunate realms, where there is no opportunity to practice Dharma.

They will be reborn in poverty and find it difficult to support themselves. They will be reborn in low castes. They will be born blind or very weak. They will also have an ugly form or a bad color."

As a result of pride, we will be reborn in the lower realms, where we will have no opportunity to practice Dharma; and even when we are eventually born again as a human being, we will still have no opportunity to practice Dharma and develop our mind toward liberation or enlightenment. We may be born into one of the lower castes, for example. In the East, birth into a low caste means that a person is not respected, so they have little power to benefit other people.

In *A Guide to the Bodhisattva's Way of Life,* Shantideva explains that being upset by suffering eliminates arrogance and causes compassion to arise for the circling ones.[1] The term *circling ones* refers to other living beings caught in the cycle of samsara. Problems make us develop compassion for other beings who are circling in the suffering realms. As Shantideva says, becoming upset when we fail at something eliminates our pride, which is what makes it difficult for us to develop our mind. We can transform our failure into happiness by reflecting that if we had succeeded, we would have developed even more pride and then would have to experience all the shortcomings of that pride from life to life. Feeling upset when we fail actually helps us to achieve the greatest success, because it enables us to actualize the path to enlightenment.

The Kadampa geshes explain that many problems occur because of pride. The Kadampas were great meditators who practiced the graduated path to enlightenment in the tradition passed down from the great Indian pandit and yogi, Lama Atisha. They saw every word from any of Buddha's teachings as a personal instruction to achieve enlightenment and were renowned as great practitioners of thought transformation.

There is a Kadampa saying, "Being praised inflates our mind and causes greater pride to arise. Being criticized instantly destroys our faults." Developing our mind in the path to enlightenment comes about through recognizing and eliminating our faults; only then can the actions of our body, speech, and mind become the constant cause of happiness. One of the benefits of criticism is that it can help us to rid ourselves of our faults.

When we are praised, we feel up; a little later, when someone criticizes us, we go down again. To protect ourselves from such emotional ups and downs and ensure stability of mind, we should remember the problems caused by praise, especially the obstacle it can become to the development of our mind. We will not cling to praise once we are aware of the problems we experience from it. In this way we will have continual peace in our heart, and the praise will not interfere with our attainment of the path to enlightenment.

This does not mean, however, that we should not praise others. Praising others, whether they are ordinary or enlightened beings, is good. Best of all is to praise someone we don't like, because it directly opposes our self-cherishing and pride, and thus becomes a powerful way to develop our mind. When we praise our enemy in front of other people, we are offering the victory to them and taking the loss upon ourselves. Praising someone we don't like or respect is a direct challenge to our pride, because we usually act arrogantly toward people we don't respect. It takes a lot of courage but is a powerful way to destroy our pride. Of course, it depends on our motivation. When discussing the nonvirtue of harsh speech, His Holiness the Dalai Lama explained that saying apparently sweet words is harsh speech if our words are meant to hurt the other person.

When we praise others, especially our enemies, we should do it sincerely from our heart by remembering their kindness. We should recall that all our past, present, and future happiness is received through the kindness of our enemy. Because holy beings such as Buddhas feel only infinite love and compassion for us, they give us no opportunity to practice patience. Because they love us, our friends and family also give us no opportunity to practice patience. Strangers neither like nor dislike us, so again they give us no opportunity to practice patience.

Among all the numberless living beings, our enemy is the only one who gives us the opportunity to practice patience. No one else gives us any opportunity at all. Our enemy is the only one who helps us to complete the realization of patience, thus enabling us to achieve enlightenment for the benefit of all living beings.

We call someone our enemy because they do not like us and show anger toward us, and when we are not trying to practice patience, we do not want anything to do with such a person. We regard them as a problem, and they appear to us to be a problem. When we are trying to practice patience, however, we appreciate the kindness of our enemy. Their anger toward us is an essential requirement if we are to develop our mind in the path to enlightenment. Rather than appearing as an unwanted problem, our enemy appears as a welcome, useful person who supports the development of the path within our mind. They no longer appear to us as a problem but as a source of happiness.

We should think deeply about the kindness of any person who is angry with us. The kindness of our enemy is as infinite as space, because through enabling us to practice patience they not only bring us peace and all the realizations of the path to enlightenment but also enable us to bring every living being to the peerless happiness of enlightenment. When we think of their kindness, we feel joy from the very depth of our heart.

Even if we offered mountains of gold or the whole sky filled with diamonds to our enemy, it would not be enough to repay their kindness. Nothing can compare to the value of the deep peace we immediately experience in our heart when we practice patience with our enemy. We cannot repay them for this peace of mind let alone for enlightenment. This makes our enemy much more precious than any material wealth.

Using Illness to Purify Negative Karma

We can use our problems to purify negative karma, the cause of problems, and also to make us careful not to create further negative actions. It follows logically from this that problems also make us happy to create good karma, the cause of happiness.

When we experience a problem and check for its cause, we find that the cause is not external but in our own mind. As I have already explained, our problems are caused by the negative imprints left on our mind by delusions and by the actions motivated by these delusions. Because the continuation of consciousness does not have a beginning, we have been accumulating the causes of problems during beginningless rebirths. Discovering this inspires us to purify the causes of problems that we have already created so many times in this life and during beginningless past lives and also inspires us to be careful to stop creating further causes of problems.

A thought transformation text mentions that "sickness is a broom," because it cleans away negative karmas and obscurations. Meditators in Tibet did not have vacuum cleaners—or even electricity—in their hermitages, but these days we could say that sickness is a vacuum cleaner that cleans away mental garbage. Through experiencing our disease, we exhaust our past negative actions, which are the cause of not only our disease but all our problems. We can then see our disease in a positive light as a source of happiness.

The same text also explains that "suffering is the blessing of the guru." (Or, if you believe in God, you could think that your illness is the blessing of God.) What does this mean? When we encounter sickness or other difficulties, we can think that it is the blessing of our guru in the sense that our guru is helping us to purify our negative karma. Whether we are working, doing retreat, or studying Dharma, we should recognize any difficulty we encounter while trying to follow the guru's advice as the blessing of the guru. Any problem that we experience, including sickness, is the blessing of the guru, who is helping us to purify our obstacles. Instead of experiencing a big disaster, we have been able to purify our negative karma through experiencing a small problem. The problem is a blessing because it purifies much negative karma and many delusions, the potential causes of many other problems.

How can we transform being poor into happiness? We simply need to think of the benefits of being poor and the shortcomings of being wealthy. This will inspire us to see our poverty as a source of happiness, because it supports our actualizing of the path to enlightenment.

When we think about the lives of wealthy people, who generally have many problems and much mental suffering, our attachment to wealth will quickly disappear. Wealthy people worry about protecting their wealth and about increasing it; they also worry about someone else becoming wealthier. The lives of wealthy people are also filled with distractions; they have so many things to do and so many sense pleasures to indulge in that they do not find time to meditate, and this makes it difficult for them to achieve realizations. If we are poor, on the other hand, we can succeed in our practice of meditation because our hardships help us to accomplish our Dharma practice.

The Kadampa geshes say that a comfortable life exhausts the merit created in the past, just as a shopping spree exhausts the money saved over many years. In reality, living a comfortable life diminishes our good karma. Even though we might be living in luxury at present, it is only for a short time; when our past good karma is exhausted, our wealth will disappear, and we will again experience a life of poverty.

Experiencing a miserable life, on the other hand, means that we are exhausting our past negative karma, the cause of our present and future problems. In this way, we can see an unhappy life as something positive; we can transform it into happiness.

Using Illness As an Inspiration to Practice Virtue

Problems such as sickness can also inspire us to perform positive actions. Understanding that problems are caused by our delusions encourages us to transform our mind and develop loving kindness, compassion, patience, wisdom, and other positive minds.

Problems can also strengthen our resolve to live in morality and inspire us to take vows, the cause of happiness now and of good rebirth in the future. Experiencing problems can encourage us to make vows not to perform the various negative actions, such as killing, stealing, and lying, that harm us and other living beings.

Using Illness to Meditate on Emptiness

We can also use any sickness we experience to meditate on the ultimate nature, or emptiness, of sickness. Realizing the ultimate nature of the I is extremely important because this realization eliminates the ignorance that is the root of all problems. We can realize the ultimate nature of sickness in the same way.

The thought transformation text that I mentioned previously also explains that "suffering is a manifestation of emptiness." I discussed this earlier when I described how "AIDS" is a label. When doctors see a particular change in the cells of a person's body, they give it the label "AIDS." The doctor does not apply the label "AIDS" before or even at the same time as he sees this change; he applies it only after he sees the change. Therefore, what the doctor initially sees is not AIDS, but the base to be labeled AIDS. Seeing this base is the reason that he applies the label "AIDS" and then believes in that label. In other words, AIDS is simply a concept, an idea. AIDS is nothing more than what is merely imputed by the doctor's mind and by the patient's mind.

Therefore, there is no inherently existent AIDS. The real AIDS that appears to us to exist from its own side is a hallucination. It doesn't exist. The real AIDS that appears to be independent, inherently existent, and have nothing whatsoever to do with our mind is a complete hallucination. It is false; it is completely empty. That inherently existent AIDS is the object to be refuted.

Meditating on the emptiness of an illness—whether it is AIDS, cancer, or simply a headache—can bring powerful healing. Recognizing the hallucination, that there is no real disease that exists from its own side, also reduces the negative emotions of anxiety and fear. And meditating on the ultimate nature of disease can help us to realize the ultimate nature of the I, thus leading us to enlightenment.

Using Illness to Develop Loving Kindness

We can use a problem such as disease to develop loving kindness by thinking, "Just like me, numberless other living beings lack temporary happiness, as well as the ultimate happiness of full enlightenment. Therefore, I will use my problem to bring all of them this happiness."

Using Illness to Develop Compassion

One of the greatest benefits of experiencing a disease or any other problem is that we can use it to develop compassion for the other beings who are suffering in samsara. To appreciate this benefit fully, we have to realize just how precious and important compassion is. Otherwise, when we hear that problems help us to generate compassion, we might not think that is important.

Compassion is incredibly important and precious because all our own happiness, now and in the future, and the happiness of every other living being, depend on our compassion. Once we appreciate how precious compassion is, we see how important it is that our problems help us to develop compassion for others. We then see our disease and other problems in a positive light.

We easily feel compassion for others who have a problem similar to ours. If we have a blinding headache, for example, we naturally feel compassion for anyone else with a headache. The same applies to any disease. We feel empathy for and want to help other people with the same disease as we have because we know how it feels. If we didn't have the disease, we wouldn't feel this strong compassion. We naturally feel compassion for such people, and we can expand this compassion more and more. This feeling of compassion and the wish to help others are benefits of our having an illness.

We have to think about problems in a more expansive way, however, and not simply focus on one problem, such as a particular illness. As I mentioned earlier, there are many different levels of problems. Disease is just one tiny problem among the thousands of problems that are in the category of the suffering of suffering; and living beings also experience the suffering of change and pervasive compounding suffering. Just as how well doctors treat a disease depends on the extent of their knowledge of disease, how well we generate compassion depends on the extent of our knowledge of suffering.

We have to look not just at our sickness but at all the shortcomings of our own samsara, our own suffering realm. We then have to look at the numberless others who have the same disease as we have, as well as many other experiences of the suffering of suffering, suffering of change, and pervasive compounding suffering. We should think, "I myself am nothing, my problem is nothing. Numberless others are experiencing not only this suffering but even worse suffering. How wonderful it would be if they were free from all their suffering. I will free them from all their suffering." In this way we use our problems to develop great compassion.

Each time we use our problems to generate great loving kindness and great compassion, we accumulate infinite merit and purify obscurations, the cause not just of disease but of all suffering. If we have great loving kindness and great compassion, we can enjoy any problem that we experience. We can enjoy having cancer or AIDS; we can even enjoy dying.

13 The Ultimate Benefit of Illness

დ

The heart practice is to use illness and all our other problems to generate bodhicitta, the altruistic thought to achieve enlightenment for the sake of other living beings. The loving, compassionate thought of bodhicitta is the very heart of the teaching of Guru Shakyamuni Buddha. Bodhicitta is the best medicine, the best meditation, the best spiritual practice. Living our life with bodhicitta is the best way to take care of our health and the best way to heal AIDS, cancer, and every other disease. It provides the best protection for our life.

Bodhicitta means letting go of the I and cherishing others. The I is the source of all our emotional problems and of all the obstacles to our own success and happiness and to our bringing success and happiness to numberless other living beings. Others are the source of all our happiness, from the temporary happiness we experience in our daily life up to the ultimate happiness of liberation and full enlightenment. Since bodhicitta, the altruistic mind that cherishes others and seeks to bring them happiness, is generated in dependence upon the existence of suffering sentient beings, we receive all our happiness through the kindness of others.

Bodhicitta is also our best friend. External friends can change, but bodhicitta is always the same. It never changes and it never cheats us; it never harms us but always benefits us and other living beings. It is the best, most reliable friend.

Bodhicitta is also the best means of gaining success, in this and future lives, especially success in attaining liberation and full enlightenment. Success is a dependent arising; it depends on causes and conditions. Success in finding happiness has to come from a particular cause, good karma, which has to come from positive intention. With bodhicitta, this thought of benefiting living beings, one collects the most extensive merit, or good karma. As Shantideva says in *A Guide to the Bodhisattva's Way of Life,* even without actually engaging in an action to benefit others, just by wishing to benefit others, one collects merit as vast as the sky.[1] Since merely wishing to benefit others collects skies of merit, bodhicitta is the best means to achieve success in finding happiness. This is the logical reasoning that explains why bodhicitta is the source of success. The same reasoning applies to finding wealth.

By having bodhicitta, we become a friend to all living beings. If we feel distant from other living beings, as if there were a wall between us and them, bodhicitta will break down the wall, so that we feel close to all living beings. With the realization of bodhicitta, we hold all living beings in our heart. Our loving kindness, compassion, and bodhicitta are the source of all our happiness and success and that of all the numberless other living beings.

Whether we are sick or healthy, with the thought of bodhicitta, our life will always be beneficial for others; everything we do will always be beneficial for other sentient beings. Our life will be useful all the time, because it is lived for other sentient beings. In this way the purpose of our living will be fulfilled.

Developing bodhicitta is the quickest, most powerful way to purify obstacles to happiness and to accumulate merit, the cause of happiness, especially the ultimate happiness of full enlightenment. Without bodhicitta, we cannot achieve enlightenment or accomplish the highest goal in life: bringing every other suffering being to enlightenment. The wish to practice bodhicitta, to exchange self for others, is the best among all wishes.

How can we use our problems to generate this thought of enlightenment? We have to consider the source of all our problems. All our problems basically come from cherishing the self, so the self is the object to be renounced forever. All our happiness comes from the kindness of others, so other living beings are the object to be cherished forever. For this reason, we should renounce the self and cherish other living beings. To train our mind in exchanging self for others, we need to analyze in detail the shortcomings of self-cherishing and the infinite benefits of cherishing others. Destroying self-cherishing allows us to develop the altruistic mind of bodhicitta, which leads us to the highest happiness of full enlightenment and enables us to lead everyone else to enlightenment. At the same time, without any expectation from our side, bodhicitta naturally brings us the temporary rewards of happiness, success, fame, wealth, and power.

The Shortcomings of Self-cherishing

Why do situations in our life become problems? Because we mistakenly identify ourselves with our self-cherishing. Take the example of relationship problems. It is the attachment that arises from self-cherishing that makes us dissatisfied with our present partner and reject him or her for someone new. We can clearly see that the problem would not have happened if we had not followed our self-cherishing. Also, if we live our life by identifying ourselves with our self-cherishing, it hurts us when our partner stops loving us. Why? Because it hurts our self-cherishing. Because we see ourselves as one with our self-cherishing, any hurt to our self-cherishing hurts us. This way of identifying ourselves is completely wrong; it is completely different from the reality of what we are. When we analyze the problems we experience in our daily life, we see that they are directly related to our self-cherishing thought. The proof of this is that when we separate ourselves from self-cherishing thought, we have no problems in our life; it doesn't bother us if our partner leaves us, for example.

When we have a disease, if we are friends with self-cherishing, our illness will bother us; if we separate ourselves from self-cherishing, it will not. Even though the external situation is the same, the way we deal with it makes a huge difference. When we are aware of the problems caused by our self-cherishing, we will blame it as the cause of our illness rather than pointing to an external cause. Separating the I from the self-cherishing thought gives us the space to see self-cherishing as our real enemy.

Even though we see the I as inherently existent, as having nothing to do with our mind, this I does not exist. The real I that appears to us—"real" in the sense of existing from its own side—is a hallucination. Earlier I discussed how the body is not the I, the mind is not the

I, and even the association of the body and the mind is not the I. Even though the I exists—it performs all the activities of sleeping, eating, walking, sitting, experiencing happiness and problems—it doesn't exist anywhere on this association of body and mind.

The I, which is merely imputed by the mind, appears to us to be inherently existent; we then believe in this inherently existent I and cherish it as the most precious and important among all the numberless living beings. Pacifying the problems of this I and obtaining happiness for it becomes the most important thing in the world. In reality, however, we are cherishing a hallucination. When we analyze the object that is the basis of our self-cherishing, we find nothing there to cherish; it is empty. When we do not check, but simply believe in the hallucination, it seems as if there is a real I that is worth cherishing. This is the nature of our self-cherishing.

Since the mind is not the I, how could the self-cherishing thought be the I? The I is not self-cherishing thought; self-cherishing thought is not the I. They are different. Self-cherishing thought is simply one of the bases to be labeled "I." We have to understand this point clearly.

Because we haven't generated wisdom through understanding the conventional and ultimate nature of phenomena, we are left with the false views of ignorance, which identifies the self-cherishing thought as the I, and we believe there is no way for the I to exist without self-cherishing. Many mistakes would follow if self-cherishing thought were indeed the I. Since there are 84,000 delusions, there would have to be 84,000 I's. In that case, we would have to buy tickets for thousands of I's whenever we traveled. We would also have thousands of mothers and fathers. Since each parent has hundreds of positive and negative thoughts, each of those thoughts would also be an I. And when we married, there would be no such thing as monogamy because we would marry thousands of wives or husbands. Obviously, this is completely contradictory to our experience.

Also, if the self-cherishing thought were the I, the I would have to cease when the self-cherishing thought ceased. This would mean an I exists that cannot actualize bodhicitta and cannot experience full enlightenment.

With our ignorant concepts, we identify the self-cherishing thought as the I and think that there is no way for the I to exist without self-cherishing thought. But self-cherishing thought is not independent. It exists in dependence upon causes and conditions, and this means it can be eliminated by other causes and conditions. For example, we can eliminate it by training our mind in exchanging self for others, by learning to renounce the self and to cherish others.

How can we exchange ourselves for others? How is it possible to cherish others instead of ourselves? Consider the fact that we have received our present body from our parents; our body was originally part of the bodies of our parents, whose bodies also came from the bodies of other people. We then labeled "I" on this body and cherished it, even though it was originally part of our parents' bodies. In the same way, since what we call "others" is merely a label our mind gives to the bodies of other people, our mind can switch from cherishing the I to cherishing others. This is the logical reasoning that explains how we can change from cherishing the self to cherishing others.

There are two ways to meditate in order to realize how all our problems come from self-cherishing thought. One analysis involves seeing how our problems come from negative karma performed out of self-cherishing. Meditation on the shortcomings of self-cherishing thought is also meditation on karma; it is an extensive and effective way to think about the cause of suffering. So many of our problems are related to the ten nonvirtuous actions, and these actions are made nonvirtuous by our attitude of self-cherishing. There is no negative karma, cause of our suffering, from its own side. It is created by our mind.

The other analysis, which is shorter, involves seeing how our present problems are directly related to our self-cherishing, how all the problems we experience have an immediate relationship with our self-cherishing. If we are friends with self-cherishing thought, we have problems in our life; but the moment we recognize self-cherishing thought for what it is and separate ourselves from it, we have no problems in our life.

When we do not analyze the reality of our life, we can think that self-cherishing thought is our friend. Western culture, in particular, advises us that self-cherishing helps and protects us. If we use our wisdom to check the truth of this, however, we see that it is a hallucination. In reality, self-cherishing constantly harms us; it destroys us and our happiness. It does not allow us to achieve temporary and, especially, ultimate success.

We create every problem that happens to us in our life. All our problems come from our self-cherishing, not from other people. The main cause of our problems, and not just of disease, is our mind. It is obvious that people with strong self-cherishing have little peace and happiness and cause many problems to others. Such people cause disharmony wherever they go.

As long as we are under the control of self-cherishing, we feel jealous of anyone who has more wealth, education, or power than we do. We feel competitive with people we regard as our equals and we feel arrogant toward those we regard as our inferiors. With everyone we meet, self-cherishing causes us to generate disturbing thoughts and to create negative karma. Our self-cherishing constantly tortures us. It never leaves us in peace, but brings us much worry and fear. It also brings us the pain that comes from anger, attachment, jealousy, pride, and the other delusions.

Healing ourselves of self-cherishing is essential, because our selfish attitude to life is the source of so much unhappiness, depression, loneliness, and stress. If we do things because we are seeking solely our own happiness, and even that just in this life, our selfish motivation brings us stress. Self-cherishing also makes us take the victory for ourselves and give the loss to others, which means it actually obliges us to create the cause of failure. It brings us failure and loss in many thousands of lifetimes and creates obstacles to enlightenment.

It is our self-cherishing that prevents us from generating compassion for others and from helping them. It also prevents us from developing wisdom. Self-cherishing has not allowed us to practice meditation and end all our suffering; it has not allowed us to achieve the ultimate happiness of full enlightenment.

We should use every problem we experience as a weapon to destroy self-cherishing thought, our real enemy. We should give every problem given to us by self-cherishing thought back to our self-cherishing thought in order to destroy it. When we are being criticized, for example, rather than taking the criticism upon ourselves, we should switch the object and use the criticism as a weapon to destroy our self-cherishing. We should immediately think, "This is exactly what I need to destroy my self-cherishing, which constantly tortures me. It interferes with my happiness, both temporary and ultimate, and causes all my problems. My self-cherishing also harms all other beings, directly or indirectly, and from life to life." If we meditate in this way, we will actually see criticism and other undesirable things as useful and necessary because they help us to develop our mind and lead a better life. Self-cherishing is a disease, and criticism is the medicine that cures this chronic disease of the mind.

We should recognize self-cherishing as our real enemy and disease, criticism, and every other problem as the weapon that can destroy it. We should welcome the problem and give it back to the self-cherishing thought in order to destroy this enemy that constantly harms us. It has harmed us in the past, it is harming us now, and it will harm us in the future. The concept that our problems are harmful to us will disappear when we give the problems back to our self-cherishing thought. Our problems will no longer bother us, because we will see that they are only benefiting us by enabling us to destroy our self-cherishing, the enemy that brings all our problems and makes us constantly unhappy and dissatisfied.

The Benefits of Cherishing Others

Other living beings are the source of all our happiness. We receive all our past, present, and future happiness through the kindness of other living beings. For example, other living beings are responsible for our having a precious human rebirth and for our being able to live for so long in a safe, peaceful environment. These conditions are the results of our past positive actions of living with the vow not to kill or harm others. As I have already explained, we experience four different types of happiness from the positive action of living this way. One happiness is that we have a precious human body. Another is that we live a long life, which is experiencing the result similar to the cause. The possessed result is that we live in a place with little fear or danger, so that we have comfortable, relaxed lives. The fourth result is that in this life we again practice the morality of not killing others, which is creating the result similar to the cause.

Each of the ten virtuous actions results in happiness in a similar way, and all the happiness that we experience in our daily life is basically related to the virtuous actions that we have practiced in the past. My point is that we receive all this happiness through the kindness of other living beings. Take the example of our perfect human rebirth, which gives us the opportunity to develop our mind and achieve any temporary or ultimate happiness that we wish, as well as allowing us to free all other living beings from suffering and its causes and to bring them happiness. We have received our perfect human rebirth and even its causes (having kept the vow not to kill, practiced charity, and dedicated merits toward receiving a perfect human rebirth) through the kindness of other living beings. If other living beings did not exist, we would have no opportunity to practice morality. When we take a vow not to kill, for example, we make the vow in relation to every single living being. Our perfect human rebirth depends upon each living beings' kindness in even existing, as does every merit we are able to accumulate and every happiness we are able to offer others while we have a perfect human rebirth. Each time we generate a motivation of bodhicitta, for example, we collect infinite merit—and this is by the kindness of each living being.

We will also achieve good rebirths in our future lives by the kindness of each living being, because creating the causes of a good rebirth depends upon the existence of living beings.

We will also achieve the ultimate, everlasting happiness of liberation, with cessation of all suffering and its causes, through the kindness of each living being. How? The fundamental path that allows us to achieve this is again morality. In dependence upon the higher training in morality, we achieve concentration. In dependence upon perfect concentration, we then achieve great insight. Therefore, we also achieve the fundamental paths to liberation in dependence upon the kindness of each living being.

We will even achieve the peerless happiness of full enlightenment, with cessation of all obscurations and completion of all realizations, through the kindness of each living being. The very root of the Mahayana path, the ultimate goal of which is full enlightenment, is bodhicitta, and bodhicitta depends on the kindness of living beings. Without the existence of suffering sentient beings, there is no way we can actualize bodhicitta. Therefore, each sentient being is extremely precious and kind.

On top of this, all the comforts and enjoyments of our daily life depend on the kindness of living beings. Numberless insects had to suffer and die so that we could live in a comfortable house, and many other living beings had to create the negative actions of harming and killing them. We received the comfort of a house to protect us from the elements through the suffering and killing of numberless living beings.

It is the same with our clothing. Many living beings had to suffer and die so that we could enjoy the comfort of our clothing, especially if it is made of silk or fur, and many other beings had to harm and kill them.

We also receive the pleasure of our food and drink in dependence upon the kindness of living beings. Even for us to enjoy one cup of tea or one bowl of soup, numberless microscopic beings have to suffer and die. Numberless insects have to suffer and die in the fields so that we can eat one grain of rice, and many other beings have to create negative karma by harming them. And each grain of rice came from a previous grain of rice, and that grain from a previous grain, and so on. When we think of the continuity of one grain of rice, we cannot even imagine the number of beings that suffered and died in the long history of one tiny grain of rice, nor can we conceive of the number of human beings who created negative karma by harming them.

Since we depend upon the kindness of other living beings for all the comforts and enjoyments in our life, there is no way we can use these things solely with the thought of our own happiness. Such an attitude would be very cruel to other living beings. Because they are the source of all our enjoyments, we have to do something to benefit the numberless living beings.

Every single living being is unbelievably precious and can benefit us so much. Cherishing and serving even one living being leads us to enlightenment, because it purifies so many obscurations and accumulates so much merit. Cherishing even one living being—whether our mother, father, child, or even our enemy—enables us to rapidly develop our mind in the path to enlightenment. They are our real teachers. By showing compassion for even one living being, we can achieve all the realizations of the Mahayana path, from bodhicitta up to enlightenment.

On the other hand, not cherishing one living being—someone who dislikes us, for example—blocks our enlightenment. It is a fundamental obstacle to our achieving the peerless happiness of full enlightenment because it blocks the door of the Mahayana path, bodhicitta.

I have already explained how all our problems come from cherishing the I. As long as there is self-cherishing, there is no enlightenment, and self-cherishing is the greatest obstacle even to our temporary happiness. It is the reason we cannot find peace of mind in our daily life. Since cherishing ourselves is the door to all problems, we have to renounce ourselves and cherish others, even if it is only one living being. Even a single other living being is more precious than we are, because all our happiness and success comes from this one living being and all our problems come from the I.

Since even a single other living being is more precious and important than we are, it follows that two living beings are even more precious and important, so we should cherish and serve them. A hundred living beings are much more precious and important than we are, so we should cherish and work for them. Now, living beings are numberless, so the numberless living beings are unbelievably precious and important; because they are so much more precious and important than we are, we should cherish them. When we consider the numberless living beings, we become completely insignificant; we become nothing.

We can now see that our problems are nothing. When we are concerned only for ourselves, we think that we have many problems. Through meditating on exchanging self for others, however, we see that no matter how many problems we have they are insignificant. There is nothing more important in our life than to cherish and work for the numberless other living beings. Work other than this is empty, meaningless.

14 *The Heart of Healing: Taking and Giving*

೩

THE BODHICITTA PRACTICE of taking and giving, or tong-len, is the quickest, most powerful way to heal ourselves. In the taking and giving meditation, by generating great compassion we take the suffering and causes of suffering of the numberless other living beings within ourselves and use them to destroy our self-cherishing thought, the source of all our problems; by generating great loving kindness, we then give other living beings everything that we have: our body, our relatives and friends, our possessions, our merit, and our happiness. We perform this practice of exchanging self for others after we have meditated on the shortcomings of self-cherishing and on the kindness of other living beings and the benefits of cherishing them. We should do the practice of taking and giving whenever we have a problem, whether it is AIDS, cancer, some other disease, the breakdown of a relationship, failure in business, or difficulty in our spiritual practice.

The taking and giving meditation is a profound and powerful practice in which we use our own pain to develop compassion for other living beings. Through this meditation, we experience our disease and all our other problems on behalf of all living beings. Doing the meditation well helps to stop our pain, and it is not uncommon for it to even heal disease. The main point of taking and giving, however, is that it purifies the causes of disease, which are in our mind.

Exchanging self for others is a brave practice, and it is far more important than visualizing light coming from healing deities or any other meditation. By taking all the suffering of others upon ourselves and giving them all our own happiness, we use our disease to generate the ultimate good heart of bodhicitta. This is the very heart of healing.

Taking

To do the actual practice of exchanging self for others, first generate compassion by thinking of how living beings constantly experience suffering even though they have no wish to do so, because they are ignorant of its causes, or because, although they know the causes of suffering, they are too lazy to abandon them. Think: "How wonderful it would be if all living beings could be free from all suffering and the causes of suffering, karma and delusions." Then generate great compassion by thinking, "I myself will free them from all their suffering and its causes."

You then relate the meditation to your breathing. As you breathe in, imagine that you take in all the suffering and causes of suffering of other living beings through your nostrils in the form of black smoke. If you have an illness or some other problem, focus first on all the numberless other beings with that same problem, then think of all the other problems experienced by living beings, as well as their causes. As you slowly breathe in the black smoke, take in all this suffering and its causes. Like plucking a thorn out of their flesh, you immediately free all the numberless living beings from all their suffering.

Next, take all the subtle obscurations from the arhats and higher bodhisattvas. There is nothing to take from the gurus and Buddhas; all you can do is make offerings to them.

The black smoke comes in through your nostrils and absorbs into the self-cherishing thought in your heart, completely destroying it. Your self-cherishing, the creator of all your problems, becomes nonexistent. Like aiming a missile right on target, aim right at your self-cherishing thought, the target in this meditation.

Self-cherishing is based on the ignorance that holds to the concept of a truly existent I. Even though no truly existent I exists, we cherish this false I and regard it as the most precious and most important among all beings.

At the same time as your self-cherishing becomes completely nonexistent, the false I that ignorance holds to be truly existent also becomes completely empty, as it is empty in reality. Meditate for as long as possible on this emptiness, the ultimate nature of the I. Meditating on emptiness in this way brings powerful purification, purifying the actual cause of disease, which is the best way to cure disease.

To do the meditation more elaborately, you can take from others all the undesirable environments that they experience. Breathe in through your nostrils in the form of black smoke all the undesirable places that sentient beings experience. For example, imagine that you are breathing in the red-hot burning ground of the hot hells, the ice of the cold hells, the inhospitable environments of the hungry ghosts and animals, and the dirty places of human beings. The black smoke comes in through your nostrils and down to your heart, where it absorbs into your self-cherishing thought and completely destroys it. Your self-cherishing becomes nonexistent. Even the object that your self-cherishing treasures, the real I that appears to exist from its own side, becomes completely empty.

Because living beings are numberless, taking on the suffering of others and the causes of their suffering accumulates infinite merit. Each time we take upon ourselves the suffering of other beings we collect skies of merit, skies of good karma. It also brings incredible purification, purifying the cause not only of disease but of all our problems. It can also purify all obstacles to the development of our mind. Meditating on emptiness is also a powerful way to accumulate merit and to purify obscurations. By performing the meditation on taking in this way, we combine the practice of conventional bodhicitta, the altruistic thought to achieve enlightenment, with the practice of absolute bodhicitta, the direct perception of emptiness. Even though we may not possess the wisdom of absolute bodhicitta, our bodhicitta practice of taking and giving is integrated with meditation on emptiness.

Giving

Next, generate loving kindness by thinking that even though living beings want to be happy, they lack happiness because they are ignorant of its causes or lazy in creating them. And even if they achieve some temporary happiness, they still lack the ultimate happiness of full enlightenment. Think: "How wonderful it would be if all living beings had happiness and the causes of happiness." Then generate great loving kindness by thinking, "I myself will bring them happiness and its causes."

Visualize your body as a wish-granting jewel, which can grant all the wishes of living beings. Then give everything you have to every living being. Give all your good karma of the three times and all the happiness that results from it up to enlightenment, your possessions, your family and friends, and your body, visualized as a wish-granting jewel. Also make offerings to all the enlightened beings.

Each time we give our body to all living beings, we collect skies of merit, skies of good karma, the cause of all happiness, including the peerless happiness of enlightenment. By giving all our good karma to all living beings, we also collect skies of merit, as we do when we give all our happiness, the result of that merit, to others. It is an incredibly powerful meditation.

Living beings receive everything that they want, including all the realizations of the path to enlightenment. Those who want a friend, find a friend; those who want a guru, find a perfect guru; those who want a job, find a job; those who want a doctor, find a qualified doctor; those who want medicine, find medicine. For those with incurable diseases, you become the medicine that cures them.

Since the main human problem is difficulty in finding the means of living, imagine that each human being is showered with millions of dollars from your body, which is a wish-granting jewel. You can also think that the environment becomes a pure land—the pure land of Amitabha or of the Buddha of Compassion, for example. You grant all human beings everything they want, including a pure land with perfect enjoyments. All these enjoyments cause them only to generate the path to enlightenment within their mind, and they all become enlightened.

By visualizing this extensive practice of charity, you incidentally create the cause of your own wealth and success in this life and in future lives. You will find jobs easily and never be poor. In addition to these temporary benefits, you will receive the ultimate benefit of enlightenment. Being generous to others creates the cause of your own success, and with that success, you can then benefit others even more.

In a similar way, give the worldly gods, the *asuras* and *suras,* everything they need, such as protective armor. They all also then become enlightened.

When you do the practice of giving to all the hell beings, you can completely transform their environment into a blissful pure land, with perfect enjoyments and no suffering at all. Visualize the hells as pure realms, as beautiful as possible. All the iron houses of the hell beings, which are one with fire, become jewel palaces and mandalas. All the hell beings receive everything they want and then become enlightened.

Do the same for the hungry ghosts. Transform their environment into a pure realm and give them thousands of different foods that all taste like nectar. The hungry ghosts receive everything they need, but the ultimate point is that they all become enlightened.

Since animals mainly need protection, manifest as Vajrapani or another wrathful deity to protect them from being attacked by other animals. They receive everything they want, and everything they receive becomes the cause for them to actualize the path and become enlightened.

Give also to the arhats and bodhisattvas. Give them whatever realizations they need to complete the path to enlightenment.

After everyone has become enlightened in this way, rejoice by thinking, "How wonderful it is that I have enlightened every single living being."

Integrating Taking and Giving with Our Life

Do the taking and giving meditation a few times in the morning and again in the evening and remember it during the rest of the day, especially when you find yourself thinking of your problems. Simply thinking over and over "I have AIDS" or "I have cancer" will make you more depressed and anxious, thus weakening your body. You will be able to transform your problem into happiness, however, if you can use the thought that you have AIDS or cancer to develop loving kindness and compassion through doing the taking and giving meditation.

Rather than becoming obsessed with your problem and depressing yourself, and thus creating more problems, remember the practice of taking and giving. Immediately think, "I have prayed to take on the problems of others, and I have now received them. I will experience this problem on behalf of all living beings." You have done the visualization and you have now received what you requested. Rather than dwelling on your problem and simply enduring it, immediately remember that you are experiencing it on behalf of others.

Think that you are experiencing the suffering of all living beings, that your illness is the illness of all living beings. Rather than thinking that you have a problem, experience the problem for others. Since you have to experience the illness, you might as well use it to develop the ultimate good heart of bodhicitta. How do you do this? You need to be aware of all the illnesses and all the other suffering experienced by other living beings. You then experience your disease on behalf of all the other people with the same disease, on behalf of all people with disease of any kind, and on behalf of all the numberless other living beings with problems. Think that your illness represents all the disease and all the other problems of all living beings and that you are experiencing your illness so that others can be free from all suffering and its causes and enjoy the peerless happiness of full enlightenment. You prayed in the past to be able to experience the problems of others and for them to experience your happiness. Now your prayers have been answered.

If you have a headache, even if you do take medicine for it, you should make your experience of the headache worthwhile by thinking, "I am experiencing this headache on behalf of all living beings. I am experiencing it on behalf of the numberless other beings who have created the cause to experience a headache now or in the future. May all their suffering be pacified. May they have the happiness that comes with the absence of this problem, and may they especially have ultimate happiness."

Relate in the same way to any disease you have, even AIDS or cancer. When the thought comes, "I have AIDS" or "I have cancer," before anxiety, fear, or any other negative emotion has the chance to arise, immediately think, "I'm experiencing this problem on behalf of all living beings." Then try to maintain this awareness. If you allow your mind to become upset and depressed, you won't be able to do any spiritual practice. Also, when your mind is depressed, you won't want to communicate with or help others. There will be no space for helping others.

Use your experience in the path to enlightenment. If you dedicate for others, your experience becomes the path to free others from problems and bring them happiness, especially ultimate happiness.

You accumulate infinite merit each time you dedicate yourself to others by experiencing your problem on behalf of all living beings. Each time you use your sickness to develop bodhicitta, you accumulate infinite merit, and each time you experience your sickness on behalf of other living beings, you perform great purification. Feeling strongly and sincerely that you are experiencing your sickness for others purifies inconceivable obscurations. One minute of pure bodhicitta practice through experiencing your disease or any other problem for the sake of other living beings can bring more powerful purification than reciting a hundred thousand Vajrasattva mantras with self-cherishing thought.

Because the living beings for whom you are experiencing the suffering are numberless, you accumulate infinite merit and purify not only the cause of disease, but the cause of all other problems. Each time you think like this you become closer to the highest happiness of full enlightenment. In this way, having a problem such as AIDS or cancer, like tantra, can be a quick path to enlightenment.

The purpose of meditating on taking and giving in the morning is to develop the capacity to actually be able to exchange yourself for others during the rest of the day. Even if you cannot meditate all day long, keep the essence of the meditation in mind. Whether your problem involves your health, your relationships, or your work, if it is something that you have to endure, you might as well make it worthwhile. Take from the numberless other living beings all their problems—especially the same problem that you have—and the causes of their problems, karma and disturbing thoughts. Take all the problems and all the causes of problems into your own heart and use them to destroy your self-cherishing.

When you are asked to do a difficult job, accept to do it rather than pushing the problem onto someone else. If someone is carrying a heavy load, carry it for them, provided you have the strength. If your employer wrongly accuses you of making a mistake, rather than allowing someone else to suffer by proving it was not your mistake, accept the blame and allow the other person to get off free. If there is hard work to do, take it upon yourself and allow other people the happiness and comfort of not having to do the work.

If you have a choice between victory and loss, give the victory to others and take the loss upon yourself. In reality, by exchanging yourself for others, you are the one who gains, because it becomes a quick path to enlightenment. The more you sacrifice yourself for others and experience suffering on their behalf, the more quickly you will achieve enlightenment. Like tantric practice, this bodhicitta practice of taking and giving is a shortcut to full enlightenment.

By practicing taking and giving, you transform your problem into happiness and constantly have happiness in your heart. While the problem is happening, you will still be able to keep your mind in a state of peace and happiness. Negative thoughts will not arise and you will not engage in negative karma, which harms not only you but also others. This bodhicitta thought is an incredible protection.

Also, when you are able to keep your mind in a constant state of happiness, you feel very free and joyful, and you then have more space to communicate with others and to help them. With your mind in this open, joyful state, you do not have personality clashes with other people. You also have inspiration and energy for your spiritual practice.

Instead of seeing your problem as something you don't need, see it as necessary, because if you did not have the problem, you would not get the chance to use it to purify your obscurations and to accumulate extensive merit. Your problem only supports you by helping you to purify the cause of suffering and to achieve enlightenment. Each time you dedicate yourself to all sentient beings, you become closer to happiness, to the peerless happiness of full enlightenment.

Integrating Taking and Giving with Our Death

We can even use the taking and giving meditation at the time of our death. The time just prior to death is crucial, and if we can manage to use this meditation to transform our mind into bodhicitta at that time, it is better than winning a million dollars in a lottery. Rather than rejecting death as something to fear, we can use it to develop our mind in the path to enlightenment. If we cannot practice this meditation at the time of our death, we miss an incredible opportunity to benefit ourselves and other living beings.

Even when we are dying, we should try to make our death beneficial for all other living beings. At the time of our death, we should think, "I prayed in the past to take upon myself the suffering of death from other living beings; I am now experiencing my death on behalf of all the other living beings who are dying now and who will have to die in the future. How wonderful it would be for all of them to be free from the suffering of death and for me alone to experience it. Let them have this ultimate happiness."

Dying with the altruistic thought that we are experiencing our death on behalf of all living beings is the best *powa,* the best way to transfer our consciousness to a pure land of Buddha. Such a pure land has no suffering of birth, old age, sickness, or death. Even though we do not expect it, our wish to experience the suffering of others becomes the best powa, enabling us to quickly achieve enlightenment.

Kadampa Geshe Chekawa prayed every day to be born in hell in place of the living beings already there and those who would have to be born there in the future. On the day Geshe Chekawa was passing away in his hermitage, even though he was still praying for this, he had a vision of a pure realm instead of a hell realm. Geshe Chekawa then told his disciple-attendant that his prayers had failed.

Until we achieve complete control over death and rebirth, the taking and giving meditation enables us to use our death as a path to enlightenment. It can help us to reincarnate in the best situation to continue the development of our mind in the path—for example, in a family with all the conditions necessary for our spiritual practice. We can then go from happiness to happiness to the peerless happiness of full enlightenment.

Or the taking and giving meditation can help us to be born in a pure land, where we can receive teachings directly from the Buddha of that pure land and thus complete the path to enlightenment. We can then manifest in billions of forms and reveal the various methods that suit the level of mind of living beings and guide them to the highest happiness of full enlightenment. For as long as space exists or for as long as it takes to bring every single living being to enlightenment, we then constantly and effortlessly work for other living beings.

PART TWO

Healing Practices

15 Simple Healing Meditations

ᘒ

E VEN THOUGH THE PSYCHOLOGICAL ASPECT, transformation of the
mind, is much more important in healing, visualization of Buddhas,
stupas, and other powerful holy objects does have power to heal. Simply seeing a holy object has much power to benefit the mind and brings
great purification. This is why I recommend using a stupa or Buddha
as the meditation object in the white light healing meditation.

In the sutra teachings Guru Shakyamuni Buddha explains that even
looking with anger at a drawing of a Buddha causes a person to eventually meet ten million Buddhas. This comes about mainly through the
power of the holy mind of a Buddha. The figure of a Buddha symbolizes a holy being with a pure mind that is completely free from gross
and even subtle obscurations and that has infinite compassion for all living beings. The only thought in such a being's mind is to benefit all living beings. Such a holy mind has healing power because its omniscient
wisdom is bound by infinite compassion. Because of the power of the
object, looking at a drawing of a Buddha, even with anger or an impure
motivation, purifies much obscuration, and the purification of obscuration enables the person to eventually see many Buddhas.

Obscurations obscure our mind just as clouds temporarily obscure
the sun. Just like clouds, our obscurations are temporary; they can be
purified. Clouds become thinner and thinner as they disappear, revealing the sun shining in a clear blue sky. In a similar way, our obscurations
become thinner and thinner, revealing more and more phenomena to
us. Though not actually new phenomena, they are new to us, since
previously we couldn't see them because of our obscurations. We are
then able to see fully enlightened beings in their pure form and to hear

teachings and receive guidance directly from them, as described in the life stories of advanced practitioners.

If you cannot accept the visualization of a Buddha because of your faith in your own religion, you can instead visualize Jesus Christ or your particular object of faith. Religious faith is like a supermarket with a wide variety of food. You can buy whatever food you like.

The main point is that when you visualize your object of faith— Jesus Christ, for example—you should believe that Jesus has the qualities of an enlightened being: omniscient mind, compassion for all living beings, and the power to work perfectly for all beings. Even though you label the figure "Jesus Christ" rather than "Buddha," you should imagine that Jesus has the same qualities as Buddha. You are then taking refuge in an unmistaken object. Since meditating on any object with these qualities is the same as meditating on Buddha, you receive the blessings of an enlightened being when you do the visualizations of purification. This is much more meaningful than looking at your object of faith as an ordinary being; your meditation then becomes no different from visualizing light or nectar coming from a cow or a tree.

Even if you do not accept any religion at all, you can still do the meditations on white light healing, compassion, and taking and giving. In the white light healing meditation, a stupa is used as the meditation object because a stupa itself has healing power. The shape of a stupa is significant. From the bottom to the top, it depicts the whole path to enlightenment. It contains the base (the two truths, conventional and ultimate), the path (method and wisdom), and the result (achievement of the completely pure holy body and holy mind of a Buddha).

If you prefer, however, you can instead visualize universal healing power coming in the form of white light from all ten directions to heal you of your disease and the causes of disease, the negative imprints on your mind. Simply concentrate on the universal healing power illuminating your body and purifying you. Your body is transformed into the nature of light and your mind becomes completely pure. If you have cancer, you can also visualize the light hitting the point where the cancer is located and immediately healing it.

Alternatively, you can visualize the healing light coming from a crystal. First visualize that universal healing power in the form of white light absorbs into the crystal. White light then radiates from the crystal to completely heal your disease.

1 WHITE LIGHT HEALING MEDITATION

DURING THE WHITE LIGHT healing meditation,[1] four things are purified: disease, spirit harm, negative actions, and the imprints of negative actions. Spirit harm is a condition for disease but not its main cause. The main cause of disease—and of every other problem we experience—is the negative imprints left on our mental continuum by negative thoughts and actions. These negative imprints then materialize as problems. Imprints are left on the mind similar to the way images are left on the negative of a film. The scenes of a movie are recorded as imprints on the negative of a film; the film is then put in a projector, the electricity is turned on, and the scenes of the movie are projected onto a screen. The happiness and problems in our life come from our own mind in a similar way. Happiness comes from our positive thoughts, and problems come from our negative thoughts. All our positive and negative thoughts and actions basically come from imprints left on our mental continuum, or consciousness.

There are six consciousnesses: consciousness of the eye, ear, nose, tongue, and body, plus mental consciousness. It is this sixth consciousness, mental consciousness, that goes from life to life, that reincarnates. The five sense consciousnesses cease at the time of death, but this sixth consciousness continues, carrying all the imprints left by our past thoughts and actions. This mental consciousness carries all the imprints from yesterday to today, from last year to this year, from our childhood to now, and from other lives to this life. Because of the mental consciousness, we can remember now the things that we did this morning, yesterday, last year, or when we were a child.

Negative thoughts and actions and the imprints they leave on our mental continuum are the cause not only of disease but of all the problems in our life; therefore, to purify ourselves of the cause of disease, we have to purify our mind of these three factors. But we should not think of purifying ourselves of only disease, because disease is just one of the thousands of problems in samsara. Samsara refers to our aggregates, our present association of body and mind; it is also known as cyclic existence, because our aggregates cycle from one life to another.

Like crops growing from a field, many problems come from our present association of body and mind: rebirth, sickness, old age, death, separation from desirable objects, meeting undesirable objects, not finding satisfaction even after finding desirable objects. Why does our present association of body and mind produce so many problems? Because it came from impure causes, from karma and ignorance of the ultimate nature of the I and other phenomena. Because its cause is impure, this present association of body and mind is suffering in nature and produces many problems, one of which is disease. We are concentrating here particularly on purifying ourselves of the cause of disease, but at the same time we are purifying the cause of all the many other problems in our life.

Motivation

Before the meditation, first generate a positive motivation. Ask yourself, What is the purpose of my life? The purpose of my life is not just to solve my own problems and find happiness only for myself. The purpose of my life is to free everyone who is suffering from all problems and their causes and to bring them happiness, especially the ultimate, everlasting happiness of full enlightenment. *This* is the purpose of my life. *This* is the meaning of my being alive.

The purpose of my life is as vast as infinite space. It is my responsibility to free everyone from all problems and their causes and to bring them temporary and, especially, ultimate happiness.

To offer this extensive service to all other living beings, I need to develop wisdom and compassion for all beings. Therefore, I need to be healthy and to have a long life. It is for this reason that I am going to do this white light healing meditation.

Meditation

Relax in whatever position you feel physically comfortable. If you need to, you can even lie down. The most important point is not your physical posture but that your mind should be meditating.

First breathe in slowly, then breathe out slowly. As you breathe out, visualize that all your present and future disease and all the causes of problems—your negative actions and thoughts and their imprints on your mind—come out through your nostrils in the form of black smoke, just like from a factory chimney. All your disease, spirit harm, negative thoughts and actions, and their imprints come out in the form of black smoke, which completely disappears far beyond this earth. Feel that you have become healthy both physically and mentally.

As you breathe in, visualize light coming like sunbeams from a stupa,[2] which symbolizes the pure holy mind of a Buddha. Think that the omniscient mind of a fully enlightened being has taken form as the stupa.

Strong white light emitted from the stupa goes straight into your heart and completely illuminates your body. Think that all your disease, spirit harm, negative thoughts and actions, and their imprints are instantly purified. Think especially that any disease you have is gone. Your whole body becomes in the nature of white light. You have no suffering at all. Feel much joy. From the top of your head down to your toes, your whole body is filled with bliss.

Think also that your life has been prolonged and that your positive energy, the cause of happiness and success, has been increased. Wisdom, compassion, and the understanding and realizations of the path to enlightenment are fully developed within you.

Again do the meditation of purifying yourself and then receiving light from the stupa. Breathe out and purify; breathe in, receive healing white light, and free yourself from all problems and their causes. Your body becomes filled with light and bliss. Repeat this meditation over and over again.

Dedication

Now sincerely dedicate to the happiness of all living beings the positive energy you have created by doing this meditation.

Due to the positive actions and imprints I have created now, those I have created in the past, and also those I will create in the future, may I develop the ultimate good heart of bodhicitta and achieve the peerless happiness of full enlightenment. May I then lead every living being to the complete peace of mind of full enlightenment.

Due to all the merit created by generating a positive motivation and by doing this positive action of meditating, may any living being just by seeing, hearing, touching, remembering, or talking about me immediately be freed from all obstacles to happiness—from disease, spirit harm, negative actions, and obscurations—and quickly achieve the highest happiness of full enlightenment.

2 A MEDITATION ON COMPASSION

Since meditating on compassion is the most important practice for healing, be mindful of this meditation in your daily life.³ When you see other people, or even animals, remember that the purpose of your life is to free all of them from suffering and to bring them happiness. When you see the members of your family, or even strangers in the street, think, "I am here to bring them happiness." Try to feel this great compassion.

Practicing in this way in your everyday life is excellent, because it will bring you happiness and satisfaction and give meaning to your life. With this attitude you will enjoy your life.

Meditation

All bodhisattvas have great compassion, and their purpose in coming into this world is to save other beings from suffering and to bring them happiness. Visualize all the compassion of the bodhisattvas entering your body in the form of white light.

Even if you do not have faith in the existence of bodhisattvas, you know that some people have more compassion than others. Some people have little compassion, some have an average amount, and others have a lot. Everyone has compassion for at least one person.

Enlightened beings have universal compassion, compassion for every living being. Imagine drawing all this compassion into your own mind, which becomes filled with universal compassion. Feel compassion for every single living being, wishing them all to be free from suffering and the causes of suffering, which are in their mind. Extend this compassion to every human being—all the people in the streets, shops, homes, restaurants, offices—and to every animal and insect.

Now meditate on great compassion by thinking, "I will take upon myself the responsibility for freeing every living being from suffering and for bringing them happiness." Compassion becomes great compassion when you take this responsibility upon yourself.

Dedication

Due to all my past, present, and future positive actions and those done by others, may compassion—the source of all healing and happiness—be generated in my mind and in the minds of all living beings, especially those who are experiencing cancer, AIDS, and other diseases. Since lack of compassion and wisdom makes disease a problem for the mind, may compassion and wisdom be generated, and may all diseases be immediately cured.

3 TAKING AND GIVING MEDITATION

Recite the usual preliminary prayers.[4] Then recite the following verse with total sincerity and a heartfelt wish to really do it. (You can recite in Tibetan or English as long as you understand and feel what you are doing.)

de-na je-tsün la-ma tug-je-chän
ma-gyur dro wä dig-drib dug-ngäl-kün
ma-lü da-ta dag-la min-pa-dang
dag-gi de-ge zhän-la tang-wa-yi
dro-kün de-dang dän-par jin gyi lob

May all motherly sentient beings' seeds of nonvirtue,
Obstructions and suffering ripen on me now,
And by giving away all my happiness and virtues,
Please bless me to give joy to all sentient beings.[5]

Imagine your virus (sickness) and your self-concern and selfishness as a dark ball at your heart.

Now imagine the beings of the six realms all around you in human form, especially those who are ill with a sickness similar to yours. Think of their suffering—the suffering of those who are either sick like you or are potentially sick, and the suffering of the other realms of existence.

Now imagine drawing all the suffering out of them in the form of a black stream of light that comes out through their right nostril and into your left nostril. It goes straight down into that black ball in your heart and completely destroys it.

Imagine that you have completely freed all those beings from their suffering. Pray that your suffering can replace theirs, and then imagine that the black ball, which is your virus (sickness) and your selfishness, has been completely destroyed.

Next imagine giving away your happiness, body, possessions, and positive energy to them. These leave you in the form of a stream of white light from your right nostril. The white light enters through their left nostril and fills them with happiness.

This is the meditation practice that accompanies the prayer. It is a very high practice and when done sincerely can have a remarkable effect on the person who does it.

16 Medicine Buddha

Deity Meditation

THE HEALING DEITY that is best for a particular person is determined by their individual karma and should be checked with a qualified lama. The person should then receive the initiation of or permission to practice that deity, which also includes an oral transmission of the deity's mantra. Because the oral transmission of the mantra comes down in an unbroken lineage, it carries the blessings of the deity and of all the highly qualified lineage lamas down to the guru from whom the lineage is received. The purpose of receiving the lineage of the blessing is to give more power to meditation on the deity and recitation of the deity's mantra.

When we do deity meditation and mantra recitation, the main healing power comes from our motivation of loving kindness, compassion, and bodhicitta. The motivation is the important factor; the mantra recitation and other practices are secondary. Of course, the additional factors of visualizing holy objects and reciting mantras do increase the healing power of the practice. My advice to the people who have recovered from serious illness was not only to do meditation practices and recitation of mantras, but also to generate a positive, altruistic motivation. However, it seems that some people have recovered from cancer simply by visualizing white light and having strong faith that it is healing them.

Sometimes people recover by doing meditation practices themselves and sometimes by having someone else do the practices for them. It is better if the sick person does the meditation; the healing takes longer when someone else does the meditation, but it does help. One Italian student, who had received the Kalachakra initiation, worked in a hospital in a cancer ward. One of her patients had breast cancer, and when she sat with her she would visualize herself in the aspect of Kalachakra and send healing light to the woman's breast. After she had done this for about three months, the woman's cancer had reduced to half its original size.

We can do healing meditations for people who cannot do them for themselves; for example, children and old people often cannot concentrate or find it difficult to understand or to accept visualization and mantra recitation. We can help such people by doing the meditations for them or by blessing water with mantras of Medicine Buddha, Chenrezig, Tara, or another Buddha. (See chapter 21.)

To heal others we should use the practice of a deity with whom we have strong karmic connection, because our close relationship with the deity will bring success more quickly. But the healing power comes more from our faith than from visualizing the deity clearly or reciting the mantra correctly. The most important point is to feel that the healing deity has an omniscient mind, infinite compassion for you and all other living beings, and perfect power to guide you. This is the essence of the practice. Visualizing the aspect clearly does not make much difference, but you must not miss the essence of the practice.

Generating strong faith that you have been completely purified of your disease and its causes is extremely important because it is this mind of faith that is the real healing mind. Wisdom and compassion are important in other practices, but in practices involving meditation on a deity and recitation of mantra, healing has a lot to do with generating strong faith that you have been purified. This mind of faith is the actual healer.

Before we use mantras to heal others, we should first do the deity's retreat, with recitation of many mantras, as this generates healing power. And the more mantras we recite as a daily practice, the more healing power we will develop.

Before reciting the mantras, motivate to be able to actualize the meaning of the healing deity's mantra—which contains the whole path to enlightenment—within your mind as quickly as possible for the benefit of all living beings. Think, "Through this mantra, may I be able to heal every living being of disease and every other problem. May anyone who hears this mantra immediately recover from disease.

May they immediately be freed from all suffering and its causes and be purified of all obscurations. May they immediately actualize the whole path contained in the mantra."

Dedicating like this can create healing power within us. Our body, speech, and mind will then have power to heal others, immediately freeing them not only from disease but from all problems and their causes.

A pure bodhicitta motivation from the side of the healer is actually the most important factor in healing, even though to the patient it might seem to be the meditation, mantra, or medicine. If we perform pujas or recite mantras for sick people, our recitation will be more powerful if we have a good heart. Even though mantras and medicines can cure disease, the greatest benefit a healer can offer is their generation of a good heart. And it is the most important factor for the healer, because it ensures that their actions of meditating and reciting mantras become pure Dharma and the cause of enlightenment.

The Benefits of Medicine Buddha Practice

Why did the particular manifestations of the seven Medicine Buddhas appear? The fully enlightened mind has the omniscience that sees all the past, present, and future, has great compassion for all living beings, and possesses perfect power to guide all beings to enlightenment. Because the pure wisdom of the omniscient mind is bound by infinite compassion for living beings, it has manifested in various aspects, including those of the seven Medicine Buddhas, in order to pacify the obstacles experienced by living beings and to bring them temporary and ultimate happiness, especially the peerless happiness of full enlightenment.

The reason that Medicine Buddha practice is so powerful in bringing success, both temporary and ultimate, is that in the past when the Medicine Buddhas were still bodhisattvas, they made extensive prayers for living beings and promised to actualize all the prayers of living beings of the degenerate time, when the teachings of Shakyamuni Buddha are in decline. They generated a very strong intention to become enlightened for this reason; this was their motivation for meditating on and actualizing the path to enlightenment.

We are living in a time when the five degenerations (the degenerations of mind, life span, sentient beings, time, and view) are flourishing. All the other degenerations basically come from the first, the *degeneration of mind.* Ignorance, anger, desire, and other delusions have increased because living beings have not developed their minds in spiritual paths.

This has resulted in the *degeneration of life span,* with the average life expectancy becoming shorter. A few thousand years ago, the majority of people lived for a hundred years and before that, for much longer. The first human beings lived for many thousands of years in relative peace and happiness. Nowadays most people live for only sixty or seventy years. This degeneration of life span comes from the degeneration of mind.

The degeneration of mind has also led to the *degeneration of sentient beings,* whose minds have become very stubborn and difficult to subdue; it is very difficult for them to practice patience, loving kindness, compassion, and so forth. Even if they receive the necessary explanations, they are either unable to practice Dharma or find it very difficult to do so. Because of their disturbed, unsubdued minds, they cannot understand the Dharma when it is explained to them.

The *degeneration of time* is shown by the increasing frequency of fighting and wars between nations and of natural disasters such as earthquakes, drought, famine, and epidemics of disease.

Degeneration of mind has also led to *degeneration of view,* with fewer people believing the truth and more people believing lies and wrong explanations. When people tell the truth sincerely from the heart, others find it difficult to understand or believe them; but when people tell lies, others find them very easy to believe. We are talking here about conventional truth, not ultimate truth. People also hold wrong views, such as that virtue is not the cause of happiness and non-virtue is not the cause of suffering. They readily accept wrong explanations of the causes of happiness and suffering, but find it difficult to understand or to believe explanations of the unmistaken causes of happiness and suffering. People also find it very difficult to understand ultimate truth.

Because of the flourishing of the five degenerations, new disease patterns have also emerged and the diagnosis of sickness has changed.

Doctors have difficulty in recognizing the new diseases and do not know how to treat them. These patterns are just as Guru Padmasambhava predicted more than a thousand years ago.

Because the minds of sentient beings have become more degenerate, everything has become more degenerate. The power of food and medicine is decreasing, and even the power of mantra has degenerated. This is why when we do deity practice we generally have to recite more mantras than formerly. However, because of the power of the promises made in the past by the Medicine Buddhas, the Medicine Buddha mantra actually becomes more powerful as the times degenerate. This is one reason why it is important to recite the Medicine Buddha's mantra.

The Medicine Buddhas promised in the past to ensure the success of the prayers made by beings in degenerate times. Each of the Medicine Buddhas made many prayers to be able to solve the problems of sentient beings, and you can understand the extensiveness of their prayers from the long and medium-length versions of the Medicine Buddha puja text. (See the appendix.)

In the sutra *Beams of Lapis Lazuli,* Guru Shakyamuni Buddha asks his attendant, "Ananda, do you believe my explanation of the qualities of the Medicine Buddha?" Ananda replies, "I do not doubt the teachings of you, the Buddha." When Buddha then asks Ananda his reason for believing him, Ananda replies, "The Buddha has inconceivable qualities. Buddha's omniscient mind can directly see everything that exists, including the level of mind and karma of every single living being. This is why I have no doubts about what the Buddha says." The Buddha then advised, "Ananda, even those who hear the holy name or the mantra of this Buddha will not be reborn in the lower realms." Therefore, it is guaranteed that if we recite the Medicine Buddha's name or mantra every day we will never be reborn in the lower realms.

Praying to the Medicine Buddhas is powerful and quick to bring success, not only in healing but in other activities. This is why it is important to pray every day to Medicine Buddha, not only for the healing of disease, but also for the success of our spiritual practice and other activities. Because of the power of the Medicine Buddhas' compassion and altruistic intention to benefit living beings, we will be successful if we do the Medicine Buddha meditation-recitation and ask the Medicine Buddhas for help. From their side, the Medicine Buddhas made many prayers for sentient beings, especially those of degenerate times, and promised to actualize our prayers. If we pray to the Medicine Buddhas we will quickly be able to accomplish everything that we wish. The ultimate benefit that they can bring us is enlightenment.

Benefiting the Dying and the Dead

The seven Medicine Buddhas are powerful not only in healing disease, but in purifying karmic obscurations of both the living and the dead. It is excellent, with a bodhicitta motivation, to recite the Medicine Buddha's holy name and mantra in the ear of a dying person or animal, because it will prevent their rebirth in the lower realms. If the dying person can no longer hear, you can recite Medicine Buddha mantras and then blow on their body or on talcum powder or perfume, which you then apply to the body.

If the person is very close to death, you can use Medicine Buddha practice to perform powa, or transference of consciousness. To do this, visualize Medicine Buddha above the crown of the dying person's head. A tubelike beam is emitted from Medicine Buddha's heart and forms a channel inside the dying person. The channel is shaped like the handle of an umbrella, hollow inside but with no hole at the end, and extends to just below the navel. Visualize the person's consciousness as a point of white light, the size of a mustard seed, at their heart. It is not concrete or heavy, but extremely light.

Red, hook-shaped beams emanate from Medicine Buddha's heart and hook the person's consciousness, which flies up through the channel to Medicine Buddha's heart. After being absorbed into Medicine Buddha's heart, the consciousness emerges in a lotus in the pure realm of Medicine Buddha. The person then receives teachings from the Medicine Buddha, as well as predictions about their enlightenment.

If you have strong compassion and stable concentration during this meditation, you can help to prevent the person from being reborn in the lower realms.

You can also use powa pills at the time of death. The pills I had made in Dharamsala contain other powa pills blessed by Pabongka Dechen Nyingpo. The pills were also blessed by His Holiness the Dalai Lama, who kept them in his room for several days, and by Kirti Tsenshab Rinpoche and other lamas. Besides the essential ingredients, these pills contain many precious substances, such as magnetic iron and relics blessed by Guru Shakyamuni Buddha himself, from the famous statue of Shakyamuni Buddha in the Ramoche Temple in Lhasa.

When the dying person ceases to breathe, place a powa pill on the crown of their head and leave it there for some time. The power of the substances in the pill, especially the relics of great yogis, affects the dying person's consciousness and causes them to have a good rebirth. When the person's body is about to be taken away, pull the hair on their crown strongly to help the consciousness exit through the central channel at the crown. If the consciousness exits at the crown, the person is usually reborn in the formless realm or in a pure realm.

Medicine Buddha practice can purify even those who have already died, and can liberate them from suffering. It is beneficial to recite the Medicine Buddha mantra and blow upon meat that you are eating, and even on dead bodies or old bones, because it purifies karmic obscurations and allows the being to be reborn in a pure realm or in the upper realms. If you eat meat, you should make it beneficial for the animal that has been killed by reciting this powerful purifying mantra before eating the meat and dedicating strongly for the animal to be transferred immediately from the lower realms to a pure realm or an upper realm and to never ever be born in the lower realms again.

Even if the animal or human being died hundreds or even thousands of years ago and their consciousness is in the lower realms, reciting the Medicine Buddha mantra and blowing on their bones can transfer the consciousness to a pure realm or to an upper realm. After reciting Medicine Buddha mantras, we can also blow on water, sand, or talcum powder and sprinkle it on the bones or skin of a dead animal or person. At the very least, it will shorten the duration of their suffering in the lower realms.

Medicine Buddha puja is also very beneficial for those who are dying or have already died. When someone is seriously ill, an elaborate Medicine Buddha puja, which contains the dedicated purposes of each of the Medicine Buddhas, is often done. It is commonly found that this puja decides whether the person lives or dies. They either recover immediately or die within one or two days with a peaceful mind rather than living in pain for a long time. While the Medicine Buddha puja is very effective in cases of serious illness, it is also performed to bring general success in business, spiritual practice, or other activities.

Medicine Buddha is also the meditation practice or puja usually done for someone in a coma. Of course, recovery is a dependent arising; it depends on how heavy the karma of the person is. If the karma is not very heavy, doing the practice even for a short time can bring about a cure. But if the karma is heavy, you may need to do the Medicine Buddha puja many times—even ten, twenty, thirty, or forty times. When the obstacles are great, recovery won't happen unless a lot of effort is put into the pujas and meditation practices.

Geshe Lama Könchog told me that he once gave a picture of Medicine Buddha to someone in Taiwan who was in a coma, a friend of one of his students. I think that Geshe-la also did the elaborate Medicine Buddha puja for the person. The Medicine Buddha picture was put next to the person's bed one night, and the next morning they woke up from their coma.

Blessing Medicine

By reciting the Medicine Buddha mantra, we can also increase the power of medicine that we are taking or giving to others. Place the medicine in a bowl in front of you and visualize a moon disc above it. Standing on the moon disc is a blue OM surrounded by the syllables of the Medicine Buddha mantra, OM BEKANDZE BEKANDZE MAHA BEKANDZE RANDZE SAMUNGATE SOHA, in a clockwise direction. As you recite the mantra, visualize that nectar flows down from all the syllables of the mantra and is absorbed into the medicine. The syllables and the moon then dissolve into the medicine, which becomes very powerful and able to cure all diseases and spirit harm, as well as their causes, negative karma and delusions. If you are treating someone with cancer, imagine that the medicine has the specific power to cure cancer. The more faith you have and the more mantras you recite, the more power the medicine will have.

After Tibetan doctors have made medicine, they use Medicine Buddha meditation and mantras to bless it. The medicine is then more effective because besides the power of all the medicinal plants and other substances it contains, it has additional spiritual power that can help bring purification of the mind and a quick recovery.

If you are a healer, it is good to do a Medicine Buddha retreat for one or two months and to recite Medicine Buddha's name or mantra every day. It is mentioned that if you do this, the medicinal goddesses and protectors will help you to make correct diagnoses of your patients' illnesses and to prescribe the right treatments. By practicing these methods, you can even gain clairvoyance. A sign of attainment is that before patients come to you in person, they come to you in your dreams, and you diagnose their illness; the next day they actually do come to see you, and you can prescribe the exact treatment they need. Another sign of attainment is that when you concentrate on a patient's pulse, you can immediately recognize their disease and prescribe the correct treatment. Also, as you are examining the pulse, goddesses can appear in space around you and tell you the nature of the disease and its treatment.

The Meaning of the Medicine Buddha Mantra

There are long, middle-length, and short versions of the Medicine Buddha mantra. The long Medicine Buddha mantra, mentioned in the Medicine Buddha sutra, is to be found in both of the Medicine Buddha practices that follow, as is the short mantra, OM BEKANDZE BEKANDZE MAHA BEKANDZE RANDZE SAMUNGATE SOHA.

In the presence of the eight Medicine Buddhas, Manjushri requested, "As you promised in the past, please grant a special mantra to bring success quickly to sentient beings of the degenerate time, who have little merit and who are overwhelmed by much suffering, including diseases and spirit harm. May these sentient beings be able to see all the Buddhas and accomplish all their wishes." Together in one voice the eight Medicine Buddhas then granted the Medicine Buddha mantra in response to Manjushri's request. (When we refer to eight Medicine Buddhas, we are including Guru Shakyamuni Buddha; otherwise, there are seven Medicine Buddhas.)

If we recite this mantra as a daily practice, all the Buddhas and bodhisattvas pay attention to us, just as a mother pays attention to her beloved child, and always guide us. Also, Vajrapani, the embodiment of the power of all the Buddhas, the Four Guardians, and other protectors will always protect and guide us. It also purifies all our negative karma and quickly pacifies diseases and spirit harm. It also brings success; everything succeeds exactly in accordance with our wishes.

In the Medicine Buddha mantra, BEKANDZE means eliminating pain, and MAHA BEKANDZE means great eliminating of pain. One explanation of the meaning of the first BEKANDZE is that it refers to eliminating the pain of true suffering, the pain not just of disease but of all the problems of body and mind. It also eliminates the pain of death and rebirth caused by karma and disturbing thoughts.

The second BEKANDZE eliminates all of the true cause of suffering, which is not external but within the mind. This refers to karma and disturbing thoughts, the inner causes that enable external factors such as food or exposure to sunlight to become conditions for disease. Scientists claim that sunbathing causes skin cancer; as I have already explained, however, it is the internal cause that enables external phenomena to become conditions for disease. Without the cause in the mind, there is nothing to make external factors become conditions for disease.

The third phrase, MAHA BEKANDZE, or great eliminating of pain, refers to eliminating even the subtle imprints left on the consciousness by disturbing thoughts.

The Medicine Buddha mantra actually contains the remedy of the whole graduated path to enlightenment from the beginning up to the peerless happiness of full enlightenment. The first BEKANDZE contains the graduated path of the being of lower capability in general; the second BEKANDZE, the graduated path of the being of middle capability in general; and MAHA BEKANDZE, the graduated path of the being of higher capability. Reciting the mantra leaves imprints on our mind, so that we are able to actualize the path contained in the mantra. It establishes the blessing of the whole path within our heart; we can then generate the whole graduated path to enlightenment, as signified by BEKANDZE BEKANDZE MAHA BEKANDZE.

The OM is composed of three separate sounds, "AH," "O," and "MA," which signify the Medicine Buddha's completely pure holy body, holy speech, and holy mind. Actualizing the whole path to enlightenment purifies our impure body, speech, and mind and transforms them into the Medicine Buddha's pure holy body, holy speech, and holy mind. We can then become a perfect guide for living beings. With our omniscient mind we are able to effortlessly, directly, and unmistakenly see the level of mind of every living being and all the methods that fit them in order to bring them from happiness to happiness, to the peerless happiness of full enlightenment. We also have the perfect power to manifest in various forms to suit every living being and reveal the necessary methods to guide them, whether giving material help, education, or Dharma teachings. Whenever an imprint left by their past positive actions ripens, without delay of even a second, we can reveal the various means to guide that living being to enlightenment.

1 MEDICINE BUDDHA PRACTICE

Introduction

When you do this Medicine Buddha practice for a person or an animal who is sick or dying, visualize the seven Medicine Buddhas, one on top of the other, above the person or animal.[1] First visualize that nectar emitted from the Medicine Buddha on the very top, Renowned Glorious King of Excellent Signs, purifies the being of all their negative karma and obscuration. Recite the name of Renowned Glorious King of Excellent Signs seven times, then allow it to absorb into the Medicine Buddha below. In the same way, recite the name of each Medicine Buddha seven times, then allow it to absorb into the Medicine Buddha below.

With the final Medicine Buddha, recite as many mantras as you wish and again visualize strong purification. Think that the person or animal has been completely purified, that no negative karma at all exists in their mental continuum. Their body has become as calm and clear as crystal.

The Medicine Buddha then melts into light, absorbs within the person or animal, and blesses their body, speech, and mind to become one with the Medicine Buddha's holy body, holy speech, and holy mind. Their mind is transformed into Medicine Buddha's holy mind. Meditate strongly on that oneness.

You can then think that beams are also emitted from the Medicine Buddha to purify all other sentient beings, especially those who are sick with cancer, AIDS, and other diseases. Or you can visualize the seven Medicine Buddhas above the crown of each sentient being's head and purify them in that way. Focus particularly on the person or animal you are praying for, but think that there are also seven Medicine Buddhas above the crown of every other sentient being's head.

Motivation

Begin by generating a pure motivation to make the meditation practice most beneficial by becoming the cause for you to achieve full enlightenment. In this way, you can then free every other living being from all their suffering and its causes and bring them to full enlightenment.

Think, "The purpose of my life is not just to solve my own problems and find happiness for myself, but to free every living being from all their suffering and its causes and bring them to the peerless happiness of full enlightenment. For this reason I need to develop my mind, to develop my wisdom and compassion. By actualizing this path of mental healing, I free my mind from all gross and subtle obscurations. To succeed in this I need to have a long life and to be free from outer obstacles, such as disease, and from inner obstacles, negative thoughts and actions and their imprints on my mind. Therefore, to benefit and bring happiness to every living being, I am going to do this meditation on the seven Medicine Buddhas."

Visualization

About four inches above the crown of your head is a lotus flower. In the center of the lotus is a white moon disc and seated on the moon disc is your root guru, the dharmakaya essence of all the Buddhas, in the form of the Medicine Buddha. He is blue in color, and his body radiates blue light. His right hand, in the mudra of granting sublime realizations, rests on his right knee and holds the stem of an *arura* plant between his thumb and index finger. His left hand, in the mudra of concentration, holds a lapis lazuli bowl filled with nectar. Seated in the *vajra* position, he is wearing the three robes of a monk. He has all the signs and qualities of a Buddha.

Taking refuge and generating bodhicitta

I go for refuge until I am enlightened,
To the Buddha, the Dharma, and the Supreme Assembly.
By the virtuous merits that I collect by practicing giving and the
    other perfections,
May I quickly attain buddhahood in order to lead each and every
    sentient being to that enlightened state. (3x)

Generating the four immeasurable thoughts

How wonderful it would be if all sentient beings were to abide
    in equanimity, free of attachment and hatred, not holding
    some close and others distant.
May they abide in equanimity.
I myself will cause them to abide in equanimity.
Please, Guru-Buddha, grant me blessings to be able to do this.

How wonderful it would be if all sentient beings had happiness
    and the cause of happiness.
May they have happiness and its cause.
I myself will bring them happiness and its cause.
Please, Guru-Buddha, grant me blessings to be able to do this.

How wonderful it would be if all sentient beings were free from
    suffering and the cause of suffering.
May they be free from suffering and its cause.
I myself will free them from suffering and its cause.
Please, Guru-Buddha, grant me blessings to be able to do this.

How wonderful it would be if all sentient beings were never
  separated from the happiness of higher rebirth and liberation.
May they never be separated from this happiness.
I myself will cause them never to be separated from this happiness.
Please, Guru-Buddha, grant me blessings to be able to do this. (3x)

Cultivating special bodhicitta

Especially for the benefit of all mother sentient beings, I will quickly,
very quickly, attain the precious state of perfect and complete buddhahood. For this reason I will practice this yoga method of Guru Medicine Buddha.

Seven-limb prayer

I prostrate to Guru Medicine Buddha.
I make clouds of offerings, both actual and mentally transformed.
I confess all negative actions accumulated during beginningless
  time.
I rejoice in the virtuous actions of all holy and ordinary beings.
Please, Guru Medicine Buddha, remain as our guide,
And turn the Wheel of Dharma until samsara ends.
Through the merits of myself and others, may the two bodhi-
  cittas ripen
And buddhahood be received for the sake of all sentient beings.

Mandala offering (optional)

This ground, anointed with perfume, strewn with flowers,
Adorned with Mount Meru, four continents, the sun and the moon:
I imagine this as a Buddha-field and offer it.
May all living beings enjoy this pure land.
IDAM GURU RATNA MANDALAKAM NIRYATAYAMI

Prayers of request

I beseech you, Bhagawan Medicine Buddha, whose sky-colored holy body of lapis lazuli signifies omniscient wisdom and compassion as vast as limitless space, please grant me your blessings.

I beseech you, Guru Medicine Buddha, Compassionate One, who holds in your right hand the king of medicines, symbolizing your vow to help the pitiful migratory beings afflicted by the 424 diseases, please grant me your blessings.

I beseech you, Guru Medicine Buddha, Compassionate One, who holds in your left hand a bowl of nectar, symbolizing your vow to give the glorious immortal nectar of Dharma to eliminate the degenerations of sickness, old age, and death, please grant me your blessings.

As you, the seven Medicine Buddhas, made extensive prayers in the past and promised that all those prayers would be actualized in the degenerate time, please directly show the truth of this to me and to all other sentient beings.

Guru Shakyamuni Buddha highly praised the practices of making offerings and requests to you, the seven Medicine Buddhas, as being very quick to bring blessings. Out of your compassion, please directly show this power to me and to all other sentient beings.

Visualization

Above the crown of Guru Medicine Buddha is a wish-granting jewel, which in essence is your guru.

Above that, on a lotus and moon disc, is the Buddha King of Clear Knowing, whose body is red. His right hand is in the mudra of bestowing sublime realizations and his left hand is in the mudra of concentration.

Above him, on a lotus and moon disc, is the Buddha Melodious

Ocean of Proclaimed Dharma, whose body is yellow and whose hands are in the same mudras.

Above him, on a lotus and moon disc, is the Buddha Supreme Glory Free from Sorrow, pink in color with both hands in the mudra of concentration.

Above him, on a lotus and moon disc, is the Buddha Stainless Excellent Gold, pale yellow color, with his right hand in the mudra of expounding Dharma and his left in the mudra of concentration.

Above him, on a lotus and moon disc, is the Buddha King of Melodious Sound, reddish-yellow in color with hands in the same mudras.

Above him, on a lotus and moon disc, is the Buddha Renowned Glorious King of Excellent Signs, yellow in color with hands in the same mudras.

Requests to the Medicine Buddhas

With your hands together in prostration, recite seven times the verse with the name of each Medicine Buddha and take strong refuge from your heart in that Buddha to ensure the quick success of your prayers, whether you are praying for someone to recover from an illness or for the success of a business or Dharma project.

If you are doing the Medicine Buddha practice for someone who is dying or who has died, keep in your heart the request for their rebirth in a pure land or in an upper realm.

After the seventh repetition, as you recite the verse of request, the Medicine Buddha above absorbs into the one below.

To the fully realized destroyer of all defilements who sees the true nature of things, perfect Buddha Renowned Glorious King of Excellent Signs,[2] I prostrate, make offerings, and go for refuge. (7x)

May all the prayers you made in the past and the prayers I am making now be actualized immediately for me and for all other sentient beings.

Think that Buddha Renowned Glorious King of Excellent Signs

accepts your request with delight and sends nectar beams that purify your body and mind of all disease, spirit harm, negative karma, and obscuration. Buddha Renowned Glorious King of Excellent Signs then melts into light and absorbs into Buddha King of Melodious Sound below.

To the fully realized destroyer of all defilements who sees the true nature of things, perfect Buddha King of Melodious Sound, Brilliant Radiance of Skill, Adorned with Jewels, Moon, and Lotus, I prostrate, make offerings, and go for refuge. (7x)

May all the prayers you made in the past and the prayers I am making now be actualized immediately for me and for all other sentient beings.

To the fully realized destroyer of all defilements who sees the true nature of things, perfect Buddha Stainless Excellent Gold, Great Jewel Who Accomplishes All Vows, I prostrate, make offerings, and go for refuge. (7x)

May all the prayers you made in the past and the prayers I am making now be actualized immediately for me and for all other sentient beings.

To the fully realized destroyer of all defilements who sees the true nature of things, perfect Buddha Supreme Glory Free from Sorrow, I prostrate, make offerings, and go for refuge. (7x)

May all the prayers you made in the past and the prayers I am making now be actualized immediately for me and for all other sentient beings.

To the fully realized destroyer of all defilements who sees the true nature of things, perfect Buddha Melodious Ocean of Proclaimed Dharma, I prostrate, make offerings, and go for refuge. (7x)

May all the prayers you made in the past and the prayers I am making now be actualized immediately for me and for all other sentient beings.

To the fully realized destroyer of all defilements who sees the true nature of things, perfect Buddha Delightful King of Clear Knowing, Supreme Wisdom of the Ocean of Dharma, I prostrate, make offerings, and go for refuge. (7x)

May all the prayers you made in the past and the prayers I am making now be actualized immediately for me and for all other sentient beings.

To the fully realized destroyer of all defilements who sees the true nature of things, perfect Buddha Medicine Guru, King of Lapis Light, I prostrate, make offerings, and go for refuge. (7x)

May all the prayers you made in the past and the prayers I am making now be actualized immediately for me and for all other sentient beings.

Visualization for the mantra recitation

To grant your requests, infinite beams of white light are emitted from the heart and holy body of Guru Medicine Buddha and fill your body from your head to your toes. The light beams completely purify you of all diseases and spirit harm, as well as their causes, all your negative karma and obscurations. Your body becomes as clear as crystal.

The light pours into you a second and third time, filling your body with great bliss. After the third time, Guru Medicine Buddha melts into white or blue light and absorbs into you through your crown. Your mental continuum is completely purified, and you become the Medicine Buddha.

(Those who have not received a great initiation of Action Tantra or Highest Yoga Tantra should visualize that Medicine Buddha melts into light, which is absorbed between their eyebrows, thus blessing their body, speech, and mind.)

At your heart appears a lotus and moon disc. Standing at the center of the moon is the blue seed syllable OM, surrounded by the syllables of the Medicine Buddha mantra.

As you recite the mantra, visualize that beams of light radiate out in all directions from the syllables at your heart and completely fill and illuminate all the sentient beings of the six realms. Through your great love, which wishes them to have happiness, and your great compassion, which wishes them to be free from all suffering, you purify them of all diseases and spirit harm, as well as their causes, negative karma and obscurations.

Long Medicine Buddha mantra

OM NAMO BHAGWATE BEKANDZE / GURU BENDURYA PRABHA RANDZAYA / TATHAGATAYA / ARHATE SAMYAKSAM BUDDHAYA / TAYATHA / OM BEKANDZE BEKANDZE / MAHA BEKANDZE RANDZA / SAMUNGATE SOHA

Short Medicine Buddha mantra

(TAYATHA)[3] / OM BEKANDZE BEKANDZE / MAHA BEKANDZE RANDZA / SAMUNGATE SOHA

At the conclusion of the mantra recitation, visualize that all sentient beings are transformed into the aspect of the Medicine Buddha. Feel great joy that you have been able to lead all sentient beings to Medicine Buddha's enlightenment.

Simplified visualization

Visualize Guru Medicine Buddha above the crown of your head and make the following request.

To the fully realized destroyer of all defilements who sees the true nature of things, perfect Buddha Medicine Guru, King of Lapis Light, I prostrate, make offerings, and go for refuge. (7x)

May all the prayers you made in the past and the prayers I am making now be actualized immediately for me and for all other sentient beings.

Then recite the mantra and visualize that purifying beams of light are emitted from the heart and holy body of Guru Medicine Buddha. Your sicknesses and spirit harm, as well as their causes, your negative karma and obscurations, are eliminated. Your body is completely filled with light and becomes as clear as crystal. The beams then radiate out in all directions to heal the sicknesses and afflictions of all mother sentient beings.

Absorption

After the mantra recitation, Guru Medicine Buddha melts into light and absorbs into your heart. Your mind becomes one with the dharmakaya, the essence of all the Buddhas.

Dedication

Due to the merit accumulated by doing this Medicine Buddha practice, may I complete the oceanlike deeds of the bodhisattvas. May I become the holy savior-refuge and guide of migratory beings, who have been kind to me numberless times in past lives.

Due to all my merit of the past, present, and future, may any living being who sees me, hears me, touches me, remembers me, or speaks about me immediately be released from all their suffering and experience perfect happiness forever.

Due to all the merit I have collected in the three times and all the merit collected by Buddhas, bodhisattvas, and other sentient beings, just as Medicine Buddha's compassion encompasses all beings, may I also become the foundation of the means of living for all sentient beings, who are as extensive as space.

Due to all this merit (which is empty), may the I (which is empty) quickly achieve Guru Medicine Buddha's enlightenment (which is empty) and lead all sentient beings (who are empty) to that enlightenment (which is empty) by myself alone (who is also empty).

2 THE HEALING BUDDHA

This simple but profound meditation on the Medicine Buddha and the four medicinal goddesses was taught by the great Indian master Padmasambhava.[4] It helps to heal any disease we already have and to protect us from future disease. Of course, no matter what meditation or other technique we use, the ultimate healing method involves our own mind, our own good heart. Ultimately, there is no escape from the need to watch our mind and protect it from disturbing thoughts. While deity meditations can help us receive blessings, the main practice is protecting our mind in our daily life.

Motivation

No matter what you do, it is essential to generate a positive motivation. Therefore, think as follows: "The purpose of my life is to free all living beings from all their problems and the causes of these problems, which are in their minds, and to bring all beings peace and happiness, especially the peerless happiness of full enlightenment, which they desperately need. For me to be able to do this, my mind and body must be perfect, pure, and healthy. Therefore, to benefit living beings equal to the extent of space, I am going to practice this healing meditation."

Meditation

Visualize yourself in your ordinary body, with your heart at the center of your chest, inverted, pointing upward. Inside your heart is a white, eight-petaled lotus. At its center is a moon disc, upon which is seated the Healing Buddha in the aspect of the supreme transformation.[5] His holy body is clear and in the nature of dark blue light, and he holds an arura plant in his right hand and a begging bowl in his left.

In front of the Healing Buddha is the white medicinal goddess, Actualized Wisdom; to his right is the yellow medicinal goddess, Simultaneous Wealth; behind him is the red forest goddess, Peacock's Throat; to his left is the green tree goddess, Radiant One. Each goddess is in the nature of blissful radiant light and has one face and two arms. An arura plant is in each goddess's right hand, with a vase adorned with various ornaments in the left. The four goddesses sit cross-legged, not in the full vajra position but in the aspect of offering respect to the Healing Buddha.

Then make this request:

O Destroyer, Complete in All Qualities and Gone Beyond and you four medicinal goddesses, please pacify immediately the illnesses that afflict me now and help me to avoid all future sickness.

Light rays of the appropriate color emanate from each of the five deities at your heart. Your heart and body are full of blissful light, which completely purifies all disease, spirit harm, and negative actions and their imprints. Beams of five-colored light radiate from all the pores of your body, while nectar flows down from the Healing Buddha's begging bowl and the vases held by the four goddesses, completely filling your heart and body. Generate the strong recognition that you have vanquished all disease forever and will never be sick again.

While concentrating single-pointedly on this visualization, recite the short or long Healing Buddha mantra seven, twenty-one, one hundred and eight, or more times.

Short Healing Buddha mantra

(TAYATHA) / OM BEKANDZE BEKANDZE / MAHA BEKANDZE RANDZE / SAMUNGATE SOHA

Long Healing Buddha mantra

OM NAMO BHAGAWATE BEKANDZE / GURU BENDURYA
PRABHA RANDZAYA / TATHAGATAYA / ARHATE SAMYAKSAM
BUDDHAYA / TAYATHA / OM BEKANDZE BEKANDZE / MAHA
BEKANDZE RANDZE / SAMUNGATE SOHA

If you are sick, after you have finished reciting the mantra, put some
saliva on your left palm, rub it with the tip of your right ring finger,
place the tip of this finger at the entrance of your right and left nostrils,
where the so-called All-Doing King Nerve can be found, and apply
the saliva to the afflicted parts of your body. Then recite as many
mantras of the Sanskrit vowels and consonants as possible, along with
the mantra of the Heart of Dependent Arising.

Sanskrit vowels

OM A AA I II U UU RI RII LI LII E AI O AU AM AH SVAHA

Sanskrit consonants

OM KA KHA GA GHA NGA / TSA TSHA DZA DZHA NYA / TA THA
DA DHA NA / TA THA DA DHA NA / PA PHA BA BHA MA / YA RA
LA VA / SA SHA SA HA KSHA SVAHA

The Heart of Dependent Arising

OM YE DHARMA HETU-PRABHAVA HETUN TESHAN TATHAGATO
HYA VADAT / TESHAN CA YO NIRODHA / EVAM-VADI / MAHA-
SRAMANAH YE SVAHA

This practice, a Dharma treasure *(terma)* of Padmasambhava, protects
you from both the illnesses troubling you now and those you have not
yet contracted.

Dedication

Due to all my positive actions of the past, present, and future, which bring happiness, may the ultimate good heart—which cherishes all living beings and is the source of the happiness of the three-times of myself and others—arise in those minds where it has not yet arisen, and increase in those minds where it already has sprung.

Due to my positive actions of the three times and those of all holy beings, whose attitude is the purest, may all the kind father and mother sentient beings have happiness. May I alone be the cause of this, and may the three lower realms be empty forever.

May the prayers of all holy beings—those who dedicate their lives to the happiness of others—succeed immediately, and may I alone be the cause of this.

Due to my positive actions of the three times and those of all holy beings, may I achieve the peerless happiness of full enlightenment—the state of mind that is free of all error and complete in all positive qualities—and lead all others to that state.

17 Liberating Animals: Introduction

‍‍‌‍‍‍

L IBERATING ANIMALS is a practical, powerful method to prolong life when an untimely death is threatening to end someone's life. The practice of White Tara, Namgyalma, or another enlightened being who helps to grant long life can also be done. The person would receive the initiation of a long-life deity from a qualified lama and then do the meditations and recitation of mantras associated with that deity. To help ensure a long life, the purification practice of making tsa-tsas is also commonly done.

Deaths are called "untimely" when people suddenly die even though they have enough merit to live longer. Through their positive karma from past lives, they have created the cause to have a longer life span; but, by performing a heavy negative action motivated by self-cherishing or one of the other delusions, they create an obstacle to their life, which can result in their death. An untimely death can come about through disease, a car accident, or some other condition.

To liberate animals you buy live animals from a place where they are definitely going to be killed and sold for food, then release them in as safe a place as possible, somewhere where they can live longer. The point is that prolonging the lives of the animals by saving them from being killed naturally prolongs your own life. By planting a particular seed, you get a particular result. If you plant a potato, a potato grows; if you plant chili, chili grows. The plant that grows naturally depends on the seed that you plant. In the same way, a positive action that causes others to have longer lives naturally prolongs your own life.

Because liberating animals is a way to prevent untimely death and to prolong life, it is usually beneficial in the case of serious illness, especially cancer. Many people who have done this practice have recovered from terminal cancer. Earlier I told you the story of Alice, the woman with cancer who liberated thousands of animals; it was one of the methods that helped to prolong her life.

Generally, if we wish to be healthy and live a long life in this and future lives, we should take vows not to kill other sentient beings. Other practices to prolong life include taking the Eight Mahayana Precepts and reciting certain powerful mantras. The practice of liberating animals is primarily for prolonging life, and the recitation of mantras is more for healing sickness or providing protection from the harmful beings that become conditions for certain diseases. Liberating animals is like eating a specific diet to build up your health, and reciting mantras is like taking medicine to destroy germs.

While pujas and many other practices can be done to prolong life, liberating animals is an especially effective practice. Serving other sentient beings is also effective. Helping sick people by giving them food, drink, clothing, shelter, or medicine creates the cause of long life, as does giving food to starving people.

It is best to liberate an animal that you are able to look after yourself. By feeding them every day, you perform the Dharma practice of giving charity and create much good karma, the cause of happiness. You not only bring happiness to the animal but also constantly create the cause of your own future happiness. Also, if the animal is carnivorous, you save it from killing other animals.

Animal liberation does not have to be done only for yourself. You can also dedicate the practice to members of your family or to other people. You can actually dedicate it to all living beings. If you don't have much money to buy animals, the cheapest and easiest option is to buy worms and liberate them. Whereas fish released into open water are in danger of being attacked and eaten by their natural predators, worms, as I said earlier, are more likely to live longer because they simply disappear under the ground. Liberating fish is generally quite difficult unless you can liberate them in a special pool of water where none of their natural enemies will attack them.

Saving the lives of animals is a very common practice among Chinese Buddhists and happens often at Chinese monasteries and temples. Temples in Singapore, Taiwan, and Hong Kong have special large enclosures for turtles. When people liberate turtles, they bring them to the monastery and put them in these enclosures. Visitors who come to the monastery to make offerings or simply look around then give bread and other food to the turtles.

Practicing Animal Liberation with the Six Perfections

When the practice of liberating animals is done perfectly, it involves all of the six perfections: generosity, morality, patience, enthusiastic perseverance, concentration, and wisdom.

The practice of generosity, or charity, has four categories: giving love, giving protection from fear, giving Dharma, and giving material objects. We are practicing the generosity of giving love because we are not only wishing the animals to have happiness but actually bringing them happiness by liberating them. We are giving them protection from fear by liberating them from the immediate fear of harm and death. Because the animal liberation ceremony also purifies the negative karma of the animals, we are also liberating them from the lower realms.

We are practicing the generosity of giving Dharma when we recite powerful mantras to bless water, which is then sprinkled on the animals; this benefits them by purifying their negative karma and bringing them a good rebirth in a deva, human, or pure realm.

Giving food to the animals we liberate is an example of the fourth type of generosity, giving material objects.

The practice of morality is abandoning harm to other beings. The practice of patience has three categories: the patience of definitely thinking about Dharma, of voluntarily bearing suffering, and of not becoming angry with either humans or animals at the time of liberation. Bearing the hardships involved in liberating animals, such as buying the animals and transporting them to the place where they will be set free, are included in the practice of enthusiastic perseverance.

The practice of concentration is maintaining continuous awareness of our motivation for doing the practice so that we keep our mind constantly positive. The practice of wisdom is seeing ourselves, the action of liberating the animals, and the animals that are liberated as being merely imputed by the mind.

The Benefits of Giving Dharma

It is important to do the practice of liberating animals in the most effective way—not just so that you or somebody else will have a long life, but so that the practice will be really beneficial for the animals. In this respect, the practice of giving Dharma is extremely important. If we simply buy animals from places where they are to be killed and release them where there is no danger to their lives, we are not bringing them much benefit. Since they had no opportunity to hear Dharma, when they die, most of them will be reborn again as animals or in one of the other lower realms. Of course, our action brings some benefit to the animals because we are prolonging their lives, but the most benefit comes from their hearing the recitation of mantras and of Buddha's teachings. Reciting teachings on emptiness, bodhicitta, and tantra leaves imprints on the minds of the animals and ensures that in the future they will receive a human body, meet and practice the Dharma, and actualize the path to enlightenment. Reciting Buddha's teachings for them to hear will not only end their samsaric suffering but enable them to reach full enlightenment. We thus bring infinite benefit to the animals, saving them from the entire suffering of samsara and its causes. This makes our practice extremely worthwhile and enjoyable.

There are many stories to illustrate the benefits of giving Dharma in this way. For example, after Guru Shakyamuni Buddha gave teachings to five hundred swans, in their next life they all became monks and arhats. In other words, they completely ended their samsara. A pigeon that used to hear Nagarjuna reciting teachings was reborn as a human and became a monk and a pandit. Also, the pandit Vasubandhu had a pet pigeon that heard him reciting teachings. In its next life the pigeon was reborn as a human, became a monk, and wrote four commentaries to the teachings he had heard as a pigeon.

There is also the story of the Indian traders whose ship was in danger of being eaten by a huge whale. When they recited the refuge formula loudly, the animal closed its mouth and died. The whale was reborn as a man called Shrijata, who eventually became a monk and an arhat. This was the same being that in a past life as a fly had circumambulated a stupa on a piece of dung, the karma of which enabled him to enter a monastery and become a monk.

Shrijata's Story: The Benefits of Circumambulations

Shrijata, who only began to practice Dharma as an old man, became an arhat in that same life. When he was eighty years old, Shrijata was living at home with his family, but he got fed up because his family did not treat him well. All the children made fun of him. One day he got completely fed up with their teasing and thought, "Oh, it would be so peaceful to leave home and go to live in the monastery."

So Shrijata left home and went to the nearby monastery, the abbot of which was Shariputra, one of Guru Shakyamuni Buddha's heart disciples. When Shariputra, an arhat who excelled in wisdom, checked whether or not the old man had the karma to become a monk, he could not find any. Shariputra told the old man, "Normally in a monastery you study or, if you cannot study, you serve the other monks by cleaning and so forth. If you became a monk you could neither study nor work because you are too old." Shariputra therefore refused to ordain the old man as a monk.

Shrijata got terribly upset about this. He cried and cried and banged his head against the monastery gate. After a while he went to a nearby park, where he continued to cry. At that time Guru Shakyamuni Buddha was in India. Buddha's omniscient mind sees all sentient beings all the time, so whenever a sentient being's karma ripens so that they are receptive to his guidance, he immediately appears to them in whatever form suits their mind and guides them.

Even though in the ordinary view Buddha was far away from Shrijata, he immediately appeared in front of the old man and asked him what was wrong. The old man explained everything, including how Shariputra hadn't accepted him into the monastery. Buddha then told him that he did have the merit to become a monk. Buddha said, "Shariputra has not yet completed the accumulation of the two types of merit, the merit of wisdom and the merit of method. I, however have completed the two types of merit and have achieved full enlightenment, and I can see that you do have the karma to become a monk."

Buddha meant that Shariputra, even though an arhat, still had obscurations and therefore could not see all subtle phenomena. Arhat means, literally, "one who has destroyed the enemy." This does not refer to an external enemy but to the inner enemy of the delusions and their seeds, which produce all suffering. Having completely destroyed the inner enemy, arhats achieve the ultimate, everlasting happiness of liberation, but because arhats have not yet completed the collection of the two types of merit, they still have subtle obscurations. Even though they have incredible psychic powers and realizations, they still cannot see all subtle phenomena.

Buddha, on the other hand, had completed the two types of merit, which means he had purified the two obscurations, had omniscient mind, and could see all subtle karma. In other words, the old man's karma to become a monk was a subtle karma that only a Buddha could see.

Buddha could see that Shrijata had created the karma to become a monk, even though it had been an inconceivable length of time ago and in a distant place. Buddha explained to Shrijata that in one of his past lives, an uncountable number of lives before, he had been a fly and had performed a circumambulation of a stupa. One explanation is that cow dung was floating on some water around a stupa; the fly landed on the cow dung and did a circumambulation when the water went around the stupa. The other explanation is that the fly followed the smell of cow dung lying around a stupa and thus had the good fortune to complete a circumambulation.

Even though the fly had no recognition of the stupa as a holy object or that circumambulating it would become a cause of enlightenment, its unintentional circumambulation purified negativities and accumulated merit and thus became the cause of happiness. The fly was acting totally out of attachment to the smell of the cow dung. Its motivation was completely nonvirtuous. Due to the power of the object, however, the circumambulation became virtue. Buddha explained that the small virtue of circumambulating the stupa created the cause for Shrijata to become a monk.

When Buddha checked to see which teacher had a karmic connection with the old man and could look after him, it turned out to be Maudgalyayana, an arhat who excelled in psychic powers. Of Buddha's two heart disciples, Shariputra excelled in wisdom and Maudgalyayana in psychic powers. For a teacher to be able to guide a disciple, there needs to be a karmic connection between them. If there is no connection, the teacher cannot really benefit the disciple. Buddha then offered the old man to Maudgalyayana, who was also the abbot of a monastery.

After Shrijata became a monk, the young monks in the monastery also teased and made fun of him. One day he again got completely fed up with being teased and ran away from the monastery. He decided that he would throw himself into a nearby river. At that time Maudgalyayana went looking for the old man. When he couldn't find him anywhere in the monastery, he used his psychic powers to check Shrijata's whereabouts and discovered that the old man had just jumped into the river. Using his psychic powers, Maudgalyayana immediately appeared there and dragged the old man from the river. Shrijata was shocked, because he hadn't told his teacher what he was planning to do. He could not speak for a while. When Maudgalyayana asked him why he had jumped into the river, he couldn't answer. In complete shock, he just stood there with his mouth open.

When Shrijata was eventually able to explain everything, Maudgalyayana said, "The reason you ran away from the monastery and jumped into the river is that you lack renunciation of samsara." Maudgalyayana told the old man to hold onto a corner of his robes and then flew up into the sky with him.

They flew on and on over an ocean until they came to a huge mountain of bones. After they landed on the mountain, the old man asked his teacher, "Whose bones are these?" Maudgalyayana replied, "Oh, these are the bones from your past life." The old man had previously been born as a whale. As soon as Shrijata heard his teacher say this, all the hairs on his body stood on end, and he generated renunciation of samsara. Realizing that samsara is suffering in nature and that nothing is definite in it, he generated the determination to be free from samsara, from all suffering and its causes.

Shrijata then entered the path and became an *arya* being in that life. Even though he began to practice Dharma only after he was eighty years old, he was able to become not only a monk but an arhat, overcoming the cycle of death and rebirth and completely freeing himself from the suffering of samsara. An arhat achieves total liberation from all suffering and its cause, including the seeds of delusion. He abides in that state for a number of eons until Buddha sees that it is the right time to persuade his mind to enter the Mahayana path. Buddha then sends light beams from his hand and recites a certain verse to the arhat, who then enters the Mahayana path and, by actualizing the arya Mahayana path, gradually ceases the subtle defilements. When all the subtle defilements are totally ceased, he completes the path and becomes enlightened; he can then enlighten numberless other sentient beings.

This old man's ability to enlighten numberless sentient beings came about through his being enlightened, which came about through his entering the Mahayana path, which came about through his becoming an arhat after entering the path to liberation, which came about through his becoming a monk. And he was able to become a monk because of the very subtle karma he created as a fly. With no idea that a stupa was a holy object that could purify the mind, just with attachment, this fly followed the smell of cow dung around a stupa and completed a circumambulation. Everything started from that small positive action of circumambulating a stupa. Everything—all the realizations of the five paths to liberation and of the Mahayana path to enlightenment—started from that tiny good karma created by the fly. This shows the power of statues, stupas, scriptures, and other holy objects in bringing realizations. They are very beneficial in purifying the mind and in bringing all happiness, up to enlightenment. A stupa is such a powerful holy object that even an unintentional circumambulation of one purifies negativities and accumulates merit.

It follows that the positive action of intentionally circumambulating a stupa, especially with a positive attitude of wishing to benefit other living beings, will be much more powerful. The good results of our action will be greater and more quickly experienced than those of the fly that circumambulated the stupa without any understanding or positive intention. Each circumambulation will bring unbelievable results. Not only will it heal disease, but it will purify our past negative actions and obscurations, which are the causes of disease. Besides bringing this deep healing, it will become the cause of actualizing the whole path to the peerless happiness of full enlightenment.

Therefore, a practical way to help liberate animals is to carry them in circumambulations of holy objects. If, for example, you carry a container with a hundred worms around a stupa or another holy object, each time you go around you are giving enlightenment, the greatest gift, to those one hundred animals. If you carry one thousand worms, each time you take them around you are giving enlightenment to one thousand of your mother sentient beings. You are also giving them liberation from samsara; you are ending their samsaric suffering, the continuity of which has no beginning—the most terrifying aspect of samsaric suffering is that it has no beginning. You are giving liberation from this beginningless samsara to one thousand of your mother sentient beings. You are also giving them good rebirths; you are giving good rebirths for hundreds or thousands of lifetimes to one thousand of your mother sentient beings. One circumambulation of holy objects can create the cause to receive hundreds or thousands of good rebirths because karma is expandable—much more expandable than external phenomena. One small seed can produce a large tree with tens of thousands of branches, flowers, and seeds, but karma increases even more than this.

During an animal liberation ceremony, while it is good to purify the animals with blessed water, it is also very good to take them in circumambulations of holy objects. In this way, you not only liberate them from the lower realms, but bring them to enlightenment by enabling them to create the cause of enlightenment.

Benefits of the Mantras Recited during Animal Liberation

Even though the stories I mentioned earlier about the results of the imprints of hearing Buddha's teachings are difficult for our ordinary minds to comprehend, reciting teachings, prayers, and mantras is unbelievably beneficial. If we recite the powerful mantras that purify negative karma, the animals that hear them will not be reborn again in the lower realms.

For example, any person or animal who hears the name of the Buddha Rin-chen Tsug-tor Chen will not be reborn in the lower realms. If a dying person is still able to hear and it will not create confusion in their mind, you can recite the prayer of prostration to Rin-chen Tsug-tor Chen in their ear.[1] If they can no longer hear, you can recite this Buddha's name or any of the powerful mantras mentioned in the animal liberation practice and blow on their bodies after the recitation. Or you can blow onto some water or talcum powder and sprinkle that on their body to purify their negative karma. In this way, they are not reborn in the lower realms and have the chance to be born in a Buddha's pure realm.

One of the best ways to benefit the animals during animal liberation is to bless water with the powerful mantras of Chenrezig, Namgyalma, Wish-granting Wheel, and other Buddhas, then purify the animals by sprinkling or pouring the water on them. These mantras have a lot of power, even if you yourself don't have any realization of bodhicitta, emptiness, and so forth. Recite the mantras with strong faith and think that you have purified all the negative karma of the animals. This is a very practical way of helping to liberate the animals from the suffering of the lower realms. If their negative karma is purified, they won't have to reincarnate again and again in the lower realms.

It may look easy to purify a being's negative karma and alter their rebirth, but actually it's not straightforward and doesn't work with everyone. The being involved has to have the karma for this to happen, and it also depends on how much faith we have in the mantras. There is power in the practice because of the truth of Buddha's teachings and because of Buddha's unbearable compassion for sentient beings, but it only works if the being has the karma for it to work. Not every being who is dying has the karma to be with a pure practitioner who can save them from the lower realms or transfer their consciousness to a pure realm. This only happens to some.

Benefits of the Chenrezig Mantra

The benefits of reciting the Chenrezig mantra, OM MANI PADME HUM, are as infinite as space.[2] It is said in the teachings that it would be impossible for Buddha to finish explaining the benefits of this mantra. Of course, the benefits you receive depend on how perfectly you recite the mantra, which is determined by your motivation and by the quality of your mind.

There are fifteen major benefits of reciting the Chenrezig mantra, and this applies to both the long and the short mantra. Besides healing disease and protecting from various harms, reciting the Chenrezig mantra has the following benefits.

In all lifetimes you will meet virtuous, or religious, kings.

You will be reborn in a virtuous place where the Dharma is practiced.

You will experience favorable conditions for Dharma practice.

You will always be able to meet spiritual teachers.

You will always receive a perfect human body.

Your mind will become familiar with the path to enlightenment.

You will not degenerate your vows.

The people around you will be harmonious with you.

You will always have wealth.

You will always be protected and served by others.

Your wealth will not be stolen.

Whatever you wish will succeed.

You will always be protected by virtuous nagas and devas.

In all lifetimes you will see Buddha and hear the Dharma.

By listening to pure Dharma, you will actualize its profound meaning, emptiness.

It is said in the teachings that anyone who recites the Chenrezig mantra with compassionate thought will receive these fifteen benefits.

Benefits of the Namgyalma Mantra

The mantra of Namgyalma, a female deity for long life and for purification, has infinite benefits. It is so powerful that any being who hears it will never again be reborn in the lower realms.

There is a story as to how the Namgyalma mantra originated. A deva's son called Extremely Stable One saw that his next six rebirths would be as different animals, such as a dog, a monkey, and so forth. When devas are about the die, they are able to remember their previous lives and see their future lives. In the deva realm, devas have lives filled with pleasure and experience little physical suffering; however, when they see that they are to be reborn in one of the lower realms, they experience incredible mental suffering.

When Extremely Stable One saw that he was to take rebirths as six different animals, he became very upset and asked Indra, the king of the devas, what he should do. Indra suggested that he consult Guru Shakyamuni Buddha. When Extremely Stable One went to see Buddha, Buddha manifested as the deity Namgyalma and gave him the Namgyalma mantra. Extremely Stable One recited the mantra six times each day, and after seven days he had purified all the causes of the six animal rebirths. This mantra brings powerful purification.

The kind, compassionate Guru Shakyamuni Buddha taught the Four Guardians the following benefits of reciting the Namgyalma mantra. If you wash your body, wear clean clothes and, while living in the eight precepts, recite the mantra one thousand times, even if your are in danger of dying because the life span accorded by past karma is exhausted, your life span can be prolonged, your obscurations can be purified, and you can be freed from disease.

If you recite the mantra in the ears of animals, it will ensure that this is their last animal rebirth. If somebody has a serious disease that doctors cannot diagnose, doing Namgyalma practice as described above will liberate them from the disease and end their rebirths in the lower realms. After death they will be reborn in a pure land. For humans, the present life becomes the last rebirth from a womb.

If you recite the Namgyalma mantra twenty-one times, blow on mustard seeds, then throw the seeds on the skin or bones of a being who has created heavy negative karma, that being will immediately be liberated from the lower realms and be reborn in one of the upper realms. Even if the being has been reborn in hell or another of the lower realms, their consciousness is purified, and they are reborn in the deva realms and so on.

If you put this mantra in a stupa or on a banner inside a house or on its roof, anyone who is touched by the shadow of the stupa or the banner will not be reborn in the lower realms. Also, when wind touches such a stupa or banner, or a statue containing the Namgyalma mantra, and then touches other beings, their karma to be reborn in the lower realms is purified. Therefore, there is no doubt that reciting this mantra or keeping it on your body will bring great purification.

Benefits of the Wish-Granting Wheel Mantra

This mantra, OM PADMO USHNISHA VIMALE HUM PHAT, has unbelievable benefits. If you recite the Wish-granting Wheel mantra seven times each day you will be reborn in a pure realm. Reciting this mantra and then blowing upon clothing or incense can purify you and other sentient beings. Recite the mantra, blow on the incense, and burn it; the incense smoke will then purify other sentient beings.

When this mantra is put above doorways, the people passing below are purified and are not reborn in the lower realms. In Tibet, this mantra is written on paper and placed on the bodies of people who have died, purifying them and preventing their rebirth in the lower realms.

Simply remembering this mantra once has the power to purify even the five uninterrupted negative karmas. It prevents rebirth in the Unbearable Suffering State, the level of the hells with the heaviest suffering. You purify all your negative karma and obscuration and are never reborn in the lower realms. It enables you to remember past lives and to see future lives. Reciting this mantra seven times each day accumulates merit equivalent to the merit of making offerings to Buddhas equal in number to all the grains of sand in the Ganges River. In the next life you are reborn in a pure realm and can achieve hundreds of levels of concentration.

If you recite this mantra, blow on sand, then sprinkle the sand on a dead body, the being is reborn in an upper realm even if they had broken vows and had already been reborn in the lower realms. If you recite this mantra and blow upon perfume or incense, everybody who smells the perfume when you wear it or the incense when you burn it is purified of their negative karma and can even be healed of contagious disease. It also helps you to achieve the complete qualities of a Buddha.

Benefits of the Mitukpa Mantra

Anyone who hears the Mitukpa mantra will not go to the lower realms. If you recite the Mitukpa mantra a hundred thousand times, then blow on water, sand, or mustard seeds and sprinkle that blessed substance on the body of a person or animal that has died, if that being has been born in one of the lower realms, it will immediately be liberated from those realms. Even though the consciousness has separated from the body and is somewhere else completely, because of its past connection with that body, the consciousness is still affected. All that is needed is for the blessed substance to touch some part of the body. Just by that, the being's consciousness is purified, liberated from the lower realms, and reborn in one of the higher realms.

Hearing or reciting the Mitukpa mantra can purify even someone with very heavy karma, even someone who has created the five uninterrupted negative karmas. Simply seeing this mantra can purify all negative karma. If you show a dying person the Mitukpa mantra written on a piece of paper, it can purify all their negative karma.

Benefits of the Kunrig Mantra

Kunrig is another powerful deity for purification. Again, hearing or reciting the Kunrig mantra prevents rebirth in the lower realms. Also, Kirti Tsenshab Rinpoche said that in Amdo it is customary to prepare for death by taking a great initiation of Kunrig, so that all the negative karma created in that life is purified.

Benefits of the Stainless Beam Deity Mantra

It is stated in the commentary to the Stainless Beam Deity mantra[3] that if you recite this mantra twenty-one times, then blow on sand and sprinkle it over a grave, those whose bones are touched by the sand, if born in any of the hell realms, are completely liberated from there and receive an upper rebirth. If they have taken rebirth in an upper realm, they receive a rainfall of flowers.

Benefits of the Milarepa Mantra

The Milarepa mantra, OM AH GURU HASA VAJRA SARVA SIDDHI
PHALA HUM, has similar benefits to those mentioned above. By reciting the Milarepa mantra every day, you will be reborn in the pure land
of Milarepa and be able to see Milarepa, as he promised. If you recite
this mantra and blow upon the bones or flesh of beings who have been
reborn in the lower realms, they will be purified of all negative karma
and be able to receive rebirth in a pure land.

18 Liberating Animals: Practice

༄༅

PREPARATION

Setting up the Altar

FOR THE ANIMAL LIBERATION ceremony, it is good to set up a large altar with as many holy objects—tsa-tsas, statues, stupas, Buddha's relics, Dharma texts—and offerings as possible. You can arrange an altar at the beach or near fresh water if you are going to liberate animals that live in salt or fresh water. One idea is to have five levels, one on top of another, with a large table as the bottom level. On the very top there should be a statue of Guru Shakyamuni Buddha, a *lamrim* or *Prajnaparamita* text, and a stupa, as normally advised in lamrim teachings for setting up an altar. Place as many tsa-tsas and statues as possible on the other levels. You can use pictures of Buddhas if you don't have tsa-tsas or statues. On the bottom level arrange sets of eight offerings,[1] with flowers in vases on the corners. The offerings to the guru, Buddha, Dharma, and Sangha are for the benefit of the animals; it's like a puja for the animals.

Buying and Caring for the Animals

Buy animals that are definitely going to be slaughtered and keep them in large containers. The animals can be large or small; larger animals experience more suffering when killed. Be careful of the relationship between the animals to ensure that you do not place together an animal and its natural predator. Place the containers close to the point of release and keep them shaded from the hot sun. The place for releasing the animals should be safe from natural predators, and you should not release animals that are prey and predator at the same place.

Be mindful of the condition of the animals you are liberating. For those that might not survive long, it is best to bless a bucket of water before going to the place where the animals will be released. When you arrive at the place of release, carry the animals around the altar as many times as possible at the very beginning, before the chanting of the prayers and mantras, in case some of the animals die. Some of the fish might die because they are piled up on top of each other and cannot breathe. If the circumambulations are done immediately, even if some of the animals die before release, they will have already purified negative karma and created many causes of enlightenment, liberation from samsara, and good rebirth. If the circumambulations have been done, you don't need to feel so much regret if some of the animals die while you are reciting the mantras, blessing the water, or doing the prayers.

Generate the motivation, recite a few mantras and blow on the animals or sprinkle them with blessed water. Then quickly release the ones that are having difficulties. You can recite more mantras and prayers before liberating the animals that are in good condition. It is important to check the condition of the animals because otherwise the weak animals may die before they can be released. Be careful not to cause any additional harm to the animals.

Blessing Water

To bless the water before the animal liberation, you can mix some *mani* pills into the water. Mani pills are very powerful, as they have been blessed by His Holiness the Dalai Lama and many highly attained meditators. First wrap the mani pills in cloth, crush them, then add them to the water.

The water can be blessed with mantras just before the animals arrive or even the day before the animal liberation. You can recite the names of the Thirty-Five Buddhas and the Medicine Buddhas and the mantras of Chenrezig, Namgyalma, Wish-granting Wheel, Milarepa, Medicine Buddha, and other deities. Bless the water by visualizing the particular

Buddha above the water containers; as you recite the mantra, visualize that nectar beams come from the heart of the deity and enter the water. At the end of the mantra recitation, visualize that the deity absorbs into the water, and then blow on the water to bless it. The water then has much power to purify negative karma and obscuration.

If you prepare the water beforehand in this way, the animals that are in danger of dying do not have to wait for the water to be blessed, and the water is also blessed with more mantras.

When the animals arrive, the animal liberation practice is performed as outlined below. Recite all the mantras loudly, as some animals are able to hear them. In my experience, frogs are able to hear, because they become quiet and look at you when you recite the mantras. And it is the same with pigeons. Visualize the corresponding deity above the head of each of the animals; nectar beams then flow down to purify each of the animals of sickness, spirit harm, negative karma, and obscurations.

After the recitation of each mantra, blow on the water and think, "May this purify all the negative karma and obscurations of these animals." At the end of the prayers and mantra recitations, sprinkle or pour the blessed water over the animals. If there is a big stack of shellfish, pour the water over them so that they are all touched by it.

I often use blessed talcum powder for sick and dying people, but it is not advisable to use it with animals as the powder may get into their eyes and harm them. Also, if animals such as shellfish or crabs are piled up on top of each other, not all of them will be touched by the blessed powder; when water is poured over them, however, even the ones on the bottom will be blessed.

Circumambulating

While you are reciting the mantras or after you have finished the recitation, you should carry the animals around the altar in a clockwise direction as many times as possible. With each circumambulation of the holy objects, you plant the seed of enlightenment for yourself and for each of the animals. As I have already explained, each circumambulation can create the cause to receive not only hundreds or thousands of good rebirths, but also liberation from samsara and enlightenment. Also, one circumambulation of a stupa purifies all the heavy negative karma to be born in the eight hot hells. You then release the animals. As part of the practice of generosity, you can also scatter food for the animals you have released.

Because most animals cannot see Buddha statues and many of them cannot hear prayers and mantras, the two most skillful ways to benefit them is by sprinkling them with blessed water and by causing them to circumambulate holy objects. Liberating animals in this way is highly meaningful because you purify their negative karma, stop the causes of their suffering, and plant the seed of their liberation and enlightenment. The best thing we can do is to help the animals to purify their negative karma and to create merit, the cause of happiness, especially the peerless happiness of full enlightenment. Even if the animals die soon after their release, their lives have become meaningful. Otherwise, no matter how long they live, they would simply create more negative karma by harming other animals.

THE ACTUAL PRACTICE

Motivation

First reflect that all these creatures have been human beings, just like you. But because they did not practice Dharma and subdue their minds, they have been reborn as animals. Their present suffering bodies are the result of their unsubdued minds. We would not want their body for even a second. We get upset when we see some small sign of aging in our body, such as one more wrinkle on our face. So how could we stand to have the body of one of these animals? There is no way we could stand it.

It is vital that we feel some connection with the animals. We should not look at them and think that their bodies have nothing to do with us. We should not think that the bodies of these animals are permanent or truly existent and have no relationship with their mind. And, most important, we should not think that our own minds could not create such bodies.

Reflect on the fact that every one of these animals has been your own mother. When they were human beings, they were extremely kind in giving you your body and in saving you from danger hundreds of times each day. Later, they bore many hardships to educate you in the ways of the world; they taught you how to speak, how to walk, and how to behave. They also created much negative karma to ensure your happiness.

Not only have they been kind to you numberless times as a human mother, but they have also been kind to you numberless times as an animal mother. As a mother dog they gave you milk and food. As a mother bird they fed you with many worms every day. Each time they have been your mother they have taken care of you selflessly, sacrificing their comfort—and even their lives—numberless times to protect you and bring you happiness. As animals, they have guarded and protected you numberless times from the attacks of other animals. They have been unbelievably kind like this many times.

Not only has each of these animals been your mother, they have been your father, brother, and sister numberless times. We are all the same, we are all one family—it's just that we have different bodies at the moment. We should feel as close to these animals as we do to our present family. We should hold them in our heart.

Think, "I must free all the hell beings from all their suffering and its causes and lead them to enlightenment. I must free all the hungry ghosts from all their suffering and its causes and lead them to enlightenment. I must free all the animal beings from all their suffering and its causes and lead them to enlightenment."

Reflect a little more on the specific suffering of animals. They are ignorant, cannot communicate, live in fear of being attacked by other animals, and are tortured and killed by human beings.

Then think, "I must free all the human beings from all their suffering and its causes and lead them to enlightenment." In addition to experiencing suffering as a result of their past negative karma, human beings create further causes of suffering, such as rebirth in the lower realms, by still being under the control of delusions.

Next think, "I must free all the deva beings, the asuras and suras, from all their suffering and its causes and lead them to enlightenment." Because they are under the control of karma and delusions, the devas are also not free from suffering.

"To free all sentient beings from their obscurations and lead them to enlightenment, I myself must achieve enlightenment. There is no other way. To do that I must practice the six perfections; therefore, I am going to liberate these animals and work for sentient beings by giving Dharma and food to them." Generate bodhicitta in this way.

Specific dedication

I dedicate the liberation of these animals to His Holiness the Dalai Lama, the Buddha of Compassion in human form, sole refuge and source of happiness of all living beings. May His Holiness have a long life and may all his holy wishes be fulfilled.

I dedicate this practice to the long and healthy lives of all other holy beings, those who work for the happiness of living beings. May all their holy wishes be accomplished immediately.

May all the members of the Sangha have long and healthy lives. May all their wishes to practice Dharma be accomplished immediately. May they be able to listen, reflect, and meditate; may they be able to live in pure morality; and may they complete the scriptural understanding and actualization of the teachings in this life.

May the benefactors who support the Dharma and take care of the Sangha have long lives, and may all their wishes succeed in accordance with the holy Dharma.

This practice of liberating animals is also dedicated to the long lives of all the people who are creating good karma and making their lives meaningful by having refuge in their minds and living in morality.

May this practice also be the medicine that frees everyone from the suffering of disease, especially AIDS and cancer, and from the suffering of death.

This practice is also dedicated to all evil beings to meet and practice Dharma and, after they find faith in refuge and karma, to have long lives. (If they don't practice Dharma, it will be harmful for them to have long lives, as they will continue to live evil lives.)

Dedicate also for the long lives of specific people who are sick, such as family members and friends.

Taking refuge and generating bodhicitta

I go for refuge until I am enlightened,
To the Buddha, the Dharma, and the Supreme Assembly.
By the virtuous merits that I collect by practicing giving and the
    other perfections,
May I quickly attain buddhahood in order to lead each and every
    sentient being to that enlightened state. (3x)

Generating the four immeasurable thoughts

How wonderful it would be if all sentient beings were to abide in
    equanimity, free from attachment and hatred, not holding some
    close and others distant.
May they abide in equanimity.
I myself will cause them to abide in equanimity.
Please, Guru-Buddha, grant me blessings to be able to do this.

How wonderful it would be if all sentient beings had happiness
    and the cause of happiness.
May they have happiness and its cause.
I myself will bring them happiness and its cause.
Please, Guru-Buddha, grant me blessings to be able to do this.

How wonderful it would be if all sentient beings were free from
   suffering and the cause of suffering.
May they be free from suffering and its cause.
I myself will free them from suffering and its cause.
Please, Guru-Buddha, grant me blessings to be able to do this.

How wonderful it would be if all sentient beings were never
   separated from the happiness of higher rebirth and liberation.
May they never be separated from this happiness.
I myself will cause them never to be separated from this happiness.
Please, Guru-Buddha, grant me blessings to be able to do this. (3x)

If you have time, you can also do the prayers for purifying the place,
blessing the offerings, and the invocation.[2]

Seven-limb prayer

I respectfully prostrate with my body, speech, and mind;
I make clouds of offerings, both actual and mentally transformed;
I confess all negative actions accumulated during beginningless time,
And rejoice in the virtuous actions of all holy and ordinary beings.
Please, virtuous teachers, remain as our guides,
And turn the Wheel of Dharma until samsara ends.
I dedicate my own merits and those of all others to the great
   enlightenment.

Mandala offering

This ground, anointed with perfume, strewn with flowers,
Adorned with Mount Meru, four continents, the sun and the moon:
I imagine this as a Buddha-field and offer it.
May all living beings enjoy this pure land.

Due to the merits of having offered this mandala, may all the
beings of the six realms, and especially these animals, be immediately reborn in a pure realm and attain enlightenment.
IDAM GURU RATNA MANDALAKAM NIRYATAYAMI

The Foundation of All Good Qualities[3]

Please bless me to see clearly that
Proper devotion to the kind and venerable guru,
The foundation of all good qualities, is the root of the path
And to devote myself with great respect and much effort.

Please bless me to understand that this opportune excellent
    human body,
Found but once, is very difficult to obtain and highly meaningful,
And to unceasingly generate the awareness of taking its essence
At all times, day and night.

Please bless me to be mindful of death,
As body and life are unstable,
Quickly decaying like a water bubble;
To find firm conviction that after death subsequent results
Follow white and black actions like a shadow follows the body;
And thus to be always conscientious in avoiding even small and
    subtle collections of faults
And to achieve all collections of virtue.

Please bless me to know the shortcomings of samsaric perfections:
There is no satisfaction in experiencing them,
They are the door to all suffering and are unreliable;
And to generate a great striving for the bliss of liberation.

Induced by that immaculate thought,
Please bless me to take the *pratimoksha,*
The root of the doctrine, as the essential practice
With great mindfulness, alertness, and conscientiousness.

Please bless me to see that just as I myself
Have fallen into the ocean of existence, likewise so have
All mother migrators, and to train in the supreme bodhicitta
That takes on the burden of liberating migrators.

Please bless me to see clearly that even if I generate the mere
   wishing mind,
Without cultivating the three kinds of morality
Enlightenment cannot be achieved,
And to train in the vows of the Conquerors' Children with intense
   effort.

Please bless me to quickly generate
The unified path of calm abiding and penetrative insight in my
   continuum
By calming distractions to wrong objects
And by properly analyzing the meaning of reality.

When I have become a vessel trained in the common path,
Please bless me to enter easily
The holy entrance of the fortunate beings,
The supreme of all vehicles, the Vajrayana.

At that time, please bless me to gain genuine conviction
In the teaching that the basis of achieving the two types
Of attainment is completely pure commitments and vows
And to guard them at the cost of my life.

Then, please bless me to realize exactly the essential points of the
   two stages,
The heart of the tantra sets, and to practice diligently
In accordance with the teachings of the holy ones,
Not wavering from the supreme yoga of the four sessions.

Please bless me that my spiritual guides who show such
A sacred path and my companions who practice it properly
Have stable long lives and that the multitude
Of outer and inner interruptions be thoroughly pacified.

In all my rebirths, may I never be separated from perfect gurus
And always enjoy the splendor of the Dharma;

Having completed the qualities of the stages and paths,
May I quickly attain the state of Vajradhara.

Reciting the names of the Thirty-Five Buddhas and the Medicine Buddhas

Visualize the Thirty-Five Buddhas above the animals. As you recite their names, nectar beams are emitted from their holy bodies and purify all the negative karma and obscurations accumulated by all sentient beings, and especially the animals that you are liberating, during beginningless rebirths. All the negative karma comes out of their bodies as black liquid.

At the end of the recitation, imagine that all their minds have become completely pure and that their bodies are as clear as crystal and in the nature of light; they have also generated all the realizations of the path and become enlightened.

Next slowly recite the names of the seven Medicine Buddhas, accompanied by the same purification meditation. Then complete the rest of the confession prayer, which contains the remedy of the four powers.

I, (say your name), throughout all times, take refuge in the gurus;
I take refuge in the Buddhas;
I take refuge in the Dharma;
I take refuge in the Sangha. (3x)

To the Founder, the Bhagavan, the Tathagata, the arhat, the fully
   enlightened one, to Guru Shakyamuni Buddha, I prostrate.
To the Tathagata, Great Destroyer, Destroying with Vajra Essence,
   I prostrate.
To the Tathagata, Jewel Radiating Light, I prostrate.
To the Tathagata, King Ruling the Naga Spirits, I prostrate.
To the Tathagata, Leader of the Warriors, I prostrate.
To the Tathagata, Supremely Blissful One, I prostrate.
To the Tathagata, Jewel Fire, I prostrate.
To the Tathagata, Jewel Moonlight, I prostrate.

To the Tathagata, Holy Sight Bringing Accomplishments, I prostrate.

To the Tathagata, Jewel Moon, I prostrate.

To the Tathagata, Stainless One, I prostrate.

To the Tathagata, Glorious Giver, I prostrate.

To the Tathagata, Pure One, I prostrate.

To the Tathagata, Bestower of Purity, I prostrate.

To the Tathagata, Celestial Waters, I prostrate.

To the Tathagata, Celestial Being of Celestial Waters, I prostrate.

To the Tathagata, Glorious Good, I prostrate.

To the Tathagata, Glorious Sandalwood, I prostrate.

To the Tathagata, One of Unlimited Splendor, I prostrate.

To the Tathagata, Glorious Light, I prostrate.

To the Tathagata, Glorious One without Sorrow, I prostrate.

To the Tathagata, Son of the Desireless One, I prostrate.

To the Tathagata, Glorious Flower, I prostrate.

To the Tathagata, Understands Reality by Enjoying the Radiant Light of Purity, I prostrate.

To the Tathagata, Understands Reality by Enjoying the Radiant Light of the Lotus, I prostrate.

To the Tathagata, Glorious Wealth, I prostrate.

To the Tathagata, Glorious Mindful One, I prostrate.

To the Tathagata, Glorious Renowned Name, I prostrate.

To the Tathagata, Holding the Banner of Victory over the Senses, I prostrate.

To the Tathagata, Suppressing All Completely, I prostrate.

To the Tathagata, Conqueror in All Battles, I prostrate.

To the Tathagata, Gone Beyond to Perfect Self-Control, I prostrate.

To the Tathagata, Arranging Appearances for All, I prostrate.

To the Tathagata, Jewel Lotus Who Suppresses All, I prostrate.

To the Tathagata, the Bhagavan, the fully enlightened one, Great Jewel Always Remaining in the Lotus, King with Power over the Mountains, I prostrate.

To the Bhagavan, the Tathagata, the arhat, the fully enlightened one, Renowned Glorious King of Excellent Signs, I prostrate.

To the Bhagavan, the Tathagata, the arhat, the fully enlightened one, King of Melodious Sound, Brilliant Radiance of Skill, Adorned with Jewels, Moon, and Lotus, I prostrate.

To the Bhagavan, the Tathagata, the arhat, the fully enlightened one, Stainless Excellent Gold, Radiant Jewel Who Accomplishes All Vows, I prostrate.

To the Bhagavan, the Tathagata, the arhat, the fully enlightened one, Supreme Glory Free from Sorrow, I prostrate.

To the Bhagavan, the Tathagata, the arhat, the fully enlightened one, Melodious Ocean of Proclaimed Dharma, I prostrate.

To the Bhagavan, the Tathagata, the arhat, the fully enlightened one, Delightful King of Clear Knowing, Supreme Wisdom of an Ocean of Dharma, I prostrate.

To the Bhagavan, the Tathagata, the arhat, the fully enlightened one, Medicine Guru, King of Lapis Light, I prostrate.

All you Thirty-five Buddhas and others, as many as there are Tathagatas, arhats, fully enlightened ones, who are existing, sustaining, and living, who are in the nature of the three holy bodies; all you Buddha-Bhagavans who live in all ten directions of sentient beings' worlds, please pay attention to me.

From life without beginning in samsara, in this life, in the life preceding this one, and in all samsaric realms of rebirth, whatever negative karma I have created, made others create, or rejoiced in the creation of negative karma, such as: selfishly taking the possessions of stupas, of the Sangha, of the Sangha of the ten directions, making others take, or rejoicing in the taking of; having created the five extreme negative actions (as well as the five negative actions that are close to the five extreme negative actions), making others create these actions, or rejoicing in the creation of these actions; or fully creating the path of the ten evil actions, making others create them, or rejoicing in the creation of these actions.

Being obscured by this karma, whatever has been created, causes me and other sentient beings to be born in the *narak* stages, in an animal rebirth, in the *preta* realm, in irreligious countries, as barbarians, as long-life gods, or as living beings with imperfect organs, holding wrong views, or not being pleased with Buddha's descent.

All these negativities I am announcing, I am accepting them as negative, I will not keep them secret by not confessing them, I will not hide them, and from now on, I will cut off and abstain from creating these negative actions in the presence of the Buddha-Bhagavans, who are the transcendental wisdom knowing all existence; who are compassionate eyes looking at all sentient beings all the time; who are witnesses, as the omniscient mind sees whatever negative and positive karma are created; and who are true knowledge, as the omniscient mind fully sees all existence and explains exactly and without mistake to all followers.

All Buddha-Bhagavans, please pay attention to me. From life without beginning in samsara, in this life, in the life preceding this one, and in all samsaric realms of rebirth, whatever merit I have created by even small actions: such as by giving just one mouthful of food to a being born in the animal realm; whatever merit I have created by keeping precepts; whatever merit I have created by following the conduct for receiving sublime nirvana; whatever merit I have created by fully ripening other beings' minds; whatever merit I have created by generating bodhicitta; and all the merit of the highest transcendental wisdom I have created—putting together my own virtues and then heaping them together with those of all others, thus totaling all our merit, I fully dedicate it all to the highest of which there is no higher, to that even above the highest, to the higher of the highest (and to the *nirmanakaya* which is higher than the Hinayana arhat). For this reason I completely dedicate to the highest, fully accomplished enlightenment

However the previous Buddha-Bhagavans have dedicated, however the as yet undescended Buddha-Bhagavans will dedicate, and however the present Buddha-Bhagavans are dedicating, in that manner I also dedicate fully.

All negative karma that result in suffering in suffering realms I confess individually. I rejoice in all merit. I implore all the Buddhas to grant my request: may I receive the highest, most sublime transcendental wisdom.

To the sublime kings of human beings—those who are living in the present time, those who have lived in the past, and those who have not descended—to all those who have qualities as vast as an infinite ocean, with hands folded in the mudra of prostration, I go for refuge.

Chenrezig practice

Visualize Thousand-armed Chenrezig above the animals. As you recite the mantras, nectar beams emitted from Chenrezig's heart purify the animals as explained before.

Long Chenrezig mantra

NAMO RATNA TRAYAYA / NAMAH ARYA JNANA SAGARA / VAIROCHANA / VYUHA RAJAYA / TATHAGATAYA / ARHATE / SAMYAKSAM BUDDHAYA / NAMAH SARVA TATHAGATEBYAH ARADBHYAH / SAMYAKSAM BUDDHEBHYAH / NAMAH ARYA AVALOKITESHVARAYA / BODHISATTVAYA / MAHASATTVAYA / MAHAKARUNIKAYA / TADYATHA / OM / DHARA DHARA / DHIRI DHIRI / DHURU DHURU / ITTI VATTE / CHALE CHALE / PRACHALE PRACHALE / KUSUME / KUSUME VARE / ILI MILI / CITI JVALAM / APANAYE SVAHA

Short Chenrezig mantra

OM MANI PADME HUM

Long Namgyalma mantra

OM NAMO BHAGAWATE / SARVA TRAILOKYA / PRATIVISHISH-TAYA / BUDDHAYA TE NAMA / TA YA THA / OM BHRUM BHRUM BHRUM / SHODHAYA SHODHAYA / VISHODHAYA VISHODHAYA / ASAMA-SAMANTA-AVABHA SPHARANA GATI / GAGANA SOMBAVA VISHUDDHE / ABHIKINTSANTU MAM / SARVA TATHAGATA SUGATA VARA VACANA AMRITA ABHISEKERA / MAHAMUDRA MANTRA PADAIH / AHARA AHARA NAMA AYUS SANDHARINI / SHODHAYA SHODHAYA / VISHODHAYA VISHODHAYA / GAGANA

SVARHAVA VISHUDDHE / USNISHA VIJAYA PARISHUDDHE /
SAHASRA RASMI SANCODITE / SARVA TATHAGATA AVALOKINI /
SAI PARAMITA PARIPURANI / SARVA TATHAGATA MATI / DASHA
BHUMI PRATISHTHITE / SARVA TATHAGATA HRIDAYA /
ADISHTHANA ADHISHTHITE / MUDRE MUDRE HAHA MUDRE /
VAJRA KAYA SAMHATANA PATISHUDDHA / SARVA KARMA AVA-
RANA VISUDDHE / PRATINI VARTAYA MAMA AYUR VISUDDHE /
SARVA TATHAGATA SAMAYA /ADHISHTHANA ADHISHTHITE /
OM MUNI MUNI / MAHA MUNI / VIMUNI VIMUNI /MAHA
VIMUNI / MATI MATI / MAHA MATI / MAMATI / SUMATI /
TATHATA / BHUTAKOTI PARISHUDDHE / VISPHUTA BUDDHI
SHUDDHE / HE HE JAYA JAYA / VIJAYA VIJAYA / SMARA SMARA /
SPHARA SPHARA / SPHARAYA SPHARAYA / SARVA BUDDHA /
ADISHTHANA ADHISHTHITE / SHUDDHE SHUDDHE / BUDDHE
BUDDHE / VAJRE VAJRE / MAHA VAJRE / SUVAJRE / VAJRA-
GARBHE / JAYAGARBHE / VIJAYAGARBHE / VAJRA DZOLA
GARBHE / VAJRODEBHAVE / VAJRA SAMBHAVE / VAJRE VAJRINI /
VAJRAM BHAVATU MAMA SHARIRAM / SARVA SATTVANANTSA
KAYA / PARI SHUDDHIR BHAVATU / ME SADA SARVA GATI
PARISHUDDHIR TSA / SARVA TATHAGATA TSAMAM SAMA-
SVAYANTU / BUDDHYA BUDDHYA / SIDDHYA SIDDHYA /
BODHAYA BODHAYA / VIBODHAYA VIBODHAYA / MOTSAYA
MOTSAYA / VIMOTSAYA VIMOTSAYA / SHODHAYA SHODHAYA /
VISHODHYA VISHODHYA / SAMANTENA MOTSAYA MOTSAYA /
SAMANTRA RASMI PARI SHUDDHE / SARVA TATHAGATA
HRIDAYA /ADHISHTHANA ADHISHITHITE / MUDRE MUDRE /
MAHA MUDRE / MAHAMUDRA MANTRA PADAIH SOHA

Short Namgyalma mantra

OM BHRUM SOHA / OM AMRITA AYUR DADE SOHA

Wish-Granting Wheel mantra

OM PADMO USHNISHA VIMALE HUM PHAT

Mitukpa mantra

NAMO RATNA TRAYAYA / OM KAMKANI KAMKANI / ROTSANI ROTSANI / TORTANI TORTANI / TRASANI TRASANI / TRATI-HANA TRATIHANA / SARWA KARMA PARAM PARANI ME SARWA SATO NENTSA SOHA

Kunrig mantra

OM NAMO BHAGAWATE SARWA DURKATE PARISHODHANA RADZAYA / TATHAGATAYA / ARHATE SAMYAKSAM BUDDHAYA / TAYATA / OM SHODHANI SHODHANI / SARWA PAPAM BISHO-DHANI SHUDDHE BISHUDDHE SARWA KARMA AHWARANA BISHODHANI SOHA

Stainless Beam Deity mantra

NAMA TREYA DHIKANAM / SARWA TATHAGATA HRIDAYA GARBHE DZOLA DZOLA / DHARMA DHATU GARBHE / SAMBHARA MAMA AHYU / SAM SHODHAYA / MAMA SARWA PAPAM SARWA TATHAGATA SAMANTO UNIKA BIMALE BISHUDDHE HUM HUM HUM HUM / AM BAM SAM DZA SOHA

Milarepa mantra

OM AH GURU HASA VAJRA SARVA SIDDHI PHALA HUM

Medicine Buddha mantra

TAYATHA / OM BEKANDZE BEKANDZE / MAHA BEKANDZE RANDZE / SAMUNGATE SOHA

Dedication

At the end, dedicate the merits in the same way as you motivated at the beginning of the practice.

I dedicate the liberation of these animals to His Holiness the Dalai Lama, the Buddha of Compassion in human form, sole refuge and source of happiness of all living beings. May His Holiness have a long life and may all his holy wishes be fulfilled.

I dedicate this practice to the long and healthy lives of all other holy beings, those who work for the happiness of living beings. May all their holy wishes be accomplished immediately.

May all the members of the Sangha have long and healthy lives. May all their wishes to practice Dharma be accomplished immediately. May they be able to listen, reflect, and meditate; may they be able to live in pure morality; and may they complete the scriptural understanding and actualization of the teachings in this life.

May the benefactors who support the Dharma and take care of the Sangha have long lives, and may all their wishes succeed in accordance with the holy Dharma.

This practice of liberating animals is also dedicated to the long lives of all the people who are creating good karma and making their lives meaningful by having refuge in their minds and living in morality.

May this practice also be the medicine that frees everyone from the sufferings of disease, especially AIDS and cancer, and from the suffering of death.

This practice is also dedicated to all evil beings to meet and practice Dharma and, after they find faith in refuge and karma, to have long lives.

Dedicate also for the long lives of specific people who are sick, such as family members and friends.

19 Dealing with Depression

ॐ

DEPRESSION can be the result of a specific situation, in which case you can apply the relevant meditation to deal with those conditions; however, depression and feelings of hopelessness can also arise for no particular reason. When you are experiencing depression, you should prepare yourself each morning by making a strong determination not to allow the situation to upset you. Making the determination to bear the situation is important because it strengthens you and gives you courage. Also make a strong determination to transform your depression into happiness. During the day, when you start to feel depressed or upset, you should immediately remember the determination you made in the morning and not let the situation overwhelm you. No matter how bad the situation seems, and even if it is commonly regarded as a serious problem, you should not allow it to make your life dark and depressed.

After making this determination, you then mentally prepare yourself for the day by thinking of the methods you will use when you start to feel depressed or upset. There are various special techniques for fighting depression.

Remember Impermanence and Death

The first technique is to think of impermanence and death. Remember that your death will definitely happen, but that when it will happen is uncertain. This life is very short; it lasts just for a minute, a second. Rather than thinking that you won't die for a long time, think that you might suddenly die today, even within the next hour—or the next minute.

Think about impermanence and death every day, every hour, every minute. After waking up in the morning, rejoice that you are still alive, that you still have a precious human body, then decide that today is the day you are going to die. Whether or not your death is going to happen today, you should think, "I am going to die today" or "I am going to die within the next hour." This helps to cut your attachment, your grasping and clinging, which bring a lot of expectations. Depression is related to attachment; you become depressed when you don't get what your attachment wants. Therefore, you need to think, "I could die today—even within the next hour." Or actually decide, "I am going to die today." Thinking that your life is very short and that it could easily end stops your strong grasping; you then have no worry and fear in your life.

Otherwise, if you don't apply this technique of thinking that your death could happen today, you will always feel dissatisfaction, loneliness, and depression. There is then a danger that you will commit suicide. When your mind is in a depressed state and your life looks very black, committing suicide is just a moment away.

Experience Your Depression on Behalf of Others

A second technique for dealing with depression, and the best way to make your depression beneficial, is to use it to generate the loving, compassionate thought of bodhicitta. In this way you transform your problem of depression into happiness and use it to bring happiness to all living beings; you use your depression in the path to enlightenment.

Numberless living beings are living with depression and numberless others have the karma to experience depression in the future. Think, "I am just one person, while others are numberless. How wonderful it would be if I, one person, could experience the depression of all living beings, as well as all their other suffering, and allow them to have all happiness and peace, up to enlightenment." If possible, when you say "all their other suffering," think of the suffering of suffering, the suffering of change (which means the temporary samsaric pleasures), and pervasive compounding suffering. This is more profound because you are not just thinking of physical pain or poverty but considering the entire suffering of samsara.

Then think, "Even if I were to be born in hell, since I am just one person, it would be nothing to get upset about. And even if I were to achieve total liberation from samsara, since it would be just for myself and the rest of the living beings would still be suffering, it would be nothing amazing. How wonderful it would be if all other beings could be free from the suffering of depression and I, one being, could take upon myself all the depression and other suffering of the numberless living beings and allow them to have all the happiness up to enlightenment. This would be the greatest achievement of my life!"

Then do the actual meditation of taking other living beings' suffering—in particular, their depression—upon yourself. By generating compassion for others, take all their depression and causes of depression, as well as all their other suffering, within you. Breathe in through your nostrils all this suffering in the form of black smoke, which then absorbs into your ego, your self-cherishing thought, the real enemy that you have to destroy. Use all this suffering as a weapon to destroy your ego, which gives you all your depression and other problems. This demon abiding in your heart, your real enemy, is completely destroyed; it becomes nonexistent.

After that, if possible, meditate on emptiness. After destroying the ego, which cherishes the I, meditate on the emptiness of the I. As the ego is totally destroyed, so also is the false I that the ego has been cherishing so strongly as the most important and precious among all beings. As the self-cherishing thought becomes nonexistent, so also does its object, the real I, which appears to you to exist from its own side. You then meditate on the emptiness, the ultimate nature, of the I. Concentrate a little while on the state of emptiness. Concentrate on the absence of the inherently existent I, which exists nowhere, neither on the base nor anywhere else.

This meditation can be very beneficial for depression, but it depends on how effectively you can meditate on emptiness. For some people meditating on emptiness is powerful medicine.

After this, by generating loving kindness toward others, do the meditation of giving. Give all living beings your body, in the form of a wish-fulfilling gem; all your wealth and possessions; all your merit, or good karma, the cause of all your happiness; and all your happiness, up to enlightenment. Other living beings receive everything they need; all the enjoyment they receive then causes them to actualize the spiritual path, and they all become enlightened.

Relate this practice of taking and giving to your breathing. In the case of depression, concentrate more on the practice of taking upon yourself the suffering of other living beings. The essential meditation is to experience your depression on behalf of all other living beings.

Do the meditation of taking and giving in the morning and evening, and during the rest of the day, while you're driving, eating, and engaged in other activities, immediately apply the antidote whenever the thought of your depression comes into your mind. As soon as you start to feel depressed, immediately think, "I am experiencing this depression on behalf of all other living beings" or "This depression that I'm experiencing is the depression of all other living beings." Thinking that the depression is not yours but that of all other living beings can be helpful. This also applies to AIDS, cancer, or any other sickness.

When you experience your depression for others, when you change your attitude from thinking "I'm depressed" to "I'm experiencing this depression for others," your depression becomes enjoyable and worthwhile. It is essential to think again and again that you are experiencing your depression for others, because this thought keeps your mind in a constant state of peace and happiness. When you practice this in your daily life, you then enjoy life and see purpose in living. You feel joy at having the opportunity to experience depression, and you see your life as worthwhile because you are living it for others.

To enjoy depression or any other problem you experience in your life, you have to think of its benefits, and the greatest benefit of depression is that you can use it to develop bodhicitta. By experiencing depression, you can see more easily the suffering of other living beings, especially the numberless other beings who are experiencing depression and have created the cause to experience it. Your own personal experience of depression enables you to appreciate how unbearable it is.

Using your depression to develop bodhicitta purifies an unimaginable amount of negative karma and collects merit as vast as space.

Each time you think, "I am experiencing this depression, this unhap-piness, on behalf of all living beings," you collect extensive merit, and the more merit you collect, the easier it is for you to realize emptiness. The merit you collect by doing this bodhicitta practice of taking oth-ers' suffering and giving them your own happiness and merit helps you to realize emptiness more easily and quickly.

When you experience depression, it is good to look at the situation as a retreat. Even though you are not in a physical retreat in the sense of keeping your body in a room, you are in a real retreat through keep-ing your mind always in bodhicitta. If your depression persuades you to practice bodhicitta, you then experience powerful purification and collect extensive merit all day long. For the weeks, months, or even years that you have the depression, it is as if you are doing a Vajrasattva retreat. This is the best retreat, because every hour, every minute, every second that you put your effort into developing bodhi-citta makes your life beneficial for all sentient beings. Using your depression to practice bodhicitta, like tantra, becomes the quick path to enlightenment.

One way to stop the experience of depression and other problems is to do strong practice of purification in your daily life, thus purify-ing the cause of depression. By purifying the cause of problems, you don't experience the problems; otherwise, you will continue to expe-rience depression from life to life. As I have just mentioned, bodhi-citta practice brings powerful purification. There are also other powerful practices of purification, such as reciting the names of the Thirty-Five Buddhas, Vajrasattva meditation and recitation, and Dorje Khadro fire puja. Purification practice is essential, because unless the negative karma is purified, you will also experience depression in future lives.

Simply accepting your depression is also helpful. You can think, "I deserve to experience this depression because of the numberless heavy negative actions I have done in the past." You can also think that by experiencing the depression you are exhausting the negative karma you have collected during beginningless rebirths. Thinking in this way can make you happy to experience depression rather than regard it as harmful. When we wash dirty clothes in soapy water, at first a lot of black dirt comes out. We see this as positive, not negative, even though the clothes do not immediately become clean. It is similar when we practice a spiritual path. Negative karma can manifest, or come out, in the form of depression and sickness. This is not bad, because it is a sign that we are exhausting our negative karma. We should rejoice that we have the depression or sickness, because instead of experiencing heavy suffering for eons in the lower realms, we are purifying our past heavy karma in the form of a small problem, a depression, in this life. Compared to suffering in the hell realm, this suffering of depression is nothing. We should feel extremely lucky to be free from that heavy suffering and look upon our depression as a sign of success.

When we practice Dharma, negative karma can manifest very quickly and be exhausted through the experience of sickness, depression, and other problems. In this case the soap and water is Dharma practice. This is why many Dharma practitioners encounter sickness and many other obstacles when they do strong practice.

Buddhist teachings emphasize the importance of always keeping your mind in a state of happiness. If you are unhappy, you also make your family and the other people around you unhappy. You are so caught up in yourself and your depression that your mind is not open to others. You cannot love or help others or make them happy. You cannot even smile at others; you cannot give others even that small pleasure.

When you are happy, on the other hand, you are relaxed and have space in your mind to think of others, to cherish and love others. You can give pleasure to others by smiling at them. You can also do your work and your spiritual practice better. If your mind is depressed, you even stop your spiritual practice. You feel so discouraged that you cannot recite even one OM MANI PADME HUM. Therefore, when your life is miserable, it is very important to keep your mind happy by utilizing your problems in the path to enlightenment.

If, however, you feel a lot of excitement upon achieving some success, again your life becomes unstable. Your mind is distracted, and a mind that is not stable cannot do spiritual practice. You need to practice thought transformation, so that neither feeling miserable nor feeling happy becomes an obstacle to achieving the path to enlightenment. You need to keep your mind happy and positive, because this will keep your mind healthy, and from that healthy mind comes a healthy body.

Of course, there are people who are very healthy and live long lives even though they engage in negative activities such as killing and butchering many thousands of beings, without engaging in any practice of purification or in any positive activities. This is not necessarily a good sign, however. All their negative karma is being stored, to be experienced in the future for an incredible length of time. This present life is very short, like a second, when compared to all the future lives and to the length of even one lifetime in the hell realms. Besides bringing suffering for an inconceivable length of time in the lower realms, this negative karma will bring them suffering in the human realm for many thousands of lifetimes.

Give Your Depression to Your Ego

The third technique for dealing with depression is to give your depression to the ego. This is similar to taking on the depression of other living beings. First examine the cause of your depression. What made you experience this depression? Your ego, your self-cherishing thought. There is an immediate connection between depression and strong cherishing of the I. You become depressed basically because the ego doesn't get what it wants or expects.

Another point to consider is that depression can happen because in the past—whether in a past life or earlier in this life—out of self-cherishing you disturbed the mind of your spiritual master and degenerated or broke your commitments. But this still means that your depression happened because of the ego. It is the ego that obliges you to experience depression.

In one of the sutras in the *Kangyur*, the collection of Buddha's teachings, when explaining the benefits of keeping the five lay precepts (abandoning killing, stealing, lying, sexual misconduct, and drinking alcohol) and the shortcomings of not keeping them, Buddha mentions that feeling suddenly depressed for no particular reason is the result of the past negative karma of sexual misconduct. The text refers to sudden depression happening in the evening, but the same applies to suddenly feeling depressed when you wake up in the morning. Even though you have no particular reason to feel depressed, you suddenly feel unhappy. Your mind can be happy and then suddenly change, like clouds obscuring the sun. I guess that it comes from the negative karma of having caused the minds of others to become unhappy. Because of the ego, attachment arose, the negative karma of sexual misconduct was then performed, and as a result, you now experience depression. However, all this is still caused by the ego.

It is good to sometimes read *The Wheel of Sharp Weapons.* The essential point to understand is that the turning of the sharp weapon of karma is created by your self-cherishing thought, and that you now need to turn the weapon on the self-cherishing thought, which gave you the depression in the first place. Instead of taking the depression upon yourself, give it back to the ego and totally destroy it. Use your depression as an atomic bomb to destroy your inner enemy, the self-cherishing thought. When you encounter your enemy in a war, you use whatever weapon you have to crush them. Here you use your depression to crush the ego, your real enemy.

In this way, your depression becomes the best medicine for the chronic disease of your mind, self-cherishing thought, the continuation of which is beginningless and the harm from which is beginningless. Your depression becomes useful, especially in generating the realization of bodhicitta, and extremely precious, something that you really need.

I have suggested three powerful techniques for dealing with depression, but you can't expect the situation to resolve spontaneously. You must realize that you will have to put a lot of effort into applying these methods, because when your mind is unhappy, you feel discouraged and don't want to do any spiritual practice.

The first technique is to think of impermanence and death, remembering especially that this life lasts for just a second and that your death could happen at any time. Because thinking in this way cuts all your expectations and grasping, you will immediately feel peace in your heart.

The second technique is to experience your depression on behalf of all living beings.

The third is to use your depression as a bomb to destroy your enemy, the ego. Since without the ego there is space to develop bodhicitta, your experience of depression can help you to actualize bodhicitta.

Eliminating the ego, the obstacle to bodhicitta, enables you to realize bodhicitta, in dependence upon which you can then complete the path to enlightenment, ceasing all gross and subtle defilements and completing all realizations. You are then able to work perfectly for all sentient beings. In this way, you use your depression to achieve the highest meaning of life, enlightenment for the benefit of all sentient beings. Just as snake venom can be used to develop antivenin to protect against snake bites, depression can be used to develop bodhicitta and protect against future depression.

20 *Purification Practice*

ॐ

THROUGH YOUR OWN individual effort you can purify your mind and transform it into something positive and pure. In this way, instead of being harmful or disturbing, your actions become beneficial for yourself and for others.

Perfect purification has to include the remedy of the four powers. Among these, *the power of regret* is extremely important, because the degree to which we can purify the negative karma we have created depends on how much regret, or repentance, we can generate by reflecting on the shortcomings of that karma. Even if we don't recite any of the mantras for purification—or even know which mantras to recite—our negative karma will become thinner in accordance with the strength of the regret we feel at having created it. Even without the other three powers, how deeply we feel regret determines how much negative karma we purify. To purify negative karma it is important to feel regret as strongly as possible.

We need to think as extensively as possible about the shortcomings of negative karma. Negative karma results in rebirth in the lower realms for an unimaginable period of time, and when we are eventually born again as a human being, our negative karma is responsible for all the problems we experience, including the obstacles to achieving realizations of the path to enlightenment. Negative karma also leaves imprints on our mind, which cause us to make the same mistake again in future lives. The stronger the regret we generate by thinking of these shortcomings, the thinner our negative karma will become.

We can also purify negative karma through *the power of the object,* which means through reliance upon holy objects—the guru, Buddha,

Dharma, and Sangha—or upon sentient beings. By taking refuge in the guru, Buddha, Dharma, and Sangha, we can purify the negative karma accumulated in relation to them; and by generating bodhicitta, we can purify the negative karma accumulated in relation to sentient beings.

The virtue that is the antidote to negative karma is called *the power of always enjoying*. Generally, any virtuous action has the power to act as a remedy to negative karma, and by creating virtue, we always experience the result of happiness. This might be the meaning of "always enjoying," though I haven't seen this particular explanation of the term in a text.

The final power is *the power of making the determination not to commit the negative karma again*.

We can also use our problems to purify negative karma. By experiencing them on behalf of all sentient beings, we can even use our difficulties in the path to enlightenment. If we have strong compassion and the thought to cherish others, experiencing our problems on behalf of other sentient beings brings powerful purification.

PURIFICATION PRACTICE FOR CANCER OR AIDS

If you prefer, you can visualize the healing deity in front of you at this point, as the object of request.[1] Make the commitment in front of the guru-deity to always try to live your life in the practice of the good heart. Otherwise, visualize the usual refuge merit field, and then visualize the deity before beginning the seven-limb prayer.

Taking refuge and generating bodhicitta

I go for refuge until I am enlightened
To the Omniscient One (who has perfect power and infinite
 compassion for all living beings);
To the Supreme Teachings (the wisdom that realizes ultimate
 reality and the cessation of suffering);
To those intending virtue (who have attained realizations or who
 are now actualizing them and who guide me in the right path). (3x)

Generate the four immeasurable thoughts (see page 191).

Special bodhicitta

For the sake of all the mother and father living beings, I shall quickly, very quickly, achieve the fully enlightened state. For this reason, I am going to do the meditation-recitation of the guru-deity to heal my body through healing my mind, through clearing my mind of all obscurations.

Next recite the seven-limb prayer (see page 192), the short mandala offering (page 192), and *The Foundation of All Good Qualities* (page 193).

The seven-limb prayer and mandala offering are powerful methods for hooking all the realizations of the path to enlightenment, thus enabling you to lead everyone to the sorrowless state. And incidentally you create the cause for your own happiness and success in this life and in all future lives. You also purify all the obstacles to achieving ultimate happiness.

The lamrim prayer is a request for the complete development of the mind in order to lead all living beings to the peerless happiness of full enlightenment. Any lamrim prayer that contains the complete path to enlightenment may be recited, and if you are already reciting a lamrim prayer every day, you don't need to recite one again here.

Mantra recitation and visualization

Now recite the mantra of the healing deity that has been recommended to you. If this practice is done with the purest motivation of wishing to bring everyone to the peerless happiness of full enlightenment, you receive ultimate mental health, with cessation of all suffering and its causes, the obscurations and their imprints. Ultimate mental health is the most important thing, because the cause of suffering is in the mind, and once the cause of suffering is eliminated, it will never return. With perfect mental and physical health, a perfectly pure body and mind, you will be able to offer all benefit to all living beings. All this benefit comes from the purest motivation of cherishing others and wishing to bring them to enlightenment, which in turn comes from the direct meditation requesting all the realizations of the complete path to enlightenment.

For half of the mantra recitation concentrate on purifying yourself, and for the other half concentrate on purifying others. In this way you bring about not only a healthy body, which exists only for a short time, but most important of all, a healthy mind.

Visualization for purifying cancer

As you recite the mantra, visualize strong white beams coming from the deity's heart and entering you. Like switching on a light in a room, your body is completely illuminated. And just as darkness in a room is instantly dispelled when you switch on a light, all your disease, spirit harm, negative karma, and obscurations are instantly purified.

Visualization for purifying AIDS

As you recite the mantra, visualize the powerful nectar emitted from the deity's heart entering you, purifying your body and mind of all disease, spirit harm, negative karma, and obscurations. Visualize that all these four things come out in the form of dirty, coal-black liquid from all the pores and orifices of your body. Do not visualize purifying only yourself, but also all the people you know who have the HIV virus, all other beings who have this virus, and then all the remaining living beings.

Dedication

Due to all my past, present, and future positive actions and those done by others, may compassion—the source of all healing and happiness—be generated in my mind and in the minds of all living beings, especially those who are experiencing cancer, AIDS, and other diseases.

Due to the positive energy accumulated in the past, present, and future by me and by others, may all the mother and father living beings have happiness. May the three lower realms be empty of beings forever. May all the prayers of the bodhisattvas be fulfilled immediately. And may I alone cause all this. (The bodhisattvas' prayers include prayers for sentient beings to be free from all disease and all other problems.)

Due to the positive energy accumulated in the past, present, and future by me and by others, may I and all other living beings be able to meet, in all lifetimes, perfectly qualified Mahayana virtuous friends and to always only please them with the actions of my body, speech, and mind. May I be able to immediately fulfill all their holy wishes by myself alone.

As the great bodhisattvas Samantabhadra and Manjugosha and all the Buddhas of the past, present, and future have dedicated, I dedicate all this positive energy in the best way possible in order

to quickly achieve enlightenment and lead all other living beings
to that enlightened state.

Through the merits of these virtuous actions
May I quickly attain the state of a guru-Buddha
And lead all living beings, without exception,
Into that enlightened state.

In this last dedication verse, you can replace "Buddha" with the name
of the healing deity that you are practicing.

21 *Blessing Water*

⌒

H EALING WITH BLESSED WATER is a very common practice in Tibet, where the lamas and meditators who are healers often bless water for people who are ill. The practice involves blessing water with meditation and with recitation of the mantras of Chenrezig, Medicine Buddha, Tara, or another deity. The blessed water is then drunk several times a day. This is especially good for young children and old people, who often cannot concentrate or find it difficult to do visualization and mantra recitation. It might be the only way to heal those with whom you cannot communicate.

You can bless the water and use it to heal yourself or others. Remember the story I told earlier of Mr. Lee from Singapore, who recovered from his stomach cancer by reciting the *Twenty-one Praises to Tara* every day and drinking blessed water.

It is a common practice to recite mantras to create power in a substance then use it for healing, especially for diseases of the bones. Creams and powders can also be blessed with meditation and mantras then applied externally to the body. The mantras are powerful not just in healing disease but in purifying the mind, which is the essential point. The mantras have the power to purify the causes of disease and of all other problems: negative actions and thoughts, as well as the imprints left by them on the mind. The blessed water is actually drunk to heal these chronic inner diseases.

To bless water, place a container of water on your altar or in front of you. Imagine that out of the compassion of the enlightened being you have visualized, milky nectar flows from their heart or their hands into the water. Recite as many mantras of the deity as possible then blow on the water. The more mantras you recite, the more power your speech will have and the more blessed your breath will be. Your breath will have power to heal because of the power of mantra; the healing power comes from the power of the Buddhas' holy minds, which have compassion for all living beings. Although the Buddhas have infinite qualities, they guide us mainly because of their compassion.

Each atom of the blessed water has incredible power to heal, and to heal not just disease, which is simply one problem, but many other problems.

CHENREZIG HEALING MEDITATION

This practice should be done with the motivation of single-pointedly cherishing other sentient beings and with unbearable compassion for their suffering.[1] Because of the power of the Chenrezig mantra, even if the practice is done with an impure motivation, there will still be benefit, and the disease will still be cured, so there is no doubt about the result if it is done with the good heart that only cherishes others.

Anyone who has done a Chenrezig retreat or who recites many thousands of Chenrezig mantras every day can help to heal very serious diseases that cannot be cured by ordinary means.

Either visualize yourself as Thousand-Armed Chenrezig or visualize Chenrezig above the container of water. Nectar flows into the container from Chenrezig's main right hand, which is in the mudra of granting sublime realizations.

With this visualization, recite the long (or short) mantra of Chenrezig as many times as possible. After each round of the mala blow on the water again and again. Think that the water is transformed into very powerful nectar that can instantly pacify disease and its cause. The more mantras you recite, the more powerful and effective the blessed water becomes.

Long *Chenrezig mantra*

NAMO RATNA TRAYAYA / NAMAH ARYA JNANA SAGARA /
VAIROCHANA / VYUHA RAJAYA / TATHAGATAYA / ARHATE /
SAMYAKSAM BUDDHAYA / NAMAH SARVA TATHAGATEBYAH
ARADBHYAH / SAMYAKSAM BUDDHEBHYAH / NAMAH ARYA
AVALOKITESHVARAYA / BODHISATTVAYA / MAHASATTVAYA /
MAHAKARUNIKAYA / TADYATHA / OM / DHARA DHARA / DHIRI
DHIRI / DHURU DHURU / ITTI VATTE / CHALE CHALE / PRACHALE
PRACHALE / KUSUME / KUSUME VARE / ILI MILI / CITI JVALAM /
APANAYE SVAHA

Short *Chenrezig mantra*

OM MANI PADME HUM

At the end of the mantra recitation make the following strong requests
to Chenrezig.

Since you, Chenrezig, have full understanding and unbearable
compassion and since sentient beings are suffering, may anyone
who drinks this water be cured of their particular disease and suffering and their minds be purified.

Please, Chenrezig, dissolve into the water and just by (name of the
person) drinking this water, may their self-cherishing mind be
transformed into the pure attitude of bodhicitta, the source of all
happiness and success for all beings. May they renounce themselves and cherish others with this loving compassionate thought.

May their anger be transformed into patience. May their dissatisfaction be transformed into satisfaction. May their ignorance
be transformed into the wisdom that understands the causes of
happiness and suffering and the wisdom that understands the
absolute nature, or emptiness, of the I and of all existence. May
their mind be transformed into a fully awakened mind.

May their body, speech, and mind have the perfect power to guide, to benefit, and to fulfill the wishes of all sentient beings.

Extremely pleased by your heartfelt request, Chenrezig melts into white light and is absorbed into the water. Imagine that the water increases and becomes extremely powerful, so powerful that anyone who drinks it will be purified of their disease and its cause, their negative karma and obscurations. Think that the water now has the power to actualize the requests you have made to Chenrezig.

22 Healing Pujas

ॐ

WHETHER MEDITATION ALONE can cure a disease depends on the number and severity of the obstacles involved. With a serious case of a disease, we may have to take a lot of medicine and a variety of other treatments; with a mild case, we may not need to take much medicine at all. It is the same with obstacles. If the obstacles are great, we will have to do more practice and a greater variety.

There are basically three categories of disease. One type of disease has no cure at all; nothing can be done about it, and we simply have to endure it until that particular karma is exhausted. With the second type of disease, we can recover only if certain pujas, meditations, or mantras are done to stop the spirit harm involved; only then can other medical treatments be effective. If the spirit harm cannot be stopped, no medicine can work, even though the disease is correctly diagnosed and the normally correct treatment is prescribed. The disease then falls into the first category. The third type of disease can easily be cured through standard medical treatment.

Like antibiotics taken to kill bacteria, meditations and mantras can be powerful in healing and in protecting from nagas and the various types of spirits, beings who can become conditions for cancer and other sicknesses. Nagas live below the earth or in water. It seems that the ancient Greeks also believed in nagas, though they called them mermaids; they had drawings of beings that were half human female and half snake. When I went on a tour of Disneyland in America, I was surprised to see a statue of a mermaid. I don't know why they had a mermaid there, because in the view of Western science such beings don't exist. Western science has yet to discover spirits and nagas, though it is possible that some scientists have themselves had strange experiences that suggest the possibility of their existence. I was very surprised to see a naga in Disneyland.

Almost every disease can be related to some external condition, such as a spirit or naga. Spirits and nagas can appear in a variety of forms, and there are meditation practices related to each type. It is said that cancer is related to harm caused by nagas, which is why taking the initiations of certain deities that are remedies to such harm and doing their meditation-recitation practice or doing naga pujas can help people recover from cancer.

The resident geshe at Nagarjuna Center in Barcelona advised a woman with breast cancer to recite mantras and then blow on her affected breast. After doing this, she recovered from the breast cancer. The geshe asked her whether she had ever urinated in the ocean when she went to the beach, and she said that she had. When we pollute the environment, we can also disturb the nagas and spirits who share that environment, and these beings can then harm us. Of course, they are simply a condition and not the main cause for our receiving harm. The main cause is our own negative thoughts and negative actions, which have harmed others. When we harmed other beings in the past, we established a connection with them, and this is why they later become conditions for us to receive harm.

Certain deities manifest to protect sentient beings from the harm of nagas. The Vajrapani-Hayagriva-Garuda deity, for example, specifically manifests to protect sentient beings from nagas as well as from harmful spirits. Vajrapani, embodiment of the perfect power of all the Buddhas, is the opponent of the spirits that cause such things as epileptic fits. Of course, the scientific explanation is that epileptic fits are caused by electrical discharges in the brain, but they are also related to the external condition of harmful spirits. Hayagriva, an extremely powerful deity in degenerate times, is a specific remedy for harm received from nagas and from the spirits known as "King." The Garuda protects from harmful nagas and landlord spirits.

Of course, we have to remember that the actual origin of harm from nagas and spirits is our own three poisonous minds of ignorance, anger, and attachment. Nagas and spirits are simply conditions for our disease; the real cause of their harm is our own mind. While Vajrapani-

Hayagriva-Garuda practice is a remedy to spirit harm, its ultimate purpose is to liberate us from the three poisonous minds. We should do the practice not just to protect ourselves from this harm but to liberate ourselves by actualizing the path of method and wisdom within our mind. Our ultimate aim, of course, is to cease karma and delusions, thus overcoming not only disease but the entire suffering of samsara, including the cycle of death and rebirth. We will then be able to complete the path to enlightenment and work perfectly for all sentient beings.

Pujas, which involve specific meditations, can also be done to control spirits and nagas, but the effectiveness of the puja for the sick person depends on the qualifications of the person doing it, just like the effectiveness of treatment from a doctor. Although the sick person and even the person doing the puja might not be able to see the particular spirit that is causing harm, those with clairvoyance can see them. If the puja is done correctly, the person recovers from their disease, which is itself proof of the existence of these external conditions for sickness. Even without taking medicine, a patient can often recover simply because a puja is done. If the puja is done perfectly, a complete cure comes more quickly.

The puja usually involves giving presents to the spirits to make them happy and then giving them teachings on not harming others. You offer the spirits a substitute for the sick person by visualizing numberless beautiful, well-dressed people or by making a symbolic representation of them. You also describe in words how huge and magnificent they are. You offer the spirits food, clothing, and any other enjoyment they might want. You can also make representations of these enjoyments. You visualize the enjoyments as extensively as possible, then give everything to the spirits. After making the spirits happy by giving them these presents, you teach them Dharma; you tell them that they should not harm others because the result will be that they themselves will receive harm and suffer. You make Dharma charity to the spirits by giving them this advice. Sometimes you also say that if the spirits will not listen to you, you will destroy them. Using wrathful actions, you can place them in situations where they can no longer harm other beings. I am just giving you a general idea of the meditations involved in such a puja.

Such pujas must not be done out of anger or any other negative mind. They have to be done with as much compassion as possible for the spirits and for the person who is sick. If you do such pujas out of anger, the wrathful actions can harm you if you are not sufficiently qualified.

The fact that these pujas help to heal people is proof that spirits and nagas do exist and do harm people. The reason such beings are able to harm us is related to our karma, to our self-cherishing thought and the actions we do out of it. Of course, any harm we receive, whether from spirits or from human beings, comes from our karma.

23 Tibetan Medicine

⋙

WHEN I WAS STAYING in Dharamsala after Lama Yeshe had passed away, I thought very deeply about how to benefit people with AIDS. I did some divinations myself and also checked with the protector associated with the Upper Tantric College and with some other protectors. Although the answers were not very clear, the arura tree was mentioned. Arura, the plant the Medicine Buddha holds in his right hand, is a powerful medicine. Just as ignorance is the foundation of all the rest of the 84,000 delusions, arura is the foundation of all Tibetan medicine. Keeping arura fruit on your body, besides protecting you and healing disease, heals your mind. A statue in one of the temples in Tibet has an offering of arura inside its heart. People lean against the statue for prolonged periods because it is said that the arura inside the statue brings great healing.

The ordinary arura that is normally used in Tibetan medicine is not as effective as the best-quality arura. A very precious and extremely rare medicine containing the best-quality arura is kept in the Tibetan government storehouse, along with precious relics of holy beings, including those of Buddha's past lives as a bodhisattva.

I heard about the benefits of the pill that contains the best-quality arura from Doctor Tsondru, a learned doctor who taught the monks at Kopan for three years. The monks memorized the entire medical text, which is a tantric root text, and also studied diagnosis, though they did not learn how to actually make medicines. When Dr. Tsondru told me that His Holiness Trijang Rinpoche had two or three of these pills, I quickly wrote a letter to His Holiness to ask if it would be possible to get some. His Holiness sent me one of his pills.

In Solu Khumbu, there are many incidents of poisoning that involve spirits and black magic. The poison can be given in various ways. In one method, the poisoner has a tiny amount of poison under their thumbnail, and they put their thumb inside the tea or *chang* that they offer to the person they wish to poison. The person who is poisoned can be sick for a long time, experiencing a lot of internal pain and becoming very thin. If they are not treated with special medicines, the poison turns into scorpions and other animals, which eat the person up inside.

In Solu Khumbu there is a hospital established by Sir Edmund Hillary and staffed by doctors mostly from New Zealand. I heard that during an operation there, they found a froglike animal inside someone's body, and when they sliced the animal's body open, there was no blood inside. Such strange stories are generally related to spirits.

I left the pill I had received from His Holiness Trijang Rinpoche at Solu Khumbu after my mother had been poisoned. The pill is swallowed, but because it is so rare and precious, it is later taken out of the feces, washed, and used again. Simply keeping the pill on the body can also help someone who has been poisoned. Such a pill is also helpful at the time of death. When I wanted the pill to mix it into some other medicine I was making, my uncle told me that he had lost it. My sister later told me that my uncle hadn't lost the pill, but wanted to keep it himself.

In terms of treating AIDS, arura was indicated as the most beneficial, and *baru* and *kyuru* would also benefit. According to Tibetan medical texts, which came from the Medicine Buddha, there are 424 diseases. The origin of all disease is the three poisonous minds of ignorance, anger, and attachment, and all diseases are branches of the three root diseases: phlegm, bile, and wind disease. The three medicines I have mentioned are the remedies to these diseases and the foundations of all Tibetan medicines.

Anna, a French student very new to Dharma, was the first person I met with AIDS. I met her briefly in Dharamsala many years ago. When someone brought me a message that Anna had AIDS, I did an observation and suggested the Tibetan medicine she should take. I also advised her to meditate on Black Garuda.

Anna obtained the medicine from the Tibetan Medical and Astrological Institute in Dharamsala. Since she had some doubts about the medicines I had suggested, she questioned the Tibetan doctor about their benefits. When the doctor mentioned the various symptoms relieved by the medicines, she was surprised to find that she had all the problems that he mentioned. She then developed a little more faith in the treatment.

While she was in Dharamsala, she took the medicines I had recommended, and her condition did improve. Anna had a close karmic connection with Kirti Tsenshab Rinpoche, from whom she received much advice and support, but she was a very new Dharma student. When she returned home to France, she stopped taking the Tibetan medicine because the people around her, especially her father, discouraged her from taking it.

Eastern methods are often regarded in the West as ignorant and wrong, while anything Western is regarded as scientific and correct. Her father could not accept Tibetan herbal medicine and preferred Western chemical medicine. Because of the strong influence of her father and of Western culture, she stopped taking the Tibetan medicine, even though it had been benefiting her. Her condition then worsened.

I made up a quantity of powder containing these three medicines— arura, baru, and kyuru—and took it with me to Vajrapani Institute, but at that time I didn't meet anyone with AIDS. It was these three medicines that I suggested Anna use to treat her AIDS.

As another treatment for AIDS, I have been trying to obtain a very precious grass that grows only in certain holy places. I think this grass could be the next LSD. I have asked a number of people to search for it on holy mountains in Tibet and also in China. It is probably growing in places that are not very accessible. It grows in Tibet at Tsa-ri, a huge mountain where indigenous people live. Tsa-ri is a holy place of Chakrasamvara, and Chakrasamvara practitioners circumambulate the mountain barefoot as purification and offer *tsog* at the many holy places on the mountain. It is said that you can achieve clairvoyance as a result. His Holiness Song Rinpoche mentions this in his life-story.

Of course, because the benefits from this grass are extraordinary, a lot of merit is needed even to be able to find it. My idea is to mix the grass with other ingredients to make medicinal pills. I believe that even a tiny bit of this grass has the power to bring incredible healing, not only of AIDS and other diseases but of the mind. The texts say that eating this plant prevents rebirth in the lower realms.

This plant is recognized by the fact that it emits smoke during the daytime and flames or light at night. It also has a strong scent that permeates many layers of cloth. I have checked through the drawings of plants in Tibetan medical texts, but I have yet to see a drawing of this particular plant. Its common name is Chinese Plant. It was mixed into old-style Chinese ink, which has a strong perfume, as I remember from when I was a child. Chinese ink is also used in Tibetan medicine.

Even a tiny piece of this plant is extremely precious. Placing it in the mouth of a dying person would prevent their rebirth in the lower realms; they would die with a positive mind because the plant itself brings great purification.

It is said that when an animal has eaten this grass, it cannot move; the yak or cow simply stays in one place and tears come out of its eyes. The villagers say, "Oh, this animal is meditating." Eating the grass somehow transforms the animal's mind; it generates renunciation, compassion, and so forth, and it cries. When the animal dies, relics even come from its body.

Medicine containing this plant would definitely bring immediate and powerful healing of diseases such as AIDS and cancer, but a lot of merit is needed even to find the plant. Because of its incredible benefits, the people who received the medicine would also need to have a lot of merit.

24 *Tangtong Gyälpo's Healing Prayer*

✣

THE PRAYER LIBERATING Sakya from Disease, a short practice composed by the great yogi Tangtong Gyälpo, was written to prevent epidemic disease and other disasters, but it can also be used for healing.[1] Tangtong Gyälpo wrote this prayer at a time when many monks were dying from a contagious disease in a Sakya monastery in Tibet. The epidemic could not be controlled even though tantric practitioners had done all kinds of wrathful pujas and distributed protections,[2] medicines, and mantras. So many monks had died from the disease that there was a danger of the monastery being completely emptied. Tangtong Gyälpo then composed this prayer, and once it was recited, the epidemic immediately stopped.

The Prayer Liberating Sakya from Disease combines taking refuge with recitation of OM MANI PADME HUM, the mantra of Chenrezig, the Buddha of Compassion. The refuge verse was given by Chenrezig to Päljor Sherab, who transmitted it to Tangtong Gyälpo. Tangtong Gyälpo did infinite work for sentient beings through doing this practice himself and through giving it to others. I received the oral transmission of this prayer, which is regarded as very precious and very blessed, from His Holiness Chogye Trichen Rinpoche, one of the main gurus of His Holiness Sakya Trizin, the head of the Sakya order of Tibetan Buddhism.

Tangtong Gyälpo also wrote a prayer to stop war, which also brings about excellent harvests, and another prayer specifically to stop famine. When Tsang, a region in central Tibet, was experiencing drought and famine, Tangtong Gyälpo composed *A Request to Alleviate the Fears of Famine* to stop the famine. He filled a bowl with grain and offered it in the main temple in Lhasa to the statue of Shakyamuni Buddha that was blessed by Buddha himself. He then recited the prayer and requested Buddha to stop the famine. At that time, some people in Tsang saw the Buddha of Compassion send down showers of grain from the sky. The weather then changed. The rain came, the crops grew, and the people in Tsang then had plenty of food.

Once when I was at Jamyang Buddhist Centre, the FPMT center in London, I suggested that it might be good to offer a large bowl filled with money to the same Buddha statue in Lhasa with a request to relieve the economic recession in London, where so many people are unemployed and living in the streets. It would be especially effective if the bowl of money was offered by a bodhisattva. Another solution to the recession would be to ask many people to take the Eight Mahayana Precepts.

THE PRAYER LIBERATING SAKYA FROM DISEASE

All sentient beings, equal to space, go for refuge to the precious Guru-Buddha. We go for refuge to the Buddha, the Dharma, and the Sangha.

This "Going for Refuge" was given by Arya Avalokiteshvara to Ka-nga-pa Päljor Sherab and by him to the mahasiddha Tangtong Gyälpo. Afterward, it provided infinite benefits for migrating beings.

We go for refuge to the assembly of gurus, meditational deities, and dakinis. We go for refuge to the empty clarity of our own minds, the dharmakaya.

Recite these verses as many times as you are able. Then recite the mantra "OM MANI PADME HUM" hundreds of times, and at the end:

May all the diseases that sadden the minds of sentient beings and that result from karma and temporary conditions, such as the harm of spirits, illnesses, and the elements, not occur in the realms of the world.

May whatever suffering that comes from life-threatening diseases—which, like a butcher leading an animal to be slaughtered, separate the body from the mind in a mere instant—not occur in the realms of the world.

May all embodied beings be unharmed by acute, chronic, and other infectious diseases, the mere sound of whose names terrifies beings as though they were placed inside the mouth of Yama, the Lord of Death.

May all embodied beings be unharmed by the 80,000 classes of harmful interferers, the 360 evil spirits that harm suddenly, the 424 diseases, and so forth.

May whatever suffering that comes from disturbances of the four elements, depriving the body and mind of every pleasure, be totally pacified, and may the body and mind have radiance and power and be endowed with long life, good health, and well-being.

By the compassion of the gurus and the Triple Gem, the power of the dakinis, Dharma protectors, and guardians, and by the strength of the infallibility of karma and its results, may these many dedications and prayers be fulfilled as soon as they are made.

Postscript: Once an epidemic was spreading at the great monastery of the Glorious Sakya (tradition). Whatever the mantric masters tried—effigies, *tormas,* medicines, mantras, protection amulets, and so forth—had no effect, and the monastery was in danger of annihilation. At that time, the master Mahasiddha (Tangtong Gyälpo) performed the "Space" refuge, recited a number of manis, and proclaimed this

prayer called "Attainment," during which the entire epidemic immediately ceased in dependence upon its performance. Thereby, it became
endowed as the vajra speech radiating masses of clouds of blessing
entitled "The Prayer Liberating Sakya from Disease."

Sarvamangalam[3]

25 Dedication

ॐ

Due to all my past, present, and future positive actions, and the positive imprints they have left on my consciousness, may bodhicitta—source of all happiness for me and for all living beings—be generated within my own heart and within the hearts of all other beings. May those who have already generated bodhicitta, develop it.

Due to all my past, present, and future positive actions, may I achieve the peerless happiness of full enlightenment and lead everyone to this state as quickly as possible.

Due to all my past, present, and future positive actions and those of others, may any living being who hears me, touches me, remembers me, talks about me, or thinks about me, never be reborn in the lower realms. From that time may they be free from all disease, spirit harm, negative karma, and obscurations, and quickly achieve enlightenment.[1]

Appendix

The following is an excerpt from *The Wish-Fulfilling Jewel: The Concise Sutra Ritual of Bhagavan Medicine Buddha,* composed by Panchen Losang Chökyi Gyaltsen and translated by David Molk.

BENEFITS OF RECITING THE SEVEN MEDICINE BUDDHAS' NAMES

Renowned Glorious King of Excellent Signs

Through force of hearing the Conqueror's name, expressing it,
    remembering, prostrating, and offering,
For all sentient beings such as ourselves
May we be freed from epidemics, execution, criminals, and spirits,
Have faculties fully complete, suffering and negativities' continuum cut,
Not fall to lower realms, experience happiness of humans and gods,
And hunger, thirst, and poverty pacified, may there be wealth.
No torments of body, such as bindings and beating,
Without harm of tigers, lions, and snakes, conflict pacified,
Endowed with loving minds, relieved from fear
Of flood as well, may we pass to fearless bliss.
And when we pass away from this life,
May we be born from lotus in that Buddha-field, qualities complete,
Become a vessel for transmission of the teachings
Of Conquerors such as Renowned Glorious King of Excellent Signs
    and cause them delight.

King of Melodious Sound

Through force of hearing the Conqueror's name, expressing it, remembering,
    prostrating, and offering,
For all sentient beings such as ourselves
May the distracted flourish in Dharma,
Have wealth and goods of human and gods,
Without torment of conception, be always born human,

Never separated from bodhicitta, increase in virtuous Dharma,
Purify obscurations and attain happiness of humans and gods.
May we be freed from separation from the spiritual guide,
From dark ages, spirit harm, death, and enemies,
And from dangers of isolated places.
May we have enthusiasm for making offerings
And performing ritual services,
May lesser beings have samadhi, mindfulness, strength,
The dharani of nonforgetfulness,
And attain supreme wisdom, and may tormenting fires be cooled.
And when we pass away from this life,
May we be born from lotus in that Buddha-field, qualities complete,
Become a vessel for transmission of the teachings
Of Conquerors such as King of Melodious Sound and cause them delight.

Stainless Excellent Gold

Through force of hearing the Conqueror's name, expressing it,
    remembering, prostrating, and offering,
For all sentient beings such as ourselves
May the short-lived gain longevity, the poor, full wealth,
May combatants come to have loving minds,
May we not be without training and fall to lower realms
But be bound by our vows and never without bodhicitta.
And when we pass away from this life,
May we be born from lotus in that Buddha-field, qualities complete,
Become a vessel for transmission of the teachings
Of Conquerors such as Stainless Excellent Gold and cause them delight.

Supreme Glory Free from Sorrow

Through force of hearing the Conqueror's name, expressing it,
    remembering, prostrating, and offering,
For all sentient beings such as ourselves
May sorrow and the like always be pacified, life be long and happy,
May the Conquerors' light increase bliss and joy in the hells,
May we have brightness, beauty, and wealth, unharmed by spirits,
May we have love for each other, and there be no disease.
And when we pass away from this life,
May we be born from lotus in that Buddha-field, qualities complete,
Become a vessel for transmission of the teachings

Of Conquerors such as Supreme Glory Free from Sorrow
and cause them delight.

Melodious Ocean of Proclaimed Dharma

Through force of hearing the Conqueror's name, expressing it,
remembering, prostrating, and offering,
For all sentient beings such as ourselves
May we always have perfect view and faith,
Hear sound of Dharma and be enriched with bodhicitta
For sake of resources may we give up negativities, may wealth increase,
May we abide in love, have long life and be content.
And when we pass away from this life,
May we be born from lotus in that Buddha-field, qualities complete,
Become a vessel for transmission of the teachings
Of Conquerors such as Melodious Ocean of Proclaimed Dharma
and cause them delight.

Delightful King of Clear Knowing

Through force of hearing the Conqueror's name, expressing it,
remembering, prostrating, and offering,
For all sentient beings such as ourselves
May the distracted be free of malice, rich in goods.
May those on bad paths to lower realms attain the ten virtues,
May those controlled by others gain perfect independence,
And all have long life, hear the names, and be virtuous.
And when we pass away from this life,
May we be born from lotus in that Buddha-field, qualities complete,
Become a vessel for transmission of the teachings
Of Conquerors such as Delightful King of Clear Knowing
and cause them delight.

Medicine Guru, King of Lapis Light

Through force of hearing the Conqueror's name, expressing it,
remembering, prostrating, and offering,
For each and every sentient being such as ourselves
May all become, like myself, graced with marks and signs,
May light dispelling darkness and enjoyment of wisdom

And skillful means be inexhaustible, may those attracted
To mistaken and lesser paths enter Mahayana paths
And all be beautified by their vows.
May we be free from pain caused by immortality, complete in faculties,
Without disease and have abundant goods.
May those disillusioned with weakest condition always have powerful faculties,
And may we be freed from Mara's noose and perverse viewpoints.
May those tormented by kings gain bliss and those who,
Out of hunger, support themselves through negativity,
Be satisfied with food received in accordance with Dharma.
May hardships of heat and cold be pacified, all good wishes be fulfilled,
And, endowed with morality pleasing the aryas, may we be liberated.
And when we pass away from this life,
May we be born from lotus in that Buddha-field, qualities complete,
Become a vessel for transmission of the teachings
Of Conquerors such as Medicine Guru, King of Lapis Light,
    and cause them delight.

Notes

Editor's Preface

1. The three main teachings that form the basis of *Ultimate Healing* are the healing course at Tara Institute in August 1991 (Lama Yeshe Wisdom Archive number 874) and discourses given in Auckland and at Mahamudra Centre, New Zealand, in February 1993 (#885 and #886, respectively). Material was also used from the following LYWA transcripts: #144, 151, 293, 303, 351, 444, 536, 652, 729, 754, 786, 808, 836, 847, 865, 873, 875, 894, 938, 962, 977, 1047, 1051, 1055, 1061, 1062, 1070, and 1072. In addition, some material was used from Lama Zopa's personal advice to students in 1998 and 1999.

2. FPMT Education Services, 125B La Posta Road, Taos, New Mexico 87571, USA. Tel: 1 (505) 758-7766.

1 The Healing Power of the Mind

1. See Carl Simonton and Margaret Lock, *The Search for Balance*, chap. 5.

2 Successful Healing

1. All names of people with illnesses in this and other chapters have been changed to protect their privacy.

2. The eight actions that are abandoned are killing; stealing; lying; sexual contact; using intoxicants; sitting on high or expensive seats; eating at the wrong time; and singing, dancing, and wearing perfumes and ornaments.

3. The middle-length Chenrezig mantra, also known as the essence mantra, is OM / DHARA DHARA / DHIRI DHIRI / DHURU DHURU / ITTI VATTE / CHALE CHALE / PRACHALE PRACHALE / KUSUME / KUSUME VARE / ILI MILI / CHITI JVALAM / APANAYE SVAHA.

5 The Nature of Compassion

1. For example, in generating compassion through the seven-point cause-and-effect instruction, one first performs the preliminary meditations on immeasurable

equanimity, on seeing all sentient beings as one's mother, on remembering their kindness, on wishing to repay their kindness, and on love.

6 The Healing Power of Compassion

1. Karmic guardians, manifestations of a being's negative karma, are terrifying guards who assist in the various tortures carried out in the hell realms.

7 Healers

1. The four traditions of Tibetan Buddhism are Nyingma, Sakya, Kagyu, and Gelug.

2. The ten nonvirtuous actions are killing, stealing, sexual misconduct, lying, slander, harsh speech, gossip, covetousness, ill will, and wrong views. See chapter 10 for more details.

9 Disease Is Just a Label

1. Unruly beings are as (unlimited) as space:
   They cannot possibly all be overcome,
   But if I overcome thoughts of anger alone
   This will be equivalent to vanquishing all foes.

   Where would I possibly find enough leather
   With which to cover the surface of the earth?
   But (wearing) leather just on the soles of my shoes
   Is equivalent to covering the earth with it.
       Shantideva, *A Guide to the Bodhisattva's Way of Life*, chap. 5, vv. 12–13.

10 Everything Comes from the Mind through Karma

1. In the case of the negative action of killing, the base is a being, other than oneself, that is killed; the thought is the intention, arising from one of the delusions, to kill that being; the action is the actual deed of killing; and the goal is the completion of the act, with the death of that being.

11 Transforming Illness into Happiness

1. Why be unhappy about something
   If it can be remedied?
   And what is the use of being unhappy about something

If it cannot be remedied?
    Shantideva, *A Guide to the Bodhisattva's Way of Life,* chap. 6, v. 10.

12 *The Benefits of Illness*

1. Furthermore, suffering has good qualities:
Through being disheartened with it, arrogance is dispelled,
Compassion arises for those in cyclic existence,
Evil is shunned and joy is found in virtue.
    Shantideva, *A Guide to the Bodhisattva's Way of Life,* chap. 6, v. 21.

13 *The Ultimate Benefit of Illness*

1. If even the thought to relieve
Living creatures of merely a headache
Is a beneficial intention
Endowed with infinite goodness,

  Then what need is there to mention
The wish to dispel their inconceivable misery,
Wishing every single one of them
To realize boundless good qualities?
    Shantideva, *A Guide to the Bodhisattva's Way of Life,* chap. 1, vv. 21–22.

15 *Simple Healing Meditations*

1. This was the very first meditation Lama Zopa led during the healing course at Tara Institute in August 1991.

2. As your meditation object, you can use an actual stupa or a statue of Buddha (or any other object of faith), a crystal, or universal healing energy. If you do not have a stupa or statue, you can use a photograph or painting or simply visualize them.

3. Lama Zopa led this meditation during one of the discourses in Auckland, New Zealand, in February 1993.

4. This meditation was composed by Rato Rinpoche for a student from Singapore who had been diagnosed as HIV+. The student was completely cured after practicing this meditation with great sincerity for just four days.
    The preliminary prayers include taking refuge and generating bodhicitta, the four immeasurable thoughts, the seven-limb prayer, and the mandala offering (see pages 191–92).

5. This verse on taking and giving is from the prayer of the graduated path to enlightenment in *Lama Chöpa,* or *Guru Puja,* a guru yoga practice performed daily by many followers of the Gelug order of Tibetan Buddhism.

16 Medicine Buddha

1. This Medicine Buddha practice, from a collection of teachings called *Jewel Treasure* by Guru Padmasambhava, was taught to enable successful diagnosis and treatment of illness, especially in times when the five degenerations are flourishing. It was translated into English by Lama Zopa Rinpoche and edited by Ven. Thubten Gyatso in January 1981. It was first published by Wisdom Publications in 1982. It was further edited in July 1999 by Ven. Constance Miller of FPMT Education Services. It was edited again for inclusion in this book, with the addition of material from the consecration of a Medicine Buddha thangka at Vajrapani Institute in September 1997.

2. The names of the seven Medicine Buddhas in Tibetan are:

   Tsen-leg-pa Yong-drag Päl-gyi Gyäl-po (Renowned Glorious King
      of Excellent Signs),
   Rin-po-che-dang Da-wa-dang Pä-mä Rab-tu Gyän-pa Ke-pa Zi-ji Dra-yang-
      gyi Gyäl-po (King of Melodious Sound, Brilliant Radiance of Skill,
      Adorned with Jewels, Moon, and Lotus),
   Ser-zang Dri-me Rin-chen Nang-tül Zhug-pa (Stainless Excellent Gold,
      Great Jewel Who Accomplishes All Vows),
   Nya-ngän Me-chog-päl (Supreme Glory Free from Sorrow),
   Chö-drag Gya-tsö Yang (Melodious Ocean of Proclaimed Dharma),
   Chö-gya-tso Chog-gi-lö Nam-par Röl-pä Ngön-par Kyän-pe Gyäl-po
      (Delightful King of Clear Knowing, Supreme Wisdom of an Ocean
      of Dharma),
   Men-gyi-lha Bäi-dur-yä Ö-gyi Gyäl-po (Medicine Guru, King of Lapis Light).

3. *Tayatha* simply means "as follows" and introduces the actual mantra. It can be recited a few times at the beginning of the mantra recitation.

4. This healing meditation practice by Padmasambhava was translated by Lama Zopa Rinpoche at Tara Institute on September 1, 1991, at the conclusion of the first healing course. The motivation and dedication have been added to the original text. It was first published by Wisdom Publications in 1994 as *The Healing Buddha: A Practice for the Prevention and Healing of Disease.*

5. This means similar in aspect to Shakyamuni Buddha.

17 Liberating Animals: Introduction

1. The prostration prayer is "Chom-dän-dä de-zhin shek-pa dra-chom-pa yang-dak-par dzog-päi sang-gye rin-chen tsug-tor chän-la chag-tsäl-lo."

2. The benefits of the Chenrezig mantra are from a teaching given by Lama Zopa Rinpoche in Singapore on January 25, 1993 (LYWA #899).

3. The benefits of the Stainless Beam Deity mantra are from *Giving Breath to the Wretched*, by Kusali Dharma Vajra, which was translated into English by Lama Zopa Rinpoche.

18 Liberating Animals: Practice

1. Traditional altar offerings in tantric practices, the eight are offerings of water for the mouth, water for bathing the feet, flowers, incense, light, scented water, food, and music.

2. *Purifying the place*
Everywhere may the ground be pure,
Free of the roughness of pebbles and so forth.
May it be the nature of lapis
And as smooth as the palm of one's hand.

Blessing the offerings
May offering substances human and divine,
Those actual and those which are emanated,
Unsurpassed Samantabhadra clouds of offerings,
Fill the entire space.

Multiplying the offerings
OM NAMO BHAGAVATE VAJRA SARA PRAMANDANA TATHAGATAYA /
ARHATE SAMYAKSAM BUDDHAYA / TAYATHA / OM VAJRE VAJRE /
MAHA VAJRE / MAHA TEDZA VAJRE / MAHA VIDYA VAJRE / MAHA
BODHICITTA VAJRE / MAHA BODHI MENDO PASAM KRAMANA
VAJRE / SARVA KARMA AVARANA / BISHO DHANA VAJRE SOHA (3x)

The power of truth
By the power of the truth of the three jewels,
The power of the blessings of all Buddhas and bodhisattvas,
The power of the great might of the completed two collections,
And the power of the intrinsically pure and inconceivable sphere of reality,
May it be just thus.

Invocation
Protector of all beings without exception;
Endless subduer of Mara's tribe and forces;
Deity, perfect knower of all things:
Bhagavan and attendants, please come here.

3. This lamrim prayer was composed by Lama Tsongkhapa and translated into English by Ven. George Churinoff.

20 Purification Practice

1. This practice was compiled by Lama Zopa Rinpoche on August 31, 1991, for participants in the healing course at Tara Institute. The original practice contained the mantras of Sitatapatra (White Umbrella Deity) and Singhanada (Lion's Roar Avalokiteshvara). However, when doing this practice, you should use the mantra of whichever healing deity has been recommended to you by a qualified lama.

21 Blessing Water

1. This practice was composed by Lama Zopa Rinpoche and lightly edited by Murray Wright. It has been further edited for inclusion in this book.

24 Tangtong Gyälpo's Healing Prayer

1. This prayer, translated into English by Ven. George Churinoff, was originally published, along with A Request to Alleviate the Fears of Famine, in a booklet titled *Healing Prayers for a Calamitous Time*. It was subsequently published in *The Healing Buddha: A Practice for the Prevention and Healing of Disease* (Wisdom Publications, 1994). Lama Zopa Rinpoche recommended that The Prayer Liberating Sakya from Disease be recited during healing courses.

2. Protective amulets, often containing a deity's mandala and mantras wrapped in colored cotton, are usually worn around the neck to protect against spirit interference.

3. A Sanskrit word that means "May all be auspicious."

25 Dedication

1. These are the dedication prayers used by Lama Zopa Rinpoche at the end of discourses during the healing course at Tara Institute.

Glossary

(Skt = Sanskrit; Tib = Tibetan)

aggregates. The association of body and mind; a person comprises five aggregates: form, feeling, recognition, compositional factors, and consciousness.

Amdo. The northeastern region of Tibet that borders on China.

Amitabha (Skt). The Buddha of Infinite Light; a male meditational deity, red in color; prayers are often made to be reborn in Amitabha's pure land.

Ananda. A cousin of Shakyamuni Buddha and his attendant for many years; renowned for his remarkable memory.

anger. The disturbing thought that exaggerates the negative qualities of an object and wishes to harm it.

arhat (Skt). Literally, foe destroyer. A being who, having ceased their karma and delusions, is completely free from all suffering and its causes and has achieved liberation from cyclic existence.

arura (Tib). Chebulic myrobalan; "the great medicine"; the plant held in Medicine Buddha's right hand; the fruit, stem, and other parts of the plant are used in Tibetan medicine.

arya (Skt). A being who has realized emptiness.

Asanga. The fifth-century Indian pandit who received directly from Maitreya Buddha the extensive, or method, lineage of Shakyamuni Buddha's teachings; his texts are still studied in Tibetan monasteries.

asura (Skt). Or demigod. A being in the god realms who enjoys greater comfort and pleasure than human beings, but who suffers from jealousy and quarreling.

attachment. The disturbing thought that exaggerates the positive qualities of an object and wishes to possess it.

Avalokiteshvara (Skt). See *Chenrezig*.

baru (Tib). Beleric myrobalan. One of the "Three Chief Fruits" in Tibetan medicine, along with arura and kyuru.

Bhagavan (Skt). Epithet of a Buddha.

Bodhgaya. The small town in north India where Shakyamuni Buddha became enlightened.

bodhicitta (Skt). The altruistic wish to achieve full enlightenment in order to free all living beings from suffering and bring them to enlightenment.

bodhisattva (Skt). One who possesses bodhicitta.

Buddha (Skt). A fully enlightened being. (See *enlightenment*.)

Buddha of Compassion. See *Chenrezig*.

Buddha-field. See *pure land*.

Buddha-nature. Refers to the emptiness, or ultimate nature, of the mind. Because of this nature, every sentient being possesses the potential to become fully enlightened, a Buddha.

butter tea. A favorite Tibetan drink made from tea, water, milk, butter, and salt.

Buxa Duar. The town in West Bengal, India, where most of the Tibetan monks who escaped to India in 1959 were accommodated.

calm abiding. See *shamatha*.

causative phenomena. Things that come about in dependence upon causes and conditions; includes all objects experienced by the senses, as well as the mind itself; impermanent phenomena.

Chakrasamvara (Skt). Heruka Chakrasamvara. A male meditational deity of Highest Yoga Tantra.

chang (Tib). Beer made from fermented grain, often barley.

Chekawa (1101–75). The Kadampa geshe who composed the famous thought transformation text *Seven-Point Mind Training*.

Chenrezig (Tib). Or, in Sanskrit, Avalokiteshvara; Buddha of Compassion; the male meditational deity that embodies the compassion of all the Buddhas. The Dalai Lamas are incarnations of this deity.

circumambulation. A practice for purifying negative karma and accumulating merit in which a person walks clockwise around a holy object such as a stupa or statue.

compassion. The wish that all beings be free from suffering and its causes.

conventional nature. Relative truth; the way things appear to exist as distinct from the way in which they actually exist; what is true for a valid mind not perceiving ultimate truth.

cyclic existence. See *samsara*.

dakini (Skt). Literally, sky-goer; a female being with tantric realizations.

deity. The form of a Buddha used as the object of meditation in tantric practices.

delusions. The negative states of mind that are the cause of suffering. The three root delusions are ignorance, anger, and attachment.

dependent arising. The way that the self and phenomena exist conventionally as relative and interdependent. They come into existence in dependence upon (1) causes and conditions, (2) their parts, and, most subtly (3) the mind imputing or labeling them.

desire realm. One of the three realms of samsara, comprising the hell beings, hungry ghosts, animals, humans, asuras, and the six lower classes of suras; beings in this realm are preoccupied with desire for objects of the six senses.

deva (Skt). A god dwelling in the desire, form, or formless realm.

Dharma (Skt). In general, spiritual practice; specifically, the teachings of Buddha, which protect from suffering and lead to liberation and full enlightenment.

dharmakaya (Skt). The omniscient mind of a Buddha.

disturbing thoughts. See *delusions.*

Dorje Khadro (Tib). Or, in Sanskrit, Vajradaka; a male deity who acts to purify negativities through a specific fire puja practice.

Drepung Monastery. The largest of the three major Gelugpa monasteries; founded near Lhasa by one of Lama Tsongkhapa's disciples. Now reestablished in exile in South India.

ego. See *self-cherishing thought.*

Eight Mahayana Precepts. One-day vows to abandon killing; stealing; lying; sexual contact; intoxicants; high seats; eating at the wrong time; and singing, dancing, and wearing perfumes and jewelry.

emptiness. The absence, or lack, of true existence. Ultimately, every phenomenon is empty of existing truly, or from its own side, or independently. (See *merely labeled.*)

enlightenment. Buddhahood; omniscience; full awakening; the ultimate goal of Mahayana Buddhist practice, attained when all faults have been removed from the mind and all realizations completed; a state of mind characterized by the perfection of compassion, wisdom, and power.

exchanging self for others. The bodhicitta practice of renouncing the self and cherishing others.

five uninterrupted negative karmas. Killing one's father, one's mother, or an arhat; maliciously drawing blood from a Buddha; causing a schism within the Sangha.

form realm. The second of samsara's three realms, with seventeen classes of gods.

formless realm. The highest of samsara's three realms, with four classes of gods involved in formless meditations.

four continents. In Buddhist cosmology, a world has four continents inhabited by human beings. We live in the Southern Continent, the most favorable for spiritual practice.

four elements. Earth, water, fire, and air, or wind.

Four Guardians. The four kings of the four cardinal directions, who offer protection against harmful influences. Drawings of them are usually found at the entrances of Tibetan temples and monasteries.

Four Noble Truths. The subject of Shakyamuni Buddha's first teaching: true suffering, true cause of suffering, true cessation of suffering, and true path to the cessation of suffering.

four powers. The four remedies that make confession effective in purifying negative karma.

Ganden Monastery. The first of the three great Gelugpa monastic universities near Lhasa, founded in 1409 by Lama Tsongkhapa. It was destroyed in the 1960s and has now been reestablished in exile in South India.

Garuda. A tantric deity in the aspect of the powerful, horned bird of Indian culture; it represents the energy that destroys negativity, especially that of anger.

geshe (Tib). Literally, virtuous spiritual friend. A term given to the great Kadampas; the title conferred on those who have completed extensive studies and examinations at Gelugpa monastic universities.

Geshe Lama Könchog. An ascetic meditator and friend of Lama Yeshe; currently lives at Kopan Monastery in Nepal.

god. A samsaric being dwelling in a state with much comfort and pleasure.

graduated path to enlightenment. Or, in Tibetan, lamrim. Originally outlined in Tibet by Lama Atisha in *Lamp on the Path to Enlightenment*, the graduated path is a step-by-step presentation of the Buddha's teachings.

great insight. The meditative understanding of impermanence and emptiness that overcomes ignorance and leads to liberation.

guru (Skt). See *lama.*

Guru Shakyamuni Buddha (563–483 B.C.). The fourth of the one thousand Buddhas of this present world age, he was born a prince of the Shakya clan in North India and taught the sutra and tantra paths to liberation and full enlightenment.

Hayagriva. The Horse-Necked One; a wrathful red protector and tantric deity; a wrathful manifestation of Chenrezig.

hell being. A samsaric being in the realm of greatest suffering.

higher training. There are three higher trainings: the trainings in morality, concentration, and wisdom.

Hinayana (Skt). Literally, the Lesser Vehicle. The path of the arhats, the goal of which is nirvana, or personal liberation from samsara.

His Holiness Trijang Rinpoche (1901–81). The late Junior Tutor of His Holiness the Fourteenth Dalai Lama and root guru of Lama Zopa Rinpoche.

hungry ghost. Or, in Sanskrit, preta. One of the six classes of samsaric beings, hungry ghosts experience the greatest suffering of hunger and thirst.

ignorance. The root of cyclic existence; not knowing the way that things actually exist.

imprints. The seeds, or potentials, left on the mind by positive or negative actions of body, speech, and mind.

inherent existence. See true existence.

initiation. Empowerment. The transmission of the practice of a particular deity from a tantric master to a disciple, which permits the disciple to engage in that practice.

interferers. Malignant spirits that can cause hindrances to health and to spiritual practice and other activities.

Kadampa geshe. A practitioner of the Buddhist tradition that originated in Tibet in the eleventh century with the teachings of Lama Atisha. Kadampa geshes are renowned for their practice of thought transformation.

Kalachakra (Skt). Literally, cycle of time. A male meditational deity of Highest Yoga Tantra.

Kangyur (Tib). The 108 volumes of the Tibetan Buddhist canon that contain the discourses of Shakyamuni Buddha.

karma (Skt). The law of cause and effect; the process whereby virtuous actions of body, speech, and mind lead to happiness and nonvirtuous ones to suffering.

Kirti Tsenshab Rinpoche (b. 1926). A highly attained lama and great ascetic yogi who lives in Dharamsala, India, and who is one of Lama Zopa Rinpoche's gurus.

Kopan Monastery. The monastery near Boudhanath in the Kathmandu valley, Nepal, founded in 1969 by Lama Thubten Yeshe and Lama Zopa Rinpoche.

Krishnacharya. Also known as Krishnachari and Kanhapa; in Tibetan, known as Nagpo Chöpa; one of the eighty-four *mahasiddhas.*

Kuan Yin. Chinese Buddhist depiction, in female aspect, of Chenrezig, Buddha of Compassion.

Kunrig (Tib). A powerful deity for purification; white in color, with three faces, and holding a dharmachakra.

kyuru (Tib). Emblic myrobalan. Sour fruit used to cure phlegm and wind disease.

lama (Tib). Or, in Sanskrit, guru; spiritual teacher, master; literally, "heavy," as in heavy with Dharma knowledge.

Lama Atisha (982–1054). The renowned Indian Buddhist master who came to Tibet to help in the revival of Buddhism and established the Kadam tradition. His text *Lamp on the Path to Enlightenment* was the first lamrim text.

Lama Tsongkhapa (1357–1419). The revered teacher and accomplished practitioner who founded the Gelug order of Tibetan Buddhism. An emanation of Manjushri, the Buddha of Wisdom.

Lama Yeshe (1935–84). Founder of the Foundation for the Preservation of the Mahayana Tradition (FPMT) and guru of Lama Zopa Rinpoche.

lamrim (Tib). See *graduated path to enlightenment.*

landlord spirit. The spirit who claims ownership of the particular place in which it resides.

Lawudo Cave. The cave in the Solu Khumbu region of Nepal where the Lawudo Lama lived and meditated for more than twenty years. Lama Zopa Rinpoche is recognized as the reincarnation of the Lawudo Lama.

liberation. The state of complete liberation from samsara; nirvana, the state beyond sorrow; the goal of the practitioner seeking individual liberation.

lineage lamas. The spiritual teachers who constitute the line of direct guru-disciple transmission of teachings, from Buddha to the teachers of the present day.

Logyönma (Tib). Or, in Sanskrit, Parnashvari. A female deity often practiced to prevent contagious disease.

loving kindness. The wish that all beings have happiness and its causes.

lower realms. The three realms of cyclic existence with the most suffering: the hell, hungry ghost, and animal realms. (See *samsara.*)

lung (Tib). Literally, wind; the state in which the wind element within the body is unbalanced. Can also refer to an oral transmission.

mahasiddha (Skt). An accomplished tantric yogi; a saint.

Mahayana (Skt). The Great Vehicle; the path of the bodhisattvas, the ultimate goal of which is buddhahood.

Maitreya Buddha (Skt). The Loving One. The future Buddha, and fifth of the thousand Buddhas of this present world age.

mala (Skt). A rosary for counting mantras.

mandala (Skt). The symbolic offering to the Buddha of the entire purified universe. Or the purified environment of a tantric deity; the diagram or painting representing this.

mani pills. Tiny pills that are blessed with the recitation of the mani mantra, OM MANI PADME HUM, one hundred million times.

Manjugosha (Skt). See *Manjushri*.

Manjushri (Skt). A male deity embodying the wisdom of all the Buddhas.

mantra (Skt). Literally, protection of the mind. Sanskrit syllables recited in conjunction with the practice of a particular meditational deity and embodying the qualities of that deity.

Maudgalyayana. One of the two chief arhat disciples of Shakyamuni Buddha, renowned for his psychic powers.

merely imputed. See *merely labeled*.

merely labeled. The subtlest meaning of dependent arising; every phenomenon exists relatively, or conventionally, as a mere label, as merely imputed by the mind. (See *emptiness*.)

merit. The positive energy accumulated in the mind as a result of virtuous actions of body, speech, and mind.

method. All aspects of the path to enlightenment associated with the development of compassion and the altruistic actions of a bodhisattva.

Milarepa (1040–1123). The great ascetic Tibetan yogi and poet, famous for his intense practice, devotion to his guru, his many songs of spiritual realization, and his attainment of enlightenment in one lifetime.

Mitukpa (Tib). Immovable Buddha; a powerful deity for purification; blue in color, with a similar aspect to Shakyamuni Buddha, except holding an upright vajra in the left hand.

Mount Meru. The center of the universe in Buddhist cosmology.

mudra (Skt). Literally, gesture. Symbolic hand gestures used in images of Buddha or in tantric rituals.

naga (Skt). Snakelike beings of the animal realm who live in or near bodies of water; commonly associated with fertility of the land, but can also function as protectors of religion.

Nagarjuna. The great Indian scholar and tantric adept who lived approximately four hundred years after Buddha's death. He clarified the ultimate meaning of Buddha's teachings on emptiness.

Namgyalma (Tib). Or, in Sanskrit, Ushnishavijaya. A tantric deity in female aspect that is practiced to prolong life.

Naropa (1016–1100). The Indian mahasiddha who transmitted many tantric lineages, including that of the renowned Six Yogas of Naropa.

nirmanakaya (Skt). Or emanation body; the form in which a Buddha appears to ordinary beings.

nonvirtue. Negative karma; that which results in suffering.

nyung-nä (Tib). A two-day Chenrezig retreat that involves fasting and prostrations.

object to be refuted. The true existence of the self and other phenomena.

obscurations. The negative imprints left on the mental continuum by negative karma and delusions.

om mani padme hum (Skt). The mani; the mantra of Chenrezig, Buddha of Compassion.

oral transmission. Or, in Tibetan, *lung*. The verbal transmission of a teaching, meditation practice, or mantra from guru to disciple, the guru having received the transmission in an unbroken lineage from the original source.

Pabongka Dechen Nyingpo (1871–1941). An influential and powerful lama of the Gelug order, Pabongka Rinpoche was the root guru of His Holiness the Dalai Lama's Senior and Junior Tutors.

Padmasambhava. The eighth-century Indian tantric master mainly responsible for the establishment of Buddhism in Tibet, revered by all Tibetan Buddhists, but especially by the Nyingmapas.

pandit (Skt). A great scholar and philosopher.

perfect human rebirth. The rare human state, qualified by eight freedoms and ten richnesses, that is the ideal condition for practicing Dharma and achieving enlightenment.

pervasive compounding suffering. The most subtle of the three types of suffering, it refers to the nature of the five aggregates, which are contaminated by karma and delusions.

powa (Tib). A tantric practice to transfer the consciousness to a pure land of Buddha at the time of death.

Prajnaparamita (Skt). Or, in English, Perfection of Wisdom; the teachings of Shakyamuni Buddha in which the wisdom of emptiness and the path of the bodhisattva are explained.

pratimoksha (Skt). The vows of individual liberation taken by monks, nuns, and lay people.

prostrations. Paying respect to the guru-deity with body, speech, and mind.

protectors. Worldly or enlightened beings who protect Buddhism and its practitioners.

puja (Skt). Literally, offering; a religious ceremony.

pure land. A pure realm of Buddha without any suffering; after birth in a pure land, the practitioner receives teachings directly from the deity of that pure land, actualizes the rest of the path, and then becomes enlightened.

purification. The removal, or cleansing, of negative karma and its imprints from the mind.

refuge. The heartfelt reliance upon Buddha, Dharma, and Sangha for guidance on the path to enlightenment.

refuge merit field. The deities and lineage lamas who are the object of meditation when taking refuge, usually with Shakyamuni Buddha as the central figure.

relics. Small, pearl-like pills that manifest spontaneously from holy objects such as statues, stupas, or the cremated bodies of great practitioners.

renunciation. The state of mind wishing to be liberated from samsara because of not having for even a second the slightest attraction to samsaric perfections.

Rinpoche (Tib). Literally, precious one. An honorific term usually given to recognized reincarnate lamas; a respectful title used for one's own lama.

ritual cake. Or, in Tibetan, *torma*. A cake, traditionally made from roasted barley flour, butter, and sugar that is offered to the Buddhas and other holy beings during religious ceremonies.

sadhu (Skt). A wandering Hindu yogi.

Sakya (Tib). One of the four principal traditions of Tibetan Buddhism, it was founded in the eleventh century by Drokmi Shakya Yeshe.

Samantabhadra (Skt). A bodhisattva renowned for his heroic aspiration and extensive offerings.

samsara (Skt). Cyclic existence; the six realms: the lower realms of the hell beings, hungry ghosts, and animals, and the upper realms of the humans, demigods, and gods; the recurring cycle of death and rebirth within one or another of the six realms under the control of karma and delusions; also refers to the contaminated aggregates of a sentient being.

Sangha (Skt). The third object of refuge; absolute Sangha are those who have directly realized emptiness; relative Sangha are ordained monks and nuns.

Saraha. An Indian tantric yogi, one of the eighty-four mahasiddhas; renowned for his realization of mahamudra, the tantric realization of emptiness.

self-cherishing thought. The self-centered attitude of considering one's own happiness to be more important than that of others; the main obstacle to the realization of bodhicitta.

sentient being. Any being who has not yet reached enlightenment.

Sera Me College. One of the two colleges within Sera Monastery; the other is Sera Je College, to which Lama Zopa Rinpoche is connected.

Sera Monastery. One of the three great Gelug monasteries near Lhasa; founded in the early fifteenth century by Jamchen Chöje, a disciple of Lama Tsongkhapa; now also established in exile in South India.

seven limbs. The seven limbs are prostrating, making offerings, confessing, rejoicing, requesting to turn the Dharma wheel, requesting the teachers to remain in the world, and dedicating.

Shakyamuni Buddha (Skt). See *Guru Shakyamuni Buddha.*

shamatha (Skt). Or, in Tibetan, *shi-né*; calm abiding; a state of concentration in which the mind is able to abide steadily, without effort and for as long as desired, on an object of meditation.

Shantideva (685–763). The great Indian bodhisattva who wrote *A Guide to the Bodhisattva's Way of Life,* one of the essential Mahayana texts.

Shariputra. An arhat renowned for his wisdom; one of Shakyamuni Buddha's two chief disciples.

Singhanada (Skt). Lion's Roar Avalokiteshvara; an aspect of Avalokiteshvara, mounted on a lion, often practiced for healing and the removal of interferences.

Sitatapatra (Skt). White Umbrella Deity; often practiced to remove interferences.

six perfections. The practices to be perfected during the ten bodhisattva levels: generosity, morality, patience, enthusiastic perseverance, concentration, and wisdom.

six realms. The three upper realms of the gods, demigods, and humans and the three lower realms of the animals, hungry ghosts, and hell beings.

spirits. Beings not usually visible to ordinary people; can belong to the hungry ghost or god realms; can be beneficent as well as harmful.

stupa (Skt). A reliquary symbolic of the Buddha's mind.

subtle dependent arising. See *merely labeled.*

suffering of change. What is normally regarded as pleasure, but which is actually unrecognized suffering.

suffering of suffering. The commonly recognized suffering experiences of pain, discomfort, and unhappiness.

Supreme Assembly. See *Sangha.*

sura (Skt). A being in the god realm who enjoys the highest pleasures to be found in cyclic existence.

sutra (Skt). The open discourses of the Buddha; a scriptural text and the teachings and practices it contains.

taking and giving. The meditation technique for developing bodhicitta, in which one takes upon oneself all the suffering and causes of suffering of all sentient beings and then gives to others one's own body, possessions, merit, and happiness.

Tangtong Gyälpo (1385–1509). Renowned mahasiddha who was considered a manifestation of Avalokiteshvara and Hayagriva; famous as a great engineer, building many temples and iron bridges, and also as a great doctor.

tantra (Skt). The secret teachings of the Buddha; a scriptural text and the teachings and practices it contains. Tantric practices generally involve identification of oneself with a fully enlightened deity in order to transform one's impure states of body, speech, and mind into the pure states of an enlightened being.

Tara (Skt). A female meditational deity, usually green in color, that embodies the enlightened activity of all the Buddhas; often referred to as the mother of the Buddhas of the past, present, and future.

Tathagata (Skt). Literally, Thus Gone; an epithet of a Buddha.

terma (Tib). A visionary, or mind, treasure; a visionary text concealed by Padmasambhava and other great masters in the early years of Buddhism's dissemination in Tibet and revealed later by practitioners known as *tertons.*

thangka (Tib). Painted or appliquéd depictions of deities, usually set in a framework of colorful brocade.

Thirty-Five Buddhas. Used in the practice of confession and purifying negative karma, the group of thirty-five Buddhas visualized while reciting *The Sutra of the Three Heaps* and performing prostrations.

thought transformation. Or, in Tibetan, lo-jong. A powerful approach to the development of bodhicitta, in which the mind is trained to use all situations, both happy and unhappy, as a means to destroy self-cherishing and self-grasping.

three poisonous minds. Ignorance, anger, and attachment.

tong-len (Tib). See *taking and giving*.

Triple Gem. The objects of Buddhist refuge: Buddha, Dharma, and Sangha.

true existence. The type of existence that everything appears to possess; in fact, everything is empty of true existence. (See *emptiness*.)

tsampa (Tib). Roasted barley flour, a Tibetan staple food.

tsa-tsa (Tib). Clay or plaster block with images of deities.

Tushita (Skt). The Joyous Land. The pure land of the thousand Buddhas of this eon, where the future Buddha Maitreya and Lama Tsongkhapa reside.

two stages. The generation and completion stages of Highest Yoga Tantra.

ultimate nature. See *ultimate reality*.

ultimate reality. The way things actually exist as distinct from how they appear to exist; emptiness; the absence of inherent existence.

unfortunate realms. See *lower realms*.

upper realms. The sura, asura, and human realms.

vajra position. Commonly known as the full lotus position. The meditation posture in which the legs are crossed with the foot, sole upward, resting on the opposite thigh.

Vajradhara (Skt). Male meditational deity; the form in which Shakyamuni Buddha revealed the tantric teachings.

Vajrapani (Skt). An extremely wrathful male meditational deity, the embodiment of the power of all the Buddhas.

Vajrasattva (Skt). A male tantric deity used especially for purification.

Vajravarahi (Skt). Or, in Tibetan, Dorje Pagmo. An aspect of Vajrayogini.

Vajrayana (Skt). Also known as Tantrayana or Mantrayana. The quickest vehicle of Buddhism, capable of leading to the attainment of full enlightenment within one lifetime.

Vajrayogini (Skt). A female deity of Highest Yoga Tantra.

Vasubandhu. An Indian Buddhist scholar of the fifth century; brother of Asanga.

virtue. Positive karma; that which results in happiness.

White Tara (Skt). An aspect of Tara, white in color, practiced to prolong life.

wind disease. See *lung*.

wisdom. All aspects of the path to enlightenment associated with the development of the realization of emptiness.

wish-granting jewel. A jewel that brings its possessor everything that they desire.

yoga (Skt). Literally, to yoke. The spiritual discipline to which one yokes oneself in order to achieve enlightenment.

yogi (Skt). A highly realized meditator.

Suggested Further Reading

Capra, Fritjof. *Uncommon Wisdom: Conversations with Remarkable People*. New York: Bantam, 1989.

Chodron, Thubten. *Open Heart, Clear Mind*. Ithaca: Snow Lion Publications, 1991.

Clifford, Terry. *Tibetan Buddhist Medicine and Psychiatry: The Diamond Healing*. York Beach: Samuel Weiser, 1984.

Dharmaraksita. *The Wheel of Sharp Weapons*. Translated by Geshe Dhargyey et al. Dharamsala: Library of Tibetan Works and Archives, 1976.

Dhonden, Yeshi. *Health through Balance: An Introduction to Tibetan Medicine*. Edited and translated by Jeffrey Hopkins. Ithaca: Snow Lion Publications, 1986.

———. *Healing from the Source: The Science and Lore of Tibetan Medicine*. Translated and edited by B. Alan Wallace. Ithaca: Snow Lion Publications, 2000.

Fenton, Peter. *Tibetan Healing: The Modern Legacy of Medicine Buddha*. Wheaton: Quest Books, 1999.

Gyatso, Tenzin, the Fourteenth Dalai Lama. *The Meaning of Life from a Buddhist Perspective*. Translated and edited by Jeffrey Hopkins. Boston: Wisdom Publications, 1992.

Khangkar, Lobsang Dolma. *Lectures on Tibetan Medicine*. Compiled and edited by K. Dhondup. Dharamsala: Library of Tibetan Works and Archives, 1986.

Levey, Joel, and Michelle Levey. *The Fine Arts of Relaxation, Concentration and Meditation*. Boston: Wisdom Publications, 1991.

Levine, Stephen. *Healing into Life and Death*. Bath: Gateway Books, 1987.

McDonald, Kathleen. *How to Meditate*. Boston: Wisdom Publications, 1984.

Moyers, Bill. *Healing and the Mind*. New York: Doubleday, 1993.

Pabongka Rinpoche. *Liberation in the Palm of Your Hand*. Translated by Michael Richards. Boston: Wisdom Publications, 1991.

Pän-ch'en Lo-zang Ch'ö-kyi Gyäl-tsän. *The Guru Puja*. Translated by Alex Berzin et al. Dharamsala: Library of Tibetan Works and Archives, 1981.

Rabten, Geshe, and Geshe Ngawang Dhargyey. *Advice from a Spiritual Friend.* Translated and edited by Brian Beresford. Boston: Wisdom Publications, 2001.

Shantideva. *A Guide to the Bodhisattva's Way of Life*. Translated by Stephen Batchelor. Dharamsala: Library of Tibetan Works and Archives, 1981.

Siegel, Bernie S. *Peace, Love and Healing*. Arrow Books, 1991.

Sogyal Rinpoche. *The Tibetan Book of Living and Dying*. Edited by Patrick Gaffney and Andrew Harvey. San Francisco: HarperCollins, 1992.

Thondup Rinpoche, Tulku. *Enlightened Living*. Boston: Shambhala Publications, 1991.

———. *The Healing Power of Mind: Simple Meditation Exercises for Health, Well-Being, and Enlightenment*. Boston: Shambhala, 1996.

Tsongkapa. *The Principal Teachings of Buddhism*. Translated by Geshe Lobsang Tharchin with Michael Roach. New Jersey: Mahayana Sutra and Tantra Press, 1988.

Vajra, Kusali Dharma. *Giving Breath to the Wretched: The Method of Benefiting Sentient Beings at the Time of Death*. Translated by Lama Thubten Zopa Rinpoche. London: Wisdom Publications, 1981.

Wallace, B. Alan. *Tibetan Buddhism from the Ground Up*. Boston: Wisdom Publications, 1993.

Wangchen, Geshe Namgyal. *Awakening the Mind of Enlightenment*. Boston: Wisdom Publications, 1987.

Wangyal, Geshe. *The Door of Liberation: Essential Teachings of the Tibetan Buddhist Tradition*. Boston: Wisdom Publications, 1995.

Yeshe, Lama Thubten and Zopa Rinpoche. *Wisdom Energy*. Edited by Jonathan Landaw with Alexander Berzin. Boston: Wisdom Publications, 2000.

Zopa Rinpoche, Lama. *Transforming Problems into Happiness*. Boston: Wisdom Publications, 2001.

———. *The Door to Satisfaction: The Heart Advice of a Tibetan Buddhist Master*. Edited by Ailsa Cameron and Robina Courtin. Boston: Wisdom Publications, 1994.

———. *The Healing Buddha: A Practice for the Prevention and Healing of Disease*. Boston: Wisdom Publications, 1994.

Index

About Wisdom Publications

WISDOM PUBLICATIONS, a not-for-profit publisher, is dedicated to making available authentic Buddhist works for the benefit of all. We publish translations of the sutras and tantras, commentaries and teachings of past and contemporary Buddhist masters, and original works by the world's leading Buddhist scholars. We publish our titles with the appreciation of Buddhism as a living philosophy and with the special commitment to preserve and transmit important works from all the major Buddhist traditions. If you would like more information or a copy of our mail-order catalog, please contact us at:

Wisdom Publications, 199 Elm Street, Somerville MA 02144 USA
Telephone: (617) 776-7416 • Fax: (617) 776-7841
Email: info@wisdompubs.org • www.wisdompubs.org

Wisdom Publications is a nonprofit, charitable 501(c)3 organization affiliated with the Foundation for the Preservation of the Mahayana Tradition (FPMT).

The Lama Yeshe Wisdom Archive

THE LAMA YESHE WISDOM ARCHIVE is the repository of the teachings of Lama Thubten Yeshe and Lama Thubten Zopa Rinpoche. We are delighted to collaborate with Wisdom Publications on this book, and several more titles are in preparation.

The Archive has published several free booklets. Currently available are: *Virtue and Reality, Making Life Meaningful, Teachings from the Mani Retreat* and *Daily Purification,* all by Lama Zopa Rinpoche, and *The Essence of Tibetan Buddhism* by Lama Yeshe. Lama Zopa Rinpoche's *Teachings from the Vajrasattva Retreat* is available for sale through Wisdom Publications. You will find these and many more teachings on our website, LamaYeshe.com.

The Lama Yeshe Wisdom Archive, PO Box 356, Weston MA 02493
(781) 899-9587 • info@LamaYeshe.com • www.LamaYeshe.com